ZOLA
AND THE THEATER

ZOLA
AND THE THEATER

BY

Lawson A. CARTER

GREENWOOD PRESS, PUBLISHERS
WESTPORT, CONNECTICUT

Library of Congress Cataloging in Publication Data

Carter, Lawson A
  Zola and the theater.

    At head of title: Institut d'études françaises de Yale
University.
    Reprint of the 1st ed. published in 1963 by Yale Uni-
versity Press, New Haven, which was issued in Yale
Romanic studies, English series.
    Originally presented as the author's thesis, Yale Uni-
versity, 1951.
    Bibliography: p.
    Includes index.
    1. Zola, Émile, 1840-1902--Dramatic works.
2. French drama--19th century--History and criticism.
I. Title. II. Series: Yale Romanic studies : English
series.
[PQ2540.C3 1977]   842'.8   77-6784
ISBN 0-8371-9659-0

© 1963, *Presses Universitaires de France*

Originally published in 1963 by Yale University Press,
New Haven

Reprinted with the permission of Yale University Press

Reprinted in 1977 by Greenwood Press, Inc.

Library of Congress catalog card number 77-6784

ISBN 0-8371-9659-0

Printed in the United States of America

TABLE OF CONTENTS

FOREWORD

The eminence of Émile Zola as a novelist has to this day cast an obscuring shadow over his labors in the theater, which, throughout his adult life, absorbed a substantial part of his energy and ambitions. Some articles in periodicals have been devoted to various aspects of his work in and for the theater, and longer works of biography and criticism have mentioned his efforts in this field, but no comprehensive study has been undertaken to weave together the various strands of Zola's theatrical endeavors into a unified pattern which might justify the title *Zola and the theater.*

From the time of his first article of theatrical criticism in 1865 — which is also the year in which he is believed to have written his first mature play, *Madeleine* — until his death in 1902, Zola was persistently haunted by the opportunities which the theater seemed to offer, either as a medium for his own expression, or as target for his reforming zeal. Although his very considerable endeavors as playwright and dramatic critic have been eclipsed by his accomplishment in the novel, this eclipse need not be, and certainly was not in his day, a total one. After publication of the first instalments of *l'Assommoir* in 1876, nothing which came from Zola's pen was ignored.

The five chapters of this book have been planned primarily on the basis of subject-matter, but, for the sake of showing the chronological sequence of Zola's thought, I have not adhered rigidly to this plan. Thus the bulk of Zola's dramatic criticism (1876-1881) is considered in Chapter III, but it has seemed logical to incorporate some of his earlier criticism in Chapter II : and the discussion of Zola's " naturalism " has been treated as chronologically as possible, with an introduction to this important and fascinating theory in Chapter I and its further development in Chapter III. The scope of this book extends only to those works written or produced in France during Zola's lifetime. No attempt has been made here to list stage presentations outside of France, or theatrical and cinematographic adaptations subsequent to his death in 1902.

This work, substantially as it now stands, was originally presented in 1951 to the Faculty of the Graduate School of Yale University as a dissertation in candidacy for the degree of

Doctor of Philosophy.   In the decade which has since elapsed, a number of valuable critical and biographical studies of Émile Zola have appeared, including those by F. W. J. Hemmings, Guy Robert, Angus Wilson, Armand Lanoux, J. H. Matthews, Calvin S. Brown, Philippe van Tieghem, Jean Fréville, Henri Guillemin; a collection of letters from J.-K. Huysmans to Zola published by Pierre Lambert; a collection of letters from Henry Céard to Zola published by C.-A. Burns; and a work on Claude Bernard by Reino Virtanen containing some important pages on Zola (1).   It has been a pleasure to consult these recent works, as well as a number of articles on Zola by these and other scholars which have appeared in periodicals during the past ten or twelve years.   In revising this book for publication, I have been able at some points to refer to relevant passages from some of these works which have appeared since 1951, and have so indicated in the footnotes.

It will be readily apparent that a large part of this book has been written by Zola himself and remains in the original French.   The passages chosen for inclusion here, many of them unavailable in volume, are so characteristic of Zola's style and revelatory of his thought that it has seemed wise to leave them untouched rather than risk a translation which might be inadequate to convey his precise meaning and vigor of expression. It is not necessary, I am sure, that a reader be a professional scholar, or completely bilingual, to derive some satisfaction from a work of this nature where the two languages follow one another throughout.   It is indeed my hope — regardless of the reader's native tongue, French or English, or of his proficiency in the other — that some part of this book may yield further insight into the nature of the remarkable novelist and humanitarian that was Émile Zola.

In the accomplishment of this study, I am particularly indebted to two members of the Yale faculty : Professor Henri Peyre, who suggested the subject to me some years ago and who has been a continuing source of advice and encouragement ; and my faculty adviser, Professor Jean Boorsch, whose wise supervision and friendly counsel have inspired my steps and added to the pleasure which this undertaking has brought me.

L. A. C.

---

(1) To these names should be added that of Henri MITTERAND for his recent book, *Zola journaliste.*

CHAPTER I

TOWARDS NATURALISM

Introduction. — The new painters. — The scientific spirit. — Conclusions.

Introduction

Émile Zola was born in Paris on 2 April 1840 during a temporary sojourn of his parents in the French capital. The father, a capable civil engineer of Italian descent, had married a much younger Frenchwoman in the preceding year and established himself in Aix-en-Provence, where he resided until his death in 1847. His widow remained in Aix with her only child for another ten years, and it was there, under the gracious skies of southern France, that young Émile passed through adolescence, reading the romantic poets in the first flush of youthful idealism, and nurturing dreams of literary glory.

Neither Zola's early poems nor the literary ideas which he held in his youth foreshadowed the naturalist doctrine of his maturity. A full and intimate record of his thought during the years 1859-1862 exists in the series of letters which he wrote from Paris to his close childhood friends, Paul Cézanne and Jean-Baptistin Baille (1). Financial distress had obliged Zola and his mother to leave Aix during the winter 1857-1858 and to settle in Paris, where the help and advice of family friends were available. Zola's letters to Aix reveal the high idealism of his youth, the romantic impetus which he had received from Hugo and Musset, and his sometimes despairing efforts to reconcile the necessity of earning a living with his vaulting ambition to achieve success as a poet.

(1) In LES ŒUVRES COMPLÈTES, *Correspondance (1858-1871)*. The painter, Paul Cézanne (1839-1906), remained on intimate terms with Zola for many years. The friendship ceased, from all outward appearances, in 1886, following publication of ZOLA's, *l'Œuvre*, the novel based on the lives and theories of the impressionist painters.

Jean-Baptistin BAILLE entered the *Ecole polytechnique* in Paris, became a civil engineer, and gradually disappeared from Zola's circle of friends.

His failure to win his *baccalauréat* (1) contributed to doubts of his capacities. To Cézanne, he wrote early in 1860 :

Je doute de tout, de moi-même le premier. Il est des journées où je me crois sans intelligence, où je me demande ce que je vaux pour avoir fait des rêves si orgueilleux. Je n'ai pas achevé mes études, je ne sais même pas parler en bon français ; j'ignore tout. Mon éducation du collège ne peut me servir à rien : un peu de théorie, aucune pratique. Que faire alors ? et mon esprit balance, et me voilà triste jusqu'au soir. — La réalité me presse et cependant je rêve encore. Si je n'avais pas ma famille, si je possédais une modique somme à dépenser par jour, je me retirerais dans un bastidon, et j'y vivrais en ermite. Le monde n'est pas mon affaire ; j'y ferai triste figure, si j'y vais quelque jour. D'autre part, je ne deviendrai jamais millionnaire, l'argent n'est pas mon élément. Aussi je ne désire que la tranquillité et une modeste aisance. Mais c'est un rêve, je ne vois devant moi que luttes, ou plutôt je ne vois rien distinctement (2).

Such doubts were temporary. Hope, and the drive of his ambition, were in youth as throughout his life capable of lifting him above moments of depression. A few days after this letter to Cézanne, he was writing to Baille :

... j'ai vingt ans, et je suis encore à la charge de ma mère, qui peut à peine se suffire à elle-même. Je suis obligé de chercher un travail pour manger, et ce travail, je ne l'ai pas encore trouvé, seulement j'espère l'avoir bientôt. Telle est donc ma position : gagner mon pain n'importe comment et, si je ne veux pas dire adieu à mes rêves, m'occuper la nuit de mon avenir. La lutte sera longue, mais elle ne m'effraye pas ; je sens en moi quelque chose et, si en réalité ce quelque chose existe, tôt ou tard il doit paraître au grand jour. Donc, point de châteaux en Espagne ; une logique serrée, manger avant tout, puis voir ce qu'il y a en moi, peut-être beaucoup, peut-être rien, et si je me suis trompé, continuer à manger avec mon emploi obscur et passer comme tant d'autres, avec mes pleurs, et mes rêves, sur cette pauvre terre (3).

The " quelque chose " which Zola felt stirring within him at that time was the gift of poetry — particularly a type of poetry, derived from romanticism, which expressed the artist's vision of

---

(1) According to Paul Alexis (1847-1901), Zola's intimate friend and biographer, Zola passed his written examination for the *baccalauréat* in Paris in 1859, but failed the literature and modern languages section of the oral test. He failed again in a second attempt later that year in Marseille (ALEXIS, *Emile Zola, notes d'un ami* (Paris, 1882), pp. 40-44).
(2) To Cézanne, dated 9 February 1860, in LES ŒUVRES COMPLÈTES, *Correspondance (1858-1871)*, p. 32.
(3) *Ibid.*, p. 40. To Baille, dated 20 February 1860.

the beautiful and the ideal. " La beauté pour moi est tout ", he writes to Baille (1), and in a later letter to his friend, affirms that he is incapable of stifling the noble impulses of his nature under the mantle of realism. Continuing, he writes to Baille :

J'avais beau te crier : « La réalité est triste, la réalité est hideuse ; voilons-la donc sous des fleurs ; n'ayons de commerce avec elle qu'autant que notre misérable humanité l'exige ; mangeons, buvons, satisfaisons tous nos appétits brutaux, mais que l'âme ait sa part, que le rêve embellisse nos heures de loisir.» Tu me répondais invariablement que je me perdais aux nues, que je ne voyais pas ce qui m'aveuglait. Ne pas le voir, bon Dieu ! Je détourne les yeux du fumier pour les porter sur les roses, non pas que je nie l'utilité du fumier qui fait éclore mes belles fleurs, mais parce que je préfère les roses, si peu utiles pourtant. Tel je me montre à l'égard de la réalité et de l'idéal. J'accepte l'une comme nécessaire, je m'y soumets selon la nature ; mais, dès que je puis m'échapper de cette ornière commune, je cours à l'autre et je m'égare dans mes prairies bien-aimées (2).

He addresses a similar reproach to Cézanne, from which it clearly appears that at the age of twenty Zola placed greater value upon poetic vision than upon the portrayal of strict reality :

Que voulez-vous dire avec ce mot de réaliste ? Vous vous vantez de ne peindre que des sujets dénués de poésie ! Mais chaque chose a la sienne, le fumier comme les fleurs. Serait-ce parce que vous prétendez imiter la nature servilement ? Mais alors, puisque vous criez tant après la poésie, c'est dire que la nature est prosaïque. Et vous en avez menti. — C'est pour toi, que je dis cela, monsieur mon ami, monsieur le grand peintre futur. C'est pour te dire que l'art est un, que spiritualiste, réaliste ne sont que des mots, que la poésie est une grande chose et que hors de la poésie il n'y a pas de salut (3).

Many other examples of Zola's idealism and of his search for spiritual values may be found in the correspondence of this epoch. The function of the poet is to express his aspirations towards God, to dip his pen in the anguish of his heart, to lose himself in the clouds in quest of new utopias (4). He should dream of the progress and regeneration of humanity (5). The

(1) *Ibid.*, p. 45. To Baille, 17 March 1860.
(2) *Ibid.*, p. 141. To Baille, July 1860.
(3) *Ibid.*, p. 53. To Cézanne, 25 March 1860.
(4) *Ibid.*, p. 85. To Baille, 2 June 1860.
(5) *Ibid.*, p. 101. To Baille, 24 June 1860.

poet seeking to improve mankind has two means at his disposal :
that of satire, " l'éclat de rire de Satan ", which combats vice by
exposing it ; and that of lyricism, " le sourire de Dieu ", which
offers a lofty and sublime ideal as an encouragement to virtue (1).
Zola, at twenty, renounces the satiric method which he was
later to embrace so avidly :

Quand on remue la fange, il reste toujours quelques souillures aux
mains... Le poète satirique, voyant toujours l'homme par ses mauvais
côtés, finit par le prendre en pitié, en mépris, en haine ; son rire, d'abord
railleur, devient amer ; son désir de corriger se change en celui de
flageller ; plus il va, plus la vase est profonde, plus il devient dur,
impitoyable ; son dernier cri est un blasphème... Mais tailler ma plume
et me mettre à noircir l'homme de parti pris, lui ôtant ses rares qualités
et faisant ressortir ses nombreux défauts, c'est ce que je ne saurais
aimer (2).

And he believes most firmly that the one great mission of the
poet is to raise the beacon of spiritual values in an age darkened
by scientific materialism :

Dans nos temps de matérialisme, dans notre siècle où le commerce
absorbe chacun, où les sciences si saines et si grandes déjà rendent
l'homme orgueilleux et lui font oublier le savant suprême, le poète a
une mission sainte : montrer à toute heure, en tout lieu, l'âme à ceux
qui ne pensent qu'au corps, et Dieu à ceux dont la science a tiré la foi.
L'art n'est autre chose : c'est un flambeau splendide qui éclaire la voie
de l'humanité, et non une misérable bougie dans le taudis d'un rimeur.
Il ne s'agit pas seulement de faire de beaux vers, il faut que ces vers
soient une sublime leçon de vertu ; dans les deux cas, on peut être un
grand artiste, mais dans le premier, on se sert mal du feu sacré donné
par Dieu ; dans le second, on devient un disciple, un apôtre de la
Divinité (3).

One can imagine no more striking antithesis to the views
which Zola was later to adopt. Indeed, the change was not long
in coming. In 1861, only one year after the foregoing letter to
Baille, Zola was insisting on the superiority of science over
contemporary poetry (4).

(1) *Ibid.*, p. 153. To Baille, 10 August 1860.
(2) *Ibid.*, pp. 154-155.
(3) *Ibid.*, p. 155.
(4) According to " Trois textes inédits d'Emile Zola ", in *Revue des Sciences
humaines*, nouv. sér., fasc. 51 (juillet-décembre 1948), pp. 181-207. The
reference is to the second of these texts by Zola, an essay entitled " Du progrès
dans les sciences et dans la poésie " (Edited by G. Robert).

At the height of his fame, Zola authorized the publication of some of his early poems in the biography which his friend, Paul Alexis, was writing of him. Zola admits in his preface to these " Vers inédits " that they are in imitation of Musset, and, with a certain mockery directed at contemporary poetry, declares of them :

... je n'ai pu relire mes vers sans sourire. Ils sont bien faibles, et de seconde main, pas plus mauvais pourtant que les vers des hommes de mon âge qui s'obstinent à rimer. Ma seule vanité est d'avoir eu conscience de ma médiocrité de poète et de m'être courageusement mis à la besogne du siècle, avec le rude outil de la prose. A vingt ans, il est beau de prendre une telle décision, surtout avant d'avoir pu se débarrasser des imitations fatales. Si donc mes vers doivent servir ici à quelque chose, je souhaite qu'ils fassent rentrer en eux les poètes inutiles, n'ayant pas le génie nécessaire pour se dégager de la formule romantique, et qu'ils les décident à être de braves prosateurs, tout bêtement (1).

These verses are, as Zola declares, imitative and rather commonplace. They do not in any sense presage the emergence of a new poet. The most significant aspect of this youthful poetry is that more than half of the total comprises a trilogy of three long poems in which, as Zola wrote to Baille, he traced the progression of love, from the carnal and brutal in the first poem, to the triumph of the ideal in the last (2). Zola's conception of this trilogy illustrates his penchant for large, massive works, leading to his creation of the *Rougon-Macquart*.

It is easy to see why Zola abandoned poetry in favor of prose. Not only were his poems unable to provide him with a needed living, but also, as he soon perceived, they were derivative, and therefore inadequate to bring him the renown which he craved. He felt that he must find a path in which he might assert his own originality. His literary motto, as he writes to Baille, was *Tout ou rien!* — therefore, he explains :

Je voudrais par conséquent ne marcher sur les traces de personne ; non pas que j'ambitionne le titre de chef d'école — d'ordinaire, un tel

---

(1) Zola's preface, dated 1 December 1881, to his " Vers inédits ", in ALEXIS, *Emile Zola, notes d'un ami*, pp. 231-233. Zola's early poems are at pp. 235-236. In LES ŒUVRES COMPLÈTES, they are to be found in the appendix to the volume *Mélanges, Préfaces et Discours*, pp. 335-383.
(2) The titles are " Rodolpho ", " L'aérienne " and " Paolo ", forming the trilogy " L'amoureuse comédie ". ZOLA comments upon the trilogy in an undated letter to Baille (believed to have been written in August 1861), in LES ŒUVRES COMPLÈTES, *Correspondance (1858-1871)*, p. 220.

homme est toujours systématique — mais je désirerais trouver quelque sentier inexploré, et sortir de la foule des écrivassiers de notre temps (1).

He was determined to find the medium of expression which was best suited to his talent. " Je cherche encore ma voie ", he says in another letter to Baille. " La meilleure forme est celle dont on se sert le mieux (2). "

In 1862, Zola was fortunate enough to secure a clerical position with the publishing firm, Hachette. Two years previously, in his only other attempt at regular employment, he had been unable to endure an obscure post in a mercantile establishment for more than a few months. Hachette, however, offered him a congenial atmosphere and the opportunity to see literature in the making. He was able to meet such authors of the house as Taine, About, Amédée Achard, Prévost Paradol (3). Beginning obscurely as a package-wrapper, he was promoted before long to chief of publicity, a position which he held until early in 1866. By this time, having published his *Contes à Ninon* and *la Confession de Claude*, fortified in addition with contracts for newspaper articles, he felt secure enough in his literary career to abandon a salaried position and to rely wholly on his pen for a livelihood.

The complete reversal of Zola's youthful principles involved far more than a switch from poetry to prose. His entire philosophy was turned upside down in a cataclysmic upheaval of his thought. From a youthful idealist, he became the avowed enemy of idealism and spirituality, and the ardent champion of positivist science and observable reality (4). Following his article

(1) *Ibid.*, p. 137. To Baille, dated July 1860.
(2) *Ibid.*, p. 157. To Baille, 10 August 1860.
(3) ALEXIS, *ibid.*, pp. 58-59.
(4) An expression of Zola's early religious faith may be found in his letter to Baille of 10 August 1860, LES ŒUVRES COMPLÈTES, *Correspondance (1858-1871)* at pp. 158-161. Zola venerates the universal God, and deprecates all sectarianism. He hesitates to pronounce as to the divinity of Christ : " Ce n'est pas que j'ai plaisir à nier sa divinité : si chrétien veut dire disciple du Christ, je prends hautement ce nom ; ses préceptes sont les miens, son Dieu le mien. C'est que cette divinité me paraît inutile, c'est qu'elle a été exploitée par mes cauchemars, les prêtres et les commentateurs, c'est que je n'en ai aucun besoin pour l'aimer et le vénérer... je me résume et je conclus que j'adore le Dieu que le Christ nous révéla " (p. 161).
About twenty years later, he was to write : " L'écrivain naturaliste estime qu'il n'a pas à se prononcer sur la question d'un Dieu. Il y a une force créatrice, voilà tout " (LES ŒUVRES COMPLÈTES, *le Roman expérimental*, " La république et la littérature, II ", p. 321) ; " On ne nie pas Dieu, on tâche de remonter à lui, en reprenant l'analyse du monde. S'il est au bout, nous le verrons bien, la science nous le dira. Pour le moment, nous le mettons à part, nous ne voulons pas d'un élément surnaturel, d'un axiome extra-humain qui nous troublerait dans nos observations exactes " (*ibid.*, " Lettre à la jeunesse, III ", p. 72).

of 1861 to which reference has been made, a further expression of this change is to be found in letters written in 1864 to his younger friend, Antony Valabrègue, in which Zola expresses a belief that an original contribution to literature may be made through a study of strict reality :

> Je crois qu'il y a dans l'étude de la nature, *telle qu'elle est*, une grande source de poésie ; je crois qu'un poète, né avec un *certain tempérament*, pourra dans les siècles futurs trouver des effets nouveaux en s'adressant à des connaissances exactes [*italics are Zola's*] (1).

In another letter of this period to Valabrègue, Zola expounds at some length, under the title *l'Écran*, a theory that a work of art is the product of the artist's imagination contemplating the world through a more or less transparent screen (2) :

> Toute œuvre d'art est comme une fenêtre ouverte sur la création ; il y a, enchâssé dans l'embrasure de la fenêtre, une sorte d'écran transparent, à travers lequel on aperçoit les objets plus ou moins déformés, souffrant des changements plus ou moins sensibles dans leurs lignes et dans leur couleur. Ces changements tiennent à la nature de l'écran. On n'a plus la création exacte et réelle, mais la création modifiée par le milieu où passe son image (pp. 249-250).

Thus the exact reproduction of reality is impossible in a work of art. There is a certain necessary deformation and falsehood. The extent of this deformation is dependent upon the nature of the " screen ", which, in Zola's analogy, represents the artist's viewpoint or method in observing the world. He then classifies the three principal " screens " — the classic, the romantic, and the realist — according to their degree of truth, and expresses a personal preference for the last :

> Toutes mes sympathies, s'il faut le dire, sont pour l'écran réaliste ; il contente ma raison, et je sens en lui des beautés immenses de solidité et de vérité... je préfère l'écran qui, serrant de plus près la réalité, se contente de mentir juste assez pour me faire sentir un homme dans une image de la creation (pp. 255-256).

His only objection to the realist school is its presumptuous claim to the representation of the exact truth. " C'est là un trop

---

(1) Letter to Valabrègue, 6 July 1864, in Les Œuvres complètes, *Correspondance (1858-1871)*, p. 244.
(2) *Ibid.*, pp. 248-257. This letter, undated in Les Œuvres complètes, is given the date of 18 August 1864 in the Bibliothèque-Charpentier edition of Zola's correspondance (Zola, *Correspondance, les lettres et les arts* (Paris, 1908), pp. 11-23).

grand orgueil. " However thin and transparent the screen which is interposed between the artist and nature, there is always a certain inevitable deformation. But the realist method does yield a greater content of truth. Here, for perhaps the first time, Zola suggests that a high degree of truth be taken as a standard for literature.

Zola soon recognized how well this point of view was suited to his individual needs and talents. Henceforth, he was able to chart a course which would impose the force of his personality on the reading public and lead eventually to the literary fame so ardently desired. Romanticism and idealism were useless to him. Notoriety and success lay in capturing the public interest with attacks on traditional ideas and with the exploitation of new-sounding principles. To his first volume of critical articles (written for the *Salut public de Lyon* during 1865), he gave the provocative title, *Mes haines.* Thereafter, the systematic exploration, analysis and revelation of the truth, however sordid and disgusting it might be, became the vehicle for his ambition. In the following decade, he chose the term " naturalism " to designate the doctrine which served him both as an inspiration and a defense for his creative work — in particular for the series of twenty novels known as the *Rougon-Macquart.* It was through naturalism that he hoped to regenerate the theater, not only by plays of his own, but also by persuading other dramatists to embrace his ideas.

Although the term " naturalism " did not come into current use until the 1870s, the essential principles were developed by Zola between 1865, when he began the series of newspaper articles published the following year in *Mes haines,* and 1868, when he made his first notes for the *Rougon-Macquart.* Two influences contributed to this development : the lesser was that of the new school of painters (known a decade later as the impressionists), from whose work Zola derived certain analogies to literature ; the predominating influence was that of the growing scientific spirit of the age, which engendered in Zola his conception of the writer as a scientist.

The new painters

Zola's interest in painting was stimulated by his intimate friendship with Cézanne. While the latter was in Paris, Zola accompanied him to the workshops of the Batignolle school of young painters, and was introduced to such future impressionists as Pissaro, Renoir, Monet, Degas, Guillemet. Later, in 1866, he met and became a stout defender of Édouard Manet, and during the next few years was an habitué of the café Guerbois in the Grande Rue des Batignolles (now avenue de Clichy) where young painters and writers held weekly reunions (1). Two articles on painting (" Proudhon et Courbet " and " Gustave Doré ") appeared in *Mes haines*. Still more important was the series of articles on the current *salon* which Zola was commissioned to write for *l'Événement* in 1866 (published under the title *Mon salon*), followed in the next year by his study of Édouard Manet which first appeared in the January number of *La Revue du XIXe siècle*. *Mon salon* created a sensation for its attack on traditional methods of painting and for its sharp criticism of the jury (2). Zola's articles on painting enhanced his reputation for advanced ideas and provide his most precise definition of a work of art.

" Ma définition d'une œuvre d'art ", writes Zola in his essay " Proudhon et Courbet ", " serait, si je le formulais : *Une œuvre d'art est un coin de la création vu à travers un tempérament* " (3). He repeats this definition in identical words in his articles " M. H. Taine, artiste " and " Les réalistes du salon " (from *Mon salon*) (4). The definition recognizes two elements in a work of art, as Zola explains in " Le moment artistique " from *Mon salon* :

Il y a selon moi, deux éléments dans une œuvre : l'élément réel, qui est la nature, et l'élément individuel, qui est l'homme.

L'élément réel, la nature, est fixe, toujours le même ; il demeure égal pour tout le monde ; je dirais qu'il peut servir de commune mesure pour toutes les œuvres produites si j'admettais qu'il puisse y avoir une commune mesure.

L'élément individuel, au contraire, l'homme, est variable à l'infini : autant d'œuvres et autant d'esprits différents ; si le tempérament

---

(1) ALEXIS, *ibid.*, p. 71. See also LE BLOND's notes in LES ŒUVRES COMPLÈTES, *Mes haines*, p. 303.

(2) ZOLA's comments on each of the 21 members of the jury, published in *l'Événement*, 30 April 1866, have been omitted from all publications of *Mon salon* in book form. According to John Rewald, Zola explained his omission as follows : " Je crois devoir supprimer cette partie de l'article. On m'a prouvé le peu de fondement de plusieurs détails dont auparavant on m'avait, à différentes reprises, affirmé l'exactitude. L'esprit général devait être vrai ; mais ne sachant où le faux commence, je trouve plus simple d'effacer le tout et de m'en tenir à mes seules opinions en matière d'art " (REWALD, *Cézanne et Zola*, Paris, 1936, p. 52, footnote).

(3) LES ŒUVRES COMPLÈTES, *Mes haines*, p. 24.

(4) *Ibid.*, pp. 176 and 230.

n'existait pas, tous les tableaux devraient être forcément de simples
photographies.

   Donc, une œuvre d'art n'est jamais que la combinaison d'un homme,
élément variable, et de la nature, élément fixe (1).

   He writes to the same effect in his essay, *Édouard Manet* :

   Chaque grand artiste est venu nous donner une traduction nouvelle
   et personnelle de la nature. La réalité est ici l'élément fixe, et les divers
   tempéraments sont les éléments créateurs qui ont donné aux œuvres
   des caractères différents... Et le thème serait toujours la même nature,
   la même réalité, et les variations seraient les façons particulières et
   originales, à l'aide desquelles les artistes auraient rendu la grande
   création de Dieu (2).

   Of these two elements, Zola considers the second to be the
more important.   " Ce que je cherche surtout dans un tableau,
c'est un homme et non pas un tableau... faites vrai, j'applaudis :
faites individuel, j'applaudis plus fort. " Similar statements
characteristic of this period are : " ... l'œuvre ne vit que par
l'originalité.   Il faut que je retrouve un homme dans chaque
œuvre, ou l'œuvre me laisse froid... l'art est la libre expression
d'un cœur et d'une intelligence... il est d'autant plus grand qu'il
est plus personnel " (3).   On the other hand, an artist may, like
Gustave Doré, soar too far from reality and risk repetition of his
inspiration by too frequent reliance on the same dream.   " La
réalité ", Zola warns him, " est une bonne mère qui nourrit ses
enfants d'aliments toujours nouveaux " (4).   The emphasis
which Zola gives in his definition to the word " tempérament "
is a survival of his early romanticism — a survival which was
particularly deep-rooted.   Neither in his own creative work nor
in his later criticisms did he ever wholly abandon this belief in
the importance of the writer's individuality.   Notwithstanding
his doctrine of scientific literature, the objectivity which the
writer, as a scientist, should bring to his task was always qualified, in Zola's opinion, by the subjectivity with which, as an
individual artist, he should reveal his genius.   It was not the
absolute truth, but the highest degree of truth compatible with
art, which Zola put forward as the goal of literature.

   As to the first part of the definition, " un coin de la création ",
it is clear that " création " is identical, in Zola's use of the word,

(1) *Ibid.*, pp. 212-213.
(2) *Ibid.*, p. 255.
(3) *Ibid.*, pp. 240 and 24.
(4) *Ibid.*, p. 71.

with " nature ". The word " nature " appears with considerable frequency in his early essays in contexts which suggest its interchangeability with " création " (1). Similarly, " nature " and " réalité " (as applied to the subject matter of a painting) have the same connotation (2). Zola did not invent the word " naturaliste " or " naturalisme ". As pointed out by Martino in his *le Naturalisme français*, " naturalisme " was, from the XVIth to the XIXth Century, a philosophical term, close to atheism, referring to the system of considering nature as first principle. Subsequently, " naturalisme " was associated with " naturaliste ", which signified a person interested in the productions of nature. The development of the natural sciences in the XIXth Century gave impetus to this later meaning. " Naturaliste " and " naturalisme " were current, moreover, in mid-century art criticism (3). Zola took over a term which was in current use and gave it certain connotations of his own which are worth examining. In connection with painting, some of his first uses of " naturaliste " are to be found in his *salon* published in *l'Événement illustré* in May and June of 1868 (4). This *salon* has recently been reprinted. Zola explains his application of the term " naturaliste " to Édouard Manet in the following passage, where he relates a conversation with Manet while sitting for the latter's portrait of him :

Ce qui m'a étonné moi-même a été la conscience extrême de l'artiste. Souvent, quand il traitait un détail secondaire, je voulais quitter la pose, je lui donnais le mauvais conseil d'inventer.

— Non, me répondait-il, je ne puis rien faire sans la nature. Je ne sais pas inventer. Tant que j'ai voulu peindre d'après des leçons apprises, je n'ai produit rien qui vaille. Si je vaux quelque chose aujourd'hui, c'est à l'interprétation exacte, à l'analyse fidèle que je la dois.

Là est tout son talent. Il est avant tout un naturaliste (5).

Zola's third article of the series is entitled " Les naturalistes " and is devoted entirely to Pissaro, whom Zola has chosen as typical of this group, " qui s'accroît chaque jour ", and which

(1) *Ibid.*, pp. 212, 220, 253, 254.
(2) See *ibid.*, p. 254.
(3) P. MARTINO, *le Naturalisme français (1870-1895)*, Paris, 1923, pp. 2-5.
(4) " Mon salon ", in *l'Evénement illustré*, 1868, issues of 2, 10, 19, 24 May, and 1, 9, 16 June, published 1959 by F. W. J. HEMMINGS and Robert J. NIESS.
(5) *Ibid.*, 10 May 1868.

stands " à la tête du mouvement artistique ". Describing
Pissaro's purpose and method, Zola writes :

> L'artiste n'a souci que de vérité, que de conscience ; il se place
> devant un pan de nature, se donnant pour tâche d'interpréter les
> horizons dans leur largeur sévère, sans chercher à y mettre le moindre
> régal de son invention ; il n'est ni poète ni philosophe, mais simplement
> naturaliste, faiseur de cieux et de terrains. Rêvez si vous voulez, voilà ce
> qu'il a vu... Une telle réalité est plus haute que le rêve (1).

His fifth article, entitled " Les paysagistes ", throws further
light upon his idea of naturalism :

> Le paysage classique est mort, tué par la vie et la vérité. Personne
> n'oserait dire aujourd'hui que la nature a besoin d'être idéalisée, que les
> cieux et les eaux sont vulgaires, et qu'il est nécessaire de rendre les
> horizons harmonieux et corrects, si l'on veut faire de belles œuvres. Nous
> avons accepté le naturalisme sans grande lutte, parce que près d'un
> demi-siècle de littérature et de goût personnel nous avait préparés à
> l'accepter. Plus tard, j'en ai la conviction, la foule admettra les vérités
> du corps humain, les tableaux de figures pris dans le réel exact, comme
> elle a déjà admis les vérités de la campagne, les paysages contenant de
> vraies maisons et de vrais arbres (2).

Zola approves the comparatively new practice of painting
landscapes directly from nature, rather than in the studio (3).
The following passage suggests the " école du plein air " of Zola's
later novel, *l'Œuvre* :

> Nos paysagistes partent dès l'aube, la boîte sur le dos, heureux
> comme des chasseurs qui aiment le plein air. Ils vont s'asseoir n'importe
> où, là-bas à la lisière de la forêt, ici au bord de l'eau, choisissant à peine
> leurs motifs, trouvant partout un horizon vivant...

Servile imitation, however, results merely in " une nature de
convention ". The talented naturalist will impregnate his work
with his own personality :

> Les naturalistes de talent, au contraire, sont des interprètes per-
> sonnels ; ils traduisent les vérités en langages originaux, ils restent
> profondément vrais, tout en gardant leur individualité... la personnalité
> féconde le vrai... un tableau est une œuvre nulle et médiocre, s'il n'est
> pas un coin de la création vu à travers un tempérament.

(1) *Ibid.*, 19 May 1868.
(2) *Ibid.*, 1 June 1868.
(3) According to Rewald, most of the landscapes of Delacroix, Daubigny,
Rousseau, Courbet and Corot had been painted in the studio, and in the case
of Corot, it was precisely those landscapes executed outdoors which Zola
most admired (REWALD, *Cézanne et Zola*, p. 63).

The last article of the series, entitled " La sculpture ", affords an example of the reasoning process through which Zola, seeking a new foundation for his esthetic standards, came to replace his youthful idealism with the scientific spirit of inquiry. It was well for the Greeks, at the dawn of civilization, to be idealists :

Le sculpteur grec est un poète, un rêveur fils de Platon, qui vit dans les gymnases, ayant toujours sous les yeux les membres parfaits des athlètes. S'il connaît la nature, il ne la copie pas, il l'idéalise, n'oubliant jamais qu'il crée des dieux et non des hommes. Une statue est pour lui un poème, un acte de foi, une tendance vers la beauté divine en passant par la beauté humaine (1).

But the modern spirit of inquiry has triumphed over the ideal :

... nous savons d'ailleurs que l'idéal est un mensonge et nous préférons fouiller la science âprement pour découvrir les lois de la réalité...
Il faut... parler notre langue artistique, notre langue contemporaine de réalité et d'analyse...
Je l'ai dit, nous ne sommes plus des croyants, des rêveurs qui se bercent dans un songe de beauté absolue. Nous sommes des savants, des imaginations blasées qui se moquent des dieux, des esprits exacts que touche la seule vérité. Notre épopée est la *Comédie humaine* de Balzac. L'art chez nous est tombé des hauteurs du mensonge dans l'âpre recherche du réel...
Notre civilisation a fait de nous des chirurgiens qui se plaisent à fouiller les vérités de l'homme, et des gourmets blasés qui recherchent l'accent personnel et rare d'un tempérament.

Greater fidelity to reality, on the part of the artist and writer, was only a part of Zola's doctrine of naturalism. The force and motive power of the doctrine was derived from the scientific spirit of the epoch. Zola, searching for a new weapon with which to open a breach for himself in the citadel of letters, drew upon the arsenal of science which furnished him with the inspiration, method and justification for his future labors.

The scientific spirit

It is not surprising, in view of the strength of Zola's early idealism, that he experienced certain misgivings before his definitive " conversion " to science. As a youth, he had written, as might be expected : " La science n'est pas mon affaire : c'est

(1) *L'Evénement illustré*, 16 June 1868.

un lourd fardeau, très difficile à mettre sur les épaules (1). ''
Five years later, he is no longer a romantic idealist and has
recognized the impact of science on his age, but he still feels a
certain trepidation in regard to the new force :

> Nous sommes au seuil d'un siècle de science et de réalité et nous
> chancelons, par instants, comme des hommes ivres, devant la grande
> lueur qui se lève en face de nous (2).

And in several articles of *Mes haines*, he has expressed the
growing pains and restlessness which scientific progress has
brought to the epoch. He writes, for example, in the article
'' La littérature et la gymnastique '' :

> Nous sommes malades, cela est bien certain, malades de progrès...
> L'humanité glisse, prise de vertige, sur la pente raide de la science ;
> elle a mordu à la pomme, et elle veut tout savoir. Ce qui nous tue, ce qui
> nous maigrit, c'est que nous devenons savants, c'est que les problèmes
> sociaux et divins vont recevoir leur solution un de ces jours. Nous
> allons voir Dieu, nous allons voir la vérité, et vous pensez alors quelle
> impatience nous tient, quelle hâte fébrile nous mettons à vivre et à
> mourir. Nous voudrions devancer les temps, nous faisons bon marché
> de nos sueurs, nous brisons le corps par la tension de l'esprit. Tout notre
> siècle est là (3).

It was undoubtedly the influence of Taine which inspired
Zola to make use of scientific laws and methods in the creation of
literature. However, Taine's system of *race, milieu, moment*
brought Zola face to face with the problem of reconciling individuality and subjectivity in art with a true and objective reproduction of creation. The problem is implicit in his definition
of a work of art as a corner of creation (the objective content)
seen through an individual temperament (the subjective content).
Zola's early romanticism and his association with the impressionist painters led him to stress the rôle of the individual artist.
Taine oriented him in the contrary direction, towards scientific
and, indeed, determinist objectivity.

Zola's first article on Taine, which appears in *Mes haines*,
reveals the contradictory ferments in the mind of the young
writer. The article contains pages of protest against the
mechanical rigidity of Taine's system and against the limited

---

(1) Letter to Baille, 2 June 1860, in LES ŒUVRES COMPLÈTES. *Correspondance (1858-1871)*, p. 86.
(2) LES ŒUVRES COMPLÈTES, *Mes haines*, Préface, p. 11.
(3) *Ibid.*, pp. 47-48.

rôle assigned to the individual writer and artist. For example, we read :

... il y a dans le système un oubli volontaire qui me blesse. M. Taine évite de parler de la personnalité... Il est emporté, malgré lui, par les nécessités de sa pensée, qui va toujours se resserrant, négligeant de plus en plus l'individu, tâchant d'expliquer l'artiste par les seules influences étrangères. Tant qu'il laissera un peu d'humanité dans le poète et dans le peintre, un peu de libre arbitre et d'élan personnel, il ne pourra le réduire entièrement à des règles mathématiques. L'idéal de la loi qu'il dit avoir trouvée serait de s'appliquer à des machines... Une œuvre, pour moi, est un homme ; je veux retrouver dans cette œuvre un tempérament, un accent particulier et unique... Pour les œuvres collectives, le système de M. Taine fonctionne avec assez de régularité ; là, en effet, l'œuvre est évidemment le produit de la race, du milieu, du moment historique ; il n'y a pas d'éléments individuels qui viennent déranger les rouages de la machine. Mais dès qu'on introduit la personnalité, l'élan humain libre et déréglé, tous les ressorts crient et le mécanisme se détraque (1).

But in the conclusion of this article, Zola affirms his own belief in the inevitability of social and scientific progress :

La nouvelle science, faite de physiologie et de psychologie, d'histoire et de philosophie, a eu son épanouissement en lui. Il est, dans notre époque, la manifestation la plus haute de nos curiosités, de nos besoins d'analyse, de nos désirs de réduire toutes choses au pur mécanisme des sciences mathématiques... Mais il y a protestation en lui, protestation de l'homme faible, écrasé par l'avenir de fer qu'il se prépare ; il aspire à la force ; il regarde en arrière ; il regrette presque ces temps où l'homme seul était fort, où la puissance du corps décidait de la royauté. S'il regardait en avant, il verrait l'homme de plus en plus diminué, l'individu s'effaçant et se perdant dans la masse, la société arrivant à la paix et au bonheur, en faisant travailler la matière pour elle. Toute son organisation d'artiste répugne à cette vue de communauté et de fraternité. Il est là, entre un passé qu'il aime et un avenir qu'il n'ose envisager, affaibli déjà et regrettant la force, obéissant malgré lui à cette folie de notre siècle, de tout savoir, de tout réduire en équations, de tout soumettre aux puissants agents mécaniques qui transformeront le monde (2).

The budding influence of Taine upon Zola came into full flower a few years later with Zola's creation of *Thérèse Raquin* (the novel) and with his conception of the *Rougon-Macquart*

(1) *Ibid.*, pp. 172-174.
(2) *Ibid.*, pp. 177-178.

series of novels.   In his preface of 1868 to the second edition of
Thérèse Raquin, Zola sets forth a doctrine of rigid determinism
and mechanization which is analogous to those very principles
of Taine denounced in *Mes haines* :

> J'ai choisi des personnages souverainement dominés par leurs nerfs
> et leur sang, dépourvus de libre arbitre, entraînés à chaque acte de
> leur vie par les fatalités de leur chair... On commence, j'espère, à
> comprendre que mon but a été un but scientifique avant tout... je me
> suis perdu dans la copie exacte et minutieuse de la vie, me donnant tout
> entier à l'analyse du mécanisme humain... A coup sûr, l'analyse scienti-
> fique que j'ai tenté d'appliquer dans *Thérèse Raquin* ne les surprendrait
> pas ; ils y retrouveraient la méthode moderne, l'outil d'enquête univer-
> selle dont le siècle se sert avec tant de fièvre pour trouer l'avenir.
> Quelles que dussent être leurs conclusions, ils admettraient mon point
> de départ, l'étude du tempérament et des modifications profondes de
> l'organisme sous la pression des milieux et des circonstances (1).

And Taine's influence is seen in Zola's preparatory notes
and plan for the *Rougon-Macquart* and in his preface of 1871
to *la Fortune des Rougon* :

> Donc deux éléments : 1. L'élément purement humain, l'élément
> physiologique, l'étude scientifique d'une famille avec les enchaînements
> et les fatalités de la descendance ; 2. Effet du moment moderne sur
> cette famille, son détraquement par les fièvres de l'époque, action
> sociale et physique des milieux.
> C'est dire que cette famille, née dans un autre temps, dans un autre
> milieu, ne se serait pas comportée de la même façon (2).
> D'un côté, je montrerais les ressorts cachés, les fils qui font mouvoir
> le pantin humain ; de l'autre, je raconterais les faits et gestes de ce
> pantin. Le cœur et le cerveau mis à nu, je démontrerais aisément
> comment et pourquoi le cœur et le cerveau ont agi de certaines façons
> déterminées, et n'ont pu agir autrement... Par l'observation, par les
> nouvelles méthodes scientifiques, j'arrive à débrouiller le fil qui conduit
> mathématiquement d'un homme à un autre (3).
> L'hérédité a ses lois, comme la pesanteur.
> Je tâcherai de trouver et de suivre, en résolvant la double question
> des tempéraments et des milieux, le fil qui conduit mathématiquement
> d'un homme à un autre homme...
> Les *Rougon-Macquart*, le groupe, la famille que je me propose d'étu-
> dier, a pour caractéristique le débordement des appétits, le large soulè-

---

(1) LES ŒUVRES COMPLÈTES, *Thérèse Raquin*, pp. VII-XV.
(2) LES ŒUVRES COMPLÈTES, *la Fortune des Rougon*, " Notes et commentaires ", p. 354. This note by Zola was probably written in 1868 or 1869.
(3) *Ibid.*, p. 358. This is an excerpt from the plan which Zola submitted
to his editor, Lacroix.

vement de notre âge, qui se rue aux jouissances. Physiologiquement, ils sont la lente succession des accidents nerveux et sanguins qui se déclarent dans une race, à la suite d'une première lésion organique, et qui déterminent selon les milieux, chez chacun des individus de cette race, les sentiments, les désirs, les passions, toutes les manifestations humaines, naturelles et instinctives, dont les produits prennent les noms convenus de vertus et de vices (1).

It is clear that during the two years from 1865 (when most of the articles of *Mes haines* were written) to 1867 (date of *Thérèse Raquin*) Zola made up his mind to base his own creative work upon scientific methods of observation. It was possible, he believed, to formulate laws of human conduct, based on the observation, analysis, and classification of facts, in the same way that a scientist proceeds to formulate laws of the natural sciences. This process was naturalism, and it is probable that Taine was the first person to whom Zola applies the term " naturaliste " (2). Writing of him in July, 1866 :

Il est le naturaliste du monde moral. Il croit qu'on peut arriver à classer les faits de la vie intellectuelle comme on classe les faits de la vie physique (3).

And a month later :

M. Taine appartient au petit groupe des novateurs qui cherchent à introduire dans l'étude des faits moraux l'observation pure, l'analyse exacte employées dans celle des faits physiques. Il y a en lui un philosophe naturaliste qui déclare que le monde intellectuel est soumis à des lois comme le monde matériel, et qu'il s'agit avant tout de trouver ces lois, si l'on veut avancer sûrement dans la connaissance de l'esprit humain (4).

Zola's statement in his preface to *la Fortune des Rougon* : " L'hérédité a ses lois, comme la pesanteur " clearly was inspired

(1) *Ibid.*, *la Fortune des Rougon*, Préface, pp. 7-8.
(2) The first use by Zola which I have found of either " naturaliste " or " naturalisme " is in his column, " Livres d'aujourd'hui et de demain ", in *l'Evénement*, 15 July 1866, where, referring to François Ponsard, he writes : " ... nous pouvons tout au moins indiquer rapidement quel a été le rôle de ce déclassé classique dans nos temps d'anarchie et de naturalisme ".
F. W. J. HEMMINGS, in the article " The origin of the terms, *Naturalisme*, *naturaliste* ", *French Studies*, vol. 8 (1954), pp. 109-121, at p. 110, cites an early use of the term " naturalistes " in ZOLA's article " les Merveilles de la Céramic ", in *l'Evénement*, 22 July 1866.
(3) " Livres d'aujourd'hui et de demain ", in *l'Evénement*, 25 July 1866. HEMMINGS, in the above-cited article, points out that for the first time Zola here applies the word " naturaliste " to a fellow-writer (*French Studies*, vol. 8, at p. 112).
(4) " Marbres et plâtres : M. H. Taine ", in *l'Evénement*, 19 August 1866.

by Taine. And for the second edition of *Thérèse Raquin*, he used as an epigraph Taine's celebrated pronouncement : " Le vice et la vertu sont des produits comme le vitriol et le sucre. " Zola used the term " naturaliste " much less frequently in this early period of his career than he was to do in the 1870s. Some other early uses of the term may be found in his preface to *Thérèse Raquin*, where he speaks of " la critique méthodique et naturaliste qui a renouvelé les sciences, l'histoire et la littérature ", and of " le groupe d'écrivains naturalistes auquel j'ai l'honneur d'appartenir " (1) ; in his preparatory notes to the *Rougon-Macquart*, where he says, " Ma grande affaire est d'être purement naturaliste, purement physiologiste " (2) ; and in a newspaper article on Flaubert, where Zola writes : " Il y a chez lui une étonnante dualité... On le sent toujours prêt à bondir d'un élan lyrique, à se perdre dans les cieux agrandis de la poésie. Et il reste à terre ; sa raison d'homme, sa volonté d'analyste exact l'attache à l'étude des infiniment petits... Un poète changé en naturaliste... (3). "

Zola's application of scientific methods and documentation to literature was not wholly original. Documentary methods had already been employed by Balzac, Flaubert, and the Goncourt brothers (4). Zola's originality (in respect to the use of science) lay in the thoroughness of his documentation and, more specifically, in his choice of medical science as the particular inspiration for much of his literary production. He appears to have been fascinated by medical works. " Les livres de médecine m'attirent ", he writes in his column in *l'Événement*. " Je n'ai aucune autorité pour en parler, je ne les comprends même pas toujours, mais je les parcours et je les juge quand même, par plaisir (5). " He was profoundly affected by the Goncourts' *Germinie Lacerteux*, and it is quite possible that this novel impregnated his mind with the possibilities of exploiting medical themes in literature. In the article of *Mes haines* which he devoted to this novel, he defends the medical aspect of the work,

---

(1) LES ŒUVRES COMPLÈTES, *Thérèse Raquin*, p. xiv.
(2) LES ŒUVRES COMPLÈTES, *la Fortune des Rougon*, " Notes et commentaires ", p. 357. This excerpt is taken from a manuscript by Zola entitled " Différences entre Balzac et moi ".
(3) " Causerie ", in *la Tribune*, 28 November 1869.
(4) See Pierre MARTINO, *le Roman réaliste sous le second Empire* (Paris, 1913), pp. 235 et seq. ; and an article by G. LOTE, " la Doctrine et la méthode naturalistes d'après Emile Zola ", in *Zeitschrift für französische Sprache und Literatur*, vol. 51 (1928), pp. 193-224 and 389-418, at p. 411.
(5) " Livres d'aujourd'hui et de demain ", in *l'Evénement*, 18 June 1866.

although in 1865 he is not yet as convinced of the value of medical analysis as he will be a year or two later :

Un reproche fondé, qui peut être fait à *Germinie Lacerteux*, est celui d'être un roman médical, un cas curieux d'hystérie. Mais je ne pense pas que les auteurs désavouent un instant la grande place qu'ils ont accordée à l'observation physiologique. Certainement leur héroïne est malade, malade de cœur et malade de corps ; ils ont tout à la fois étudié la maladie de son corps et celle de son cœur. Où est le mal, je vous prie ? Un roman n'est-il pas la peinture de la vie, et ce pauvre corps est-il si damnable pour qu'on ne s'occupe pas de lui (1) ?

The following year, reviewing a novel by Dumas *fils*, *l'Affaire Clemenceau*, Zola enthusiastically compares Dumas to an anatomist and surgeon :

Il est l'œuvre d'un anatomiste impitoyable qui fouille courageusement en pleine fange humaine... M. Dumas fils a mis en présence deux natures tarées, deux êtres qui ont en eux le vice à l'état natif et il n'a reculé devant aucunes plaies, il a mis à nu toutes les hontes et toutes les misères.

Le roman n'est pas autre chose que l'étude exacte d'Ina et de Pierre, de deux créatures jetées dans le mal par le sang et par le milieu social...

Le talent de l'auteur est un talent froid et sobre, emportant le morceau. L'écrivain est un chirurgien qui, pour aller jusqu'au cœur, coupe dans la chair d'une main paisible et ferme, sans fièvre aucune. Il garde son sang-froid tant que dure l'opération. Il scie et taille avec un plaisir tranquille. Il n'a d'ailleurs ni dégoût ni enthousiasme, et il semble remuer toute cette pourriture humaine avec le calme du médecin qui connaît la toute-puissance de la mort (2).

One may read into this passage an expression of Zola's own literary ambitions. In an article on Sainte-Beuve, he stresses the importance of Sainte-Beuve's early medical studies upon his later work as critic :

En choisissant pour métier la médecine, il n'avait pas prévu qu'il prenait un chemin de traverse qui le ramènerait à la littérature. Dès qu'il eut le scalpel à la main, il éprouva toutes les curiosités de l'analyste ; il aima d'amour le cadavre humain et en fouilla les chairs, en chercha les ressorts avec passion... Voilà comme quoi M. Sainte-Beuve, qui a failli être poète, est devenu critique, sans en avoir conscience, en se faisant médecin et anatomiste. Selon moi, il travaillait déjà aux Causeries du lundi, lorsqu'il était interne à Saint-Louis... il se dit que, puisqu'il a étudié l'anatomie, il doit se servir de la plume comme d'un scalpel...

(1) LES ŒUVRES COMPLÈTES, *Mes haines*, pp. 65-66.
(2) " Livres d'aujourd'hui et de demain ", in *l'Evénement*, 29 June 1866.

Il a appliqué, en critique, la méthode anatomique dont il avait appris l'usage pendant ses études médicales. Il dissèque les intelligences, il interroge l'homme pour connaître l'œuvre, et il interroge le milieu pour connaître l'homme (1).

In his early novel, *Madeleine Férat*, Zola made use of a most curious principle of medical " science " which he encountered in Michelet's *l'Amour*, one of the favorite books of his youth (2). Michelet advanced as scientific fact — citing as his authority a treatise on heredity by Dr. Prosper Lucas (3) — the startling proposition that a woman, once impregnated, carries the seeds of this first impregnation for an indefinite period of time, and gives to subsequent children, whenever and by whomever conceived, the hereditary traits of her first husband or lover (4). This was Zola's first application of a " scientific " principle to literature. Although this particular application is unimportant in itself, it is a significant illustration of his early penchant for science, and foreshadows his conception of the *Rougon-Macquart*. It was Michelet's book which drew Zola's attention to Dr. Lucas' treatise, upon which Zola relied for the hereditary aspects of his great series of novels. A modern critic even suggests that Taine's influence upon Zola might not have been so great had not the latter been to some extent prepared for it by Michelet (5). Certainly Zola, as a young idealist, must have felt a tremor upon reading these lines by one of the favorite authors of his youth :

La science est la maîtresse du monde. Elle règne, sans même avoir besoin de commander. L'église et la loi doivent s'informer de ses arrêts, et se reformer d'après elle (6).

---

(1) " Marbres et plâtres : M. Sainte-Beuve ", in *le Figaro*, 9 February 1867.
(2) J. MICHELET, *l'Amour*, Paris, 1859 (4ᵉ éd.). For Zola's enthusiastic comments on this book, see his letter to Baille of 14 February 1860 (LES ŒUVRES COMPLÈTES *(1858-1871)*, p. 36).
(3) Dʳ Prosper LUCAS, *Traité philosophique et physiologique de l'hérédité naturelle dans les états de santé et de maladie du système nerveux*, 2 vol., Paris, 1847 and 1850.
(4) MICHELET, *ibid.*, pp. 17, 325-326 and 449-452. Michelet appears to have misinterpreted Dr. Lucas. An examination of the relevant pages of the *Traité... de l'hérédité naturelle* (vol. II, pp. 53-65) discloses that the worthy doctor, after examining the effects of impregnation on butterflies, fleas, hens, and other lower animals, placed considerable doubt upon the extension of the principle to the higher animals and to mankind. At least he reached no positive conclusions. Michelet, however, applies the principle of " impregna-tion " to the human species in categorical terms, citing Lucas as his authority.
(5) Marcel CRESSOT, " Zola et Michelet ", in *Revue d'Histoire littéraire de la France*, 35ᵉ année, 1928, pp. 382-389, at p. 388. See also F. W. J. HEMMINGS, *Emile Zola*, p. 21.
(6) MICHELET, *ibid.*, p. 439.

For his first important novel, *Thérèse Raquin*, Zola claimed a scientific purpose and relied upon medical analogies to defend the work. " Mon but ", he writes in a preface to the second edition, " a été un but scientifique avant tout... j'ai montré les troubles profonds d'une nature sanguine au contact d'une nature nerveuse... chaque chapitre est l'étude d'un cas curieux de physiologie... J'ai simplement fait sur deux corps vivants le travail analytique que les chirurgiens font sur des cadavres (1). " His application of medical science to literature reached its culmination in his conception of the *Rougon-Macquart* series of novels, which was to be " l'Histoire naturelle et sociale d'une famille sous le Second Empire " (2). The plan submitted to his editor shows that the series was based upon two main ideas : a study of hereditary and physiological influences upon the members of a family ; and a study of society during the *Second Empire* (3). According to his contemporary biographer, Paul Alexis, Zola spent eight months in 1868-1869 working on this plan, making almost daily visits to the *Bibliothèque impériale*, where he steeped himself in scientific works and took voluminous notes (4). He consulted studies by Letourneau, Berthelot and Darwin, as well as the treatise on heredity by Dr. Lucas (5). With this great project under way, Zola was thoroughly committed to the principle of observing society in the manner of a scientist.

Conclusions

Two major influences contributed to the body of esthetic principles which Zola came to call naturalism. From the influence of the impressionist painters came the definition of a work of art as " un coin de la création vu à travers un tempérament ". From Taine and positivist science came the belief that literature should portray the inter-action of human beings

(1) LES ŒUVRES COMPLÈTES, *Thérèse Raquin*, p. IX.
(2) LES ŒUVRES COMPLÈTES, *la Fortune des Rougon*, Préface, p. 9. This was the first novel of the series. According to the editor of LES ŒUVRES COMPLÈTES (*la Fortune des Rougon*, p. 363), it was completed in May of 1869. Publication was begun serially the following year in *le Siècle* and interrupted by the Franco-Prussian war. The first book edition of the novel was in 1871.
(3) *Ibid.*, " Notes et commentaires ", pp. 357-358.
(4) ALEXIS, *Emile Zola, notes d'un ami*, pp. 85-86.
(5) For the scientific sources used by ZOLA in preparation for the *Rougon-Macquart*, see, in addition to ALEXIS : MARTINO, *le Roman réaliste sous le second Empire*, pp. 268-269 ; the same author's *le Naturalisme français (1870-1895)*, pp. 39-45 ; and DOUCET, *l'Esthétique d'Emile Zola et son application à la critique*, pp. 123 and 141-147.

and environment working upon each other according to physiological and sociological laws which, through scientific methods
of observation, analysis and classification, could be and should
be discovered by the writer. Zola's doctrine required the
presence of both elements in a literary work : the subjectivity
of an individual mind, and the objectivity of a scientist. The
perfect conciliation of these mutually contradictory elements
was of course impossible. Usually, Zola himself recognized that
a certain deformation of the truth was inevitable in a work of
art. But there were occasions during his career when he abused
his system, and claimed scientific accuracy for the literary products of naturalism (1).

As a working theory, Zola's doctrine was of immense practical
value. In offering himself as a scientist undertaking a study of
society, Zola provided himself with a justification for breaking
down conventions and taboos relating to sex, society, and the
portrayal of unpleasant subjects. Naturalism was partly a
mission to open the eyes of the public to a greater measure of
truth, and partly a defense against charges of indecency. Fortified with this doctrine, Zola was able to enlarge the scope of the
novel and to extend realism to wider horizons than had been
attained by Balzac, Flaubert and de Goncourt. At the same
time, his system was flexible enough to allow him great latitude
as a subjective artist. He was free to express his individuality
without violating his principles. The many romantic and lyric
traits of his novels are in full accord with his precept of observing
nature " à travers un tempérament ". The flexibility of Zola's
doctrine applied also to his standards of criticism. The merit
of a work — novel, play or painting — was dependent upon its
objective fidelity to life and upon the subjective originality and
individuality of the artist.

Zola succeeded in liberalizing the novel. His campaign in
the theater was an effort to extend his principles to the stage.

---

(1) See my comments on ZOLA's article *le Roman naturaliste, infra,*
Chapter III.

CHAPTER II

PLAYS OF THE NATURALIST PERIOD
BY ZOLA ALONE

Introduction. — Early theatrical criticisms. — *Madeleine.* — *Thérèse Raquin.* — *Les Héritiers Rabourdin.* — *Le Bouton de Rose.* — *Renée.* — Conclusions.

Introduction

Zola's interest in the drama goes back to his schooldays at Aix, where, stimulated by romantic melodramas of the local theater, he began a verse comedy of his own, *Enfoncé le pion!* when he was perhaps 16 (1). This play was finished in Paris some two years later (2), as well as two other short verse plays written while Zola was attending the *lycée Saint-Louis* in Paris : *Perrette,* a *proverbe* based on La Fontaine's *la Laitière et le Pot au lait* ; and *Il faut hurler avec les loups* (3). During this period, Zola also drew up plans for plays which remained uncompleted : *Rollon l'archer, Annibal à Capoue, la Mascarade* (4). None of these early efforts were played or published.

Zola was far from stage-struck, however, when he arrived in Paris. During his first few years in the capital, he seldom

---

(1) ALEXIS, *Emile Zola, notes d'un ami,* pp. 25, 31, and 130.
(2) So stated by Zola in his letter to Cézanne 14 June 1858, LES ŒUVRES COMPLÈTES, *Correspondance (1858-1871),* p. 9. Cézanne shared Zola's interest in playwriting. He wrote to Zola a month later : " J'ai conçu l'idée d'un drame en 5 actes que nous intitulerons (toi et moi) : *Henry VIII d'Angleterre* ! Nous ferons ça ensemble, aux vacances. " Paul CÉZANNE, *Correspondance, recueillie, annotée et préfacée par John Rewald* (Paris, 1937), p. 37.
(3) ALEXIS, *ibid.,* p. 131. ZOLA refers to *Perrette* in letters to Cézanne and Baille, LES ŒUVRES COMPLÈTES, *Correspondance (1858-1871),* pp. 75, 170 and 215.
(4) ALEXIS, *ibid.,* p. 130. Denise LE BLOND-ZOLA, " Zola et Cézanne ", in *Mercure de France,* vol. 225 (1931), pp. 39-58, at p. 45. (The author of this article is Zola's daughter.)

went to the theater, abstaining, perhaps, for lack of funds rather than of interest. " Parfois je vais dans un théâtre ", he writes Baille in May, 1860, and a few months later, speaking of his difficulty in finding his proper means of expression, he concludes that he is unsuited to the drama : " ... mon esprit ne se prête pas à ce genre ; ce n'est donc pas le moyen que je peux choisir ". Two years later, he would like to be a pupil of Molière, but feels that he should wait another six or eight years before writing for the theater : " ... plus je vais et plus Molière devient mon maître ; le soleil, la lune, les fleurs, etc., c'est fort beau, mais une pensée vraie dite sans emphase a bien son mérite. Je crois décidément que je tourne au vers comique ; je travaillerai sans doute pour le théâtre, mais je ne veux rien écrire pour la scène avant vingt-huit ou trente ans " (1). These first years in Paris, while Zola was struggling for a chance to demonstrate the talent of which he felt himself capable, were among the most discouraging of his life. The turn in his fortunes came with the publication of his first book, *Contes à Ninon*, in 1864, followed in the next year by *la Confession de Claude* and by regular newspaper assignments for the *Petit Journal* and the *Salut public* (of Lyon) (2). By 1865, his interest in the theater had revived. A one-act comedy, *la Laide*, written originally in verse and turned subsequently into prose, was rejected by the *Odéon* and remains unpublished and unproduced (3). In the same year 1865 (4), Zola wrote his short 3-act drama *Madeleine*, which, in date of composition, was the first of his produced plays, although the actual production did not take place until 1889.

The published plays which are wholly of Zola's authorship (5) comprise two groups : 1) five plays of his naturalist period written or produced between 1865 and 1887 ; 2) six operatic librettos written in lyric prose during the last decade of his life, of which three were produced in Paris with music by Alfred Bruneau (6). In addition, Zola collaborated to a greater or lesser extent upon

---

(1) Letters to Baille 14 May and 10 August 1860, and 18 September 1862, in LES ŒUVRES COMPLÈTES, *Correspondance (1858-1872)*, at pp. 79, 158, and 228.
(2) See his letter to Antony Valabrègue 6 February 1865, *ibid.*, p. 265.
(3) ALEXIS, *ibid.*, pp. 76-77.
(4) According to ALEXIS, *ibid.*, p. 77.
(5) These plays and these plays only, are published in LES ŒUVRES COMPLÈTES, *Théâtre*, vol. I and II.
(6) After Zola's death, BRUNEAU adapted three other works of Zola to the stage, writing both words and music, to wit : *Naïs Micoulin* (1907, théâtre de Monte-Carlo), *la Faute de l'abbé Mouret* (1907, l'Odéon), and *les Quatre Journées* (1916, Opéra-Comique).

a number of plays adapted to the stage from his novels and stories. The most important of these adaptations are a group of five plays upon which he worked in collaboration with William Busnach between 1877 and 1888.

Before discussing Zola's five plays of his naturalist period, it will be helpful to examine his early opinions of the theater as expressed in occasional theatrical criticisms during the years 1865-1872 (1).

Early theatrical criticisms

A minor *querelle* between two celebrated writers provided the occasion for Zola's first remarks on the theater, written for a newspaper in June and September 1865 and reprinted in *Mes haines* under the title " Le supplice d'une femme et les deux sœurs ". Émile de Girardin (2) had written a play, *le Supplice d'une femme*, which, because of his high position in the newspaper world, was read at once by the *Théâtre-Français*. The need of a collaborator was manifest, and the services were secured of Alexandre Dumas *fils* (3) : The play opened in April 1865 and was an immediate success, but neither author chose to acknowledge his collaboration in the theater program — Dumas because his contract with the *Gymnase* prevented him from signing his name to productions at another theater, de Girardin because he felt that the play had been distorted and was no longer his own. The play dealt with the problem of a wife who, though loving her husband, had given birth to another man's child through a single act of infidelity. While Dumas made many revisions throughout the play, the principal point of disagreement was in the solution of the problem. De Girardin wanted the wife forgiven, whereas Dumas' husband keeps the child and sends the wife away, leaving open the possibility of an eventual reconciliation. Both authors published mutual accusations of bad faith. In his articles on the subject, Zola considers only the contrasting points of view of Dumas and de Girardin, and leaves

---

(1) For an account and analysis of Zola's journalistic output during these years, see the following articles : L. W. TANCOCK, " Some early critical work of Emile Zola : Livres d'aujourd'hui et de demain ", in *The Modern Language Review*, vol. XLII, 1947, pp. 43-57 ; F. W. J. HEMMINGS, " Zola on the Staff of Le Gaulois ", in *The Modern Language Review*, vol. L, Jan. 1955, pp. 25-29 ; HEMMINGS, " Zola's Apprenticeship to Journalism (1865-1870) ", in *PMLA*, vol. 71, June 1956, pp. 340-354. And see *Zola journaliste*, by Henri MITTERAND.
(2) Emile de GIRARDIN, 1806-1881. Liberal publisher and writer, founder of *la Presse*, the first low-priced political newspaper in France.
(3) Alexandre DUMAS *fils*, 1824-1895.

aside any effort to evaluate the slight merits of the play itself (1). An impartial analysis of the documents in the *querelle* yields the conclusion that Dumas had the better of the argument (2). Zola, however, was not impartial. He must have seen in de Girardin's efforts to write for the stage a situation analogous to his own — that of a writer ignorant of stage conventions, or indifferent to them, attempting to bring to the theater his vision of the truth. It is possible, too, that Zola was influenced by material considerations. He was dependent upon newspaper articles for his livelihood, and may have felt that he would earn valuable patronage by flattering the influential journalist. At all events, he embraced wholeheartedly the cause of de Girardin :

> Voici tout le procès, tel que je le comprends : d'un côté, un novateur, un penseur qui n'a pas l'expérience des planches et qui fait une tentative pour y porter la vérité brutale et implacable, le drame de la vie avec tous ses développements et toutes ses audaces ; de l'autre côté, un auteur dramatique de mérite, un maître qui a remporté de grands succès, un homme habile et expérimenté, qui déclare que la tentative est maladroite, que la vérité brutale et implacable est impossible au théâtre et qu'on ne saurait y jouer le drame de la vie dans sa réalité. Je le déclare, avant tout, je suis *a priori* pour le penseur, le novateur ; mon instinct me pousse à applaudir les esprits avides de franchise (3).

He then pleads for the application to the stage of that zest of analysis and psychology which is currently producing a new generation of novelist. In the paste-board world of the theater, there is too much reliance on conventions, with the result that the public writes the plays. The truth is softened and made flattering. A sort of foolish timidity pervades a group of men and women gathered together in an audience, imbuing them with an indefinable sense of shame and a need of watching the triumph

---

(1) The documents in the case are : de GIRARDIN's prefaces to his plays *le Supplice d'une femme* and *les Deux Sœurs* (both published by Michel Lévy Frères, Paris, 1865) ; DUMAS' booklet, *Histoire du supplice d'une femme*, first published in 1865, reprinted among DUMAS' collected works in *Entractes*, vol. II, pp. 1-126. *Le Supplice d'une femme* is printed also among DUMAS' collected works in vol. I of *Théâtre des autres*, but without de GIRARDIN's preface. Instead, there is a short preface by Dumas dated March 1894, from which it appears that his quarrel with de Girardin was of short duration and that their cordial relations were resumed two or three years later. For further references to *le Supplice d'une femme*, see also DUMAS' general preface at pp. I-XII of *Théâtre des autres*, I.

(2) Dumas defends himself on the ground that de Girardin's play was hopelessly inept, and that (contrary to de Girardin's claim) the latter had consented to the revisions.

(3) LES ŒUVRES COMPLÈTES, *Mes haines*, p. 128.

of virtue and nobility. The reader of a novel may, in the solitude of his study, accept scenes of brutal truth against which, as a member of an audience, he would protest if they were shown on a stage. " L'expérience de la scène consiste à savoir mentir, à savoir donner au public le faux qui lui plaît (1). " Zola shows himself fully aware of the practical value of yielding to convention in the interest of success, but he does not despair of the public's eventual willingness to place truth above convention and banality. When that day comes, the clever technicians of the stage will no longer be entitled to lay the blame for conventionality on the public. " On leur répondra que ce sont eux qui maintiennent le théâtre dans la routine, en se laissant, crainte d'une chute, guider par le public au lieu de le guider (2)."

A few months after the opening of *le Supplice d'une femme*, de Girardin's *les Deux Sœurs*, which he had written alone, was presented, and failed (3). Zola carefully refrains from discussing the play on its merits. But, again seeming to associate his own situation with that of de Girardin, he sympathizes with this author who, without theatrical experience, has dared enter the hallowed precincts of the stage. " Mais le grand crime se trouvait surtout dans la rare imprudence d'un journaliste, d'un simple publiciste, qui se permettait de faire une pièce de théâtre, cette chose terrible (4). " It is probable that Zola ascribes to de Girardin some of his own ambitions in the theater : " ... l'étude franche du cœur humain... le drame vivant qui naît des fatalités sociales... la moralisation indirecte par l'exposé logique et puissant de la vérité... le théâtre agrandi, le théâtre doté de mille sujets nouveaux ". The theater must be renovated, and to that end, there should be new efforts at originality and new subjects. The discovery of new subjects and ideas, expressed frankly on the stage, should weigh as heavily in critical esteem as the

(1) *Ibid.*, pp. 129-130.
(2) *Ibid.*, p. 131.
(3) According to de Girardin's preface, this was the second of a trilogy of thesis plays relating to the marriage relationship. In *les Deux Sœurs*, he considers the problem of the duel. In the acted version, ending with Act III, the husband challenges his wife's lover to a duel. The lover refuses to defend himself, on the ground that since he is at fault it would be dishonorable to do so. The husband threatens to kill both the lover and himself. The lover persists in his refusal to fight, and the husband carries out his threat. In Act IV (deleted from the production), it is discovered that the lover has been only wounded. He is tried for murder of the husband, and acquitted. The wife, however, dies of grief or shock at the end of the play.
(4) *Mes haines*, p. 134.

technique of the stage (1). Courage and sincerity should be as important as skillful manipulation of scenes and characters.

Zola made use of the two plays of de Girardin to set forth certain ideas of his own, without finding any particular merit in the plays themselves. Quite otherwise was his admiration for the Goncourts' *Henriette Maréchal*, which raised a storm of protest when it was produced in December 1865. In a letter thanking the brothers Goncourt for a seat to their play, he wrote them :

J'ai vécu toute une vie de luttes et de passion et je ne saurais trop vous féliciter de ce drame exquis et terrible, trivial et délicat, qui a été pour moi l'image de cette vie moderne que nous vivons désespérément (2).

Among the many book reviews which Zola wrote for various newspapers from 1866 on, may be found a few relating to published plays and to stage productions. He admires the heart-felt sincerity of a Breton Middle Age mystery, *le Grand Mystère de Jésus*, recently published in a second edition, but doubts that a modern audience could be found for the play. " Il a passé un vent terrible sur la France qui a emporté toute la foi et toute la naïveté nécessaires (3). "

Taine's theory of *race, milieu, moment* was used to explain the failure of Ponsard (4) to revive more than briefly the classic form of Corneille and Racine :

Chaque époque, chaque société a sa littérature distincte qui naît naturellement des nouvelles mœurs et des nouvelles intelligences.

Toute l'histoire littéraire est là pour prouver l'entière liberté des manifestations humaines et l'éternel changement des formes du beau. Il n'y a pas de cadre à imposer à l'artiste, pas de règles, pas de méthode. Les œuvres vraiment grandes, vraiment vivantes, se produisent d'une façon toute naïve, sans que l'écrivain ait songé à telle ou telle manière d'être ; car l'œuvre d'art est toujours le produit d'un certain homme mis dans un certain milieu (5).

---

(1) *Ibid.*, pp. 136-139.
(2) Letter dated 7 December 1865, in LES ŒUVRES COMPLÈTES, *Correspondance (1858-1871)*, p. 271.
(3) *L'Evénement*, 19 May 1866, " Livres d'aujourd'hui et de demain ". By " vent terrible ", Zola is probably referring to the scientific spirit of the age which had been instrumental in the loss of his own Christian faith. Elsewhere in this same article, reviewing a book of religious inspiration, he writes : " Je recommande le livre à ceux, surtout à celles qui croient encore. Je regrette sincèrement qu'il ne puisse plus rien pour moi. "
(4) François Ponsard, 1814-1867.
(5) *L'Evénement*, 15 July 1866, " Livres d'aujourd'hui et de demain ".

Zola's novel, *Thérèse Raquin*, provoked violent reactions from the critics, notably from " Ferragus " (1), who classified this novel and the Goncourt's *Germinie Lacerteux* under the heading of " la littérature putride " and defied the authors to place their " nightmares of reality " on the stage (2). Replying to this attack, Zola remarked :

Vous avez émis, Monsieur, une étrange théorie qui inaugure une esthétique toute nouvelle. Vous prétendez que si un personnage dans un roman ne peut être mis au théâtre, ce personnage est monstrueux, impossible, en dehors du vrai. Je prends note de cette incroyable façon de juger deux genres de littérature si différents. Le roman, cadre souple, s'élargissant pour toutes les vérités et toutes les audaces, et la pièce de théâtre qui vit surtout de conventions et de restrictions...

Sans plaisanter davantage, Monsieur, comment n'avez-vous pas compris que notre théâtre se meurt, que la scène française tend à devenir un tremplin pour les paillasses et les sauteuses ?... Nos foules demandent de beaux mensonges, des sentiments tout faits, des situations clichées ; elles descendent souvent jusqu'aux indécences, mais elles ne montent jamais jusqu'aux réalités...

Ah ! Monsieur, si le théâtre se meurt, laissez vivre le roman (3).

Zola was convinced that timidity and conventionality had reduced the theater to a moribund condition, and that new and courageous themes were needed to rejuvenate it. The theater required more truth, and it is not surprising that Zola found the popularity of the " féeries " particularly objectionable, describing them as " ces misérables pièces qui sont en train de tuer chez nous l'art dramatique " (4). He writes to the same effect a few weeks later :

... nos scènes ne sont plus que des tremplins sur lesquels sautent nos paillasses déguenillés. Il y a une actrice, à Paris, qui s'est fait une réputation européenne par la façon poissarde dont elle donne un coup de hanche (5).

The following extract from Zola's " Causerie " in *la Tribune* reveals his ideals for the theater more clearly than any other

(1) Pseudonym for Louis Ulbach, novelist and journalist, who, incidentally, published ZOLA's novel, *la Curée*, in the newspaper *la Cloche* two years later.
(2) ZOLA adapted *Thérèse Raquin* to the stage in 1873.
(3) *Le Figaro*, 31 January 1868. This article, together with the criticism by Ferragus, is reprinted in LES ŒUVRES COMPLÈTES, *Thérèse Raquin*, Notes et commentaires, pp. 240-248.
(4) *La Tribune*, 14 July 1868, " M. Duruy et le rapport sur le progrès des lettres ". Compare, however, some later views expressed by ZOLA (see *infra*, Chapter III : " Laughter and Fantasy ").
(5) *La Tribune*, 27 September 1868, " Causerie ".

single quotation from his early criticisms.   As it is unavailable in book from, it is quoted here at some length :

Je ne sais si je suis pratique en matières théâtrales, mais je désire ardemment voir nos scènes s'élargir et le public prendre goût aux œuvres d'analyse humaine. J'ai entendu dire du *Drame de la rue de la Paix* : « Cette pièce n'est pas scénique, elle est maladroitement menée, elle contient des scènes qui font mauvais effet.» J'entends : les ficelles manquent, n'est-ce pas ? l'action est nue, le dénouement du sujet est trop logique, trop naturel. Puis le grand crime de l'auteur est de ne pas s'être souvenu du moule dans lequel les faiseurs coulent les personnages typiques, le traître, la victime, les bons et les méchants. L'originalité est, dit-on, l'épouvantail du public. Il faut ressembler au voisin, sous peine d'être tué. La critique elle-même en est venue à constater simplement le succès ; rarement elle casse les jugements de la foule ; à peine se permet-elle quelques regrets : « Que voulez-vous, le théâtre est ainsi, la vérité ne saurait paraître toute nue ; le mensonge seul a droit de cité sur les planches. Il faut être auteur dramatique comme on est menuisier, savoir poser les chevilles, raboter les angles, ajuster mécaniquement chaque pièce. Apprenez votre métier, car tout est métier dans ce genre littéraire. Eussiez-vous du génie, nous vous sifflerions si vous ne colliez pas proprement votre ouvrage. Travaillez uniquement pour la foule qui est reine au théâtre.»
Et la critique se perd dans la discussion des ficelles, dans la question de savoir si telle ou telle situation est ou n'est pas scénique, dans le programme de ce qui est permis et de ce qui n'est point permis sur la scène ; on dirait une boutique de géomètre où l'on mesurerait, avec des compas et des règles, l'espace limité dont le talent ne peut sortir sous peine d'amende. Certes, si je crois que la foule est reine et qu'un apprentissage est nécessaire pour écrire un drame, je crois aussi qu'il nous faut essayer de conduire la foule et qu'une pièce faite médiocrement avec science ne vaut pas une pièce grandement maladroite. Au lieu d'épouvanter le mérite et de le menacer de la muselière, la critique devrait pousser nos auteurs à tout oser, à tout risquer, à mettre au théâtre la vie telle qu'elle est. La foule s'accoutumerait peut-être aux vérités du cœur et de l'esprit, les leçons qu'elle en recevrait seraient fortes et profondes (1).

Thus Zola believed that an audience, while currently addicted to conventional banalities, could eventually be led to accept a greater degree of truth on the stage, and this belief was the foundation for his own plays and for the campaign of crit. :ism which he was to undertake in the *Bien public* and the *Voltaire* some ten years later (2).

(1) *La Tribune*, 15 November 1868, " Causerie ".
(2) The main body of Zola's theatrical criticism will be examined in Chapter III.

« Madeleine »

Zola's first noteworthy play, *Madeleine*, had a curious history. Written, according to Alexis, in 1865, it was refused by two theaters — the *Gymnase* and the *Vaudeville* — in the following year (1). Then, reversing the usual process, Zola adapted it into a novel, published under the title *la Honte* in *l'Événement* in 1868, and subsequently in book form with the title of *Madeleine Férat*. It appears that later, with Zola's rise to fame, several theater managers requested the privilege of producing the play, but that the manuscript remained lost until 1889 (2). In that year, Zola made the script available to Antoine for a single performance as part of the sixteenth production of the *Théâtre-Libre*. The play was produced as Zola had first written it, without changes (3), and first published in Les Œuvres complètes, *Théâtre I*.

Madeleine, although divided into three acts, is a short, compact work having the magnitude, in length and substance, of a one-act play. In this small compass, Zola created a drama of poignant simplicity containing several passages in which genuine human feelings are unaffectedly revealed. To be sure, the plot is artificially contrived and there are traces of romantic posturing. The tragic outcome is far from inevitable. Nevertheless, the youthful spontaneity of the work gives it considerable interest. The story is that of a young woman with a " past ", of which her husband is ignorant, although husband and lover had been close friends. She is happily married until the day that her former lover, believed dead, returns to visit his old friend. Madeleine avoids meeting her lover the night of his return, and feels herself obliged to confess the facts to her husband. The husband forgives her and the young couple decide to leave at once on a second honeymoon. Unfortunately, they choose an inn, and, indeed, the very room in which Madeleine had spent a week with her lover. The room is filled with memories. The innkeeper recognizes her. Chance even brings to her room two persons out of her old life — a former girl companion, and the lover himself, who has visited the inn to renew his own memories. The scenes in which Madeleine tries

---

(1) Alexis, *ibid.*, p. 77.
(2) See Le Blond's, *avertissement* in Les Œuvres complètes. *Théâtre I*, p. 8, and the article by " Parisis ", in *le Figaro*, 1 May 1889, reprinted in *Les Œuvres complètes, Théâtre II*, pp. 678-680.
(3) According to the article by Parisis referred to in the preceding note.

to convince her old friends that she has reformed are told with eloquent simplicity. Madeleine realizes that one cannot find refuge in attempting to flee from the past. Her last hope is to be forgiven by her husband's mother, symbol of the peace and respectability for which she longs. However, an old family servant, whose sense of righteousness requires punishment for the guilty, leads Madeleine to believe that the mother has withheld forgiveness. Her last hope gone, Madeleine takes poison and dies. In this play, Zola has adapted to his purposes, in a very human way, Dr. Lucas' theory of impregnation as interpreted by Michelet, to which reference has already been made (1). Michelet believed that a woman's first lover conveyed his own hereditary traits to her children, even to those born years after relationship with the lover had ceased. In this respect, a woman is in eternal bondage to her past. Zola extended the theory, which he believed scientific, to include the realm of conscience. Madeleine is pursued relentlessly by the impurity of her former life, from which all her remorse and shame cannot free her.

... le passé d'une femme ne meurt jamais et revit tôt ou tard.

(Act I, scene IV.)

Mais voilà que le passé vient me trouver et me menacer... On dit : le passé est mort... Le passé ne meurt jamais.

(Act I, scene v.)

Ah ! les souvenirs sont lâchés. Je les sens derrière moi qui me poursuivent.

(End of Act I.)

... tu ne pourras tuer les souvenirs.

(Act II, scene III.)

Il ne voyait pas le passé qui était là, autour de nous.

(Act II, scene vi.)

On n'échappe point aux souvenirs... Jamais plus nous ne serons seuls, Francis... Le passé était ici, dans cette chambre à nous attendre... C'est une effroyable souffrance que de penser. Oh ! par pitié, tue, tue ma pensée !... Tu souffres parce que tu m'aimes et que je ne puis plus être à toi.

(Act II, scene x.)

The connection of Michelet and Lucas to this theme becomes indisputable in the expansion which Zola made of it when he adapted his play into the novel, *Madeleine Férat*. There is no question, in the play, of a resemblance between Madeleine's

(1) See Chapter I, n. 4, p. 22.

child and her lover. But in the novel, this resemblance becomes
an important element, although, since the lover had disappeared
long before conception of the child, he could not be its actual
father. The husband of the novel, ignorant of the " scientific "
reason for the resemblance, accuses Madeleine of having had the
lover in her thoughts at the moment of conception. Zola gives
what he believes to be the true explanation :

> L'idée que la ressemblance de Lucie avec le premier amant de sa
> mère était un cas assez fréquent, tenant à certaines lois physiologiques
> inconnues encore, ne pouvait lui venir, en un pareil moment
> d'angoisse (1).

Madeleine, in the novel, is herself physiologically marked for
life by the union with her first lover, Jacques :

> Ce penchant à l'imitation, qui donne à toute femme, au bout de
> quelque temps, une parenté de manières avec l'homme dans les bras
> duquel elle vit, la mena jusqu'à modifier certains de ses traits, jusqu'à
> prendre l'expression habituelle du visage de Jacques. C'était là, d'ailleurs,
> une conséquence des fatalités physiologiques qui la liaient à lui : tandis
> qu'il mûrissait sa virginité, qu'il la faisait sienne pour la vie, il dégageait
> de la vierge une femme, marquait cette femme à son empreinte...
> Elle ne s'expliquait pas les fatalités physiologiques qui soustrayaient
> son corps à l'action de sa volonté ; elle ne pénétrait pas ce travail secret
> de son sang et de ses nerfs qui l'avait rendue pour la vie la femme de
> Jacques (2).

In the three years which intervened between the composition
of the short play, *Madeleine*, and its expansion into a full-length
novel, Zola had become increasingly devoted to the application
of science to literature. Moreover, the greater space and freedom
of the novel form gave him the opportunity to develop ideas
more fully than in the play. Both novel and play contain,
however, the same theme that the past is a fatal, determinist
force overhanging the present and future.

As a corollary to this principal theme is the subordinate one
of forgiveness. The mother wants to forgive her daughter-in-
law, but is opposed by Véronique, the puritannical servant
strong in her righteousness :

MADAME HUBERT
Croyez-vous donc qu'il ne faut pas pardonner ?

VÉRONIQUE
Pardonner, c'est encourager le mal.

(1) LES ŒUVRES COMPLÈTES, *Madeleine Férat*, p. 172.
(2) *Ibid.*, pp. 242 and 245.

MADAME HUBERT
Pardonner, Véronique, c'est tuer le mal.

VÉRONIQUE
Vous êtes faible, vous dis-je. Il faudra chasser cette femme, si elle ose jamais remettre les pieds dans cette maison. Elle n'a pas droit au bonheur. Que penseraient les méchants, s'ils apprenaient qu'une pécheresse a été récompensée ici du bien qu'elle n'a pas fait ?

(Act III, scene II.)

Thus Madeleine is defeated not only by her past, but by her unrequited need of forgiveness :

J'ai rencontré sur le grand chemin mon passé de vice qui m'a rendue folle, et je trouve ici la vertu qui m'achève...

(Act III, scene III.)

" Dieu le père n'aurait pas pardonné ", says the old serving woman at the beginning of the play, commenting on Christ's forgiveness of the adulterous woman. And at the end of the tragedy, she speaks the final line : " Dieu le père n'a pas pardonné. "

In his review of the play when it was finally produced in 1889, Sarcey (1) wrote :

Madeleine témoigne d'un certain tempérament dramatique, et je suis convaincu que M. Zola, s'il eût porté dès l'abord vers le théâtre sa puissante faculté de travail, à une époque où il n'avait pas encore des partis pris de théorie nouvelle sur l'art dramatique, se serait, dans ce genre, taillé d'aussi grands succès que ceux qu'il a obtenus dans le roman (2).

In speaking of Zola's " théorie nouvelle sur l'art dramatique ", Sarcey is thinking particularly of Zola's well-publicized campaign for a new theater art which he conducted in the press during the years 1876-1880. Sarcey is mistaken in believing that Zola had no ideas of a rejuvenated theater at the time he wrote *Madeleine*. The ideas for a new dramatic art which Zola expressed in his maturity were substantially the same as those which he held at the beginning of his career. If Zola had devoted himself solely to the theater, his plays would surely have been cast in a new mold. The spirit of innovation was firmly rooted in him and would have found expression in whatever form he chose to write.

(1) Francisque Sarcey, 1827-1899.
(2) *Le Temps*, 6 May 1889, reprinted in LES ŒUVRES COMPLÈTES, *Théâtre II*, p. 683.

« Thérèse Raquin »

Early in 1872, Zola wrote to a friend : " Avez-vous remarqué la chute fatale des romanciers au théâtre ? Ils font plus noir, plus vieux, plus ficelé que le dernier des faiseurs. Cela m'effraye un peu pour moi (1). Zola was thinking of his own stage adaptation of his novel, *Thérèse Raquin*, and the letter is singularly prophetic of what was to be his own experience in July of the following year, although the play deserved a better fate than it received at the hands of the critics. In his preface to the drama, Zola gives his reasons for making the adaptation : first, because critics of the novel had defied him to put such " garbage " on the stage ; and secondly, because the subject offered an opportunity to attempt an interesting theatrical experiment. The second reason was, as he states, the determining one.

According to Alexis (2), Zola returned to Paris after the Franco-Prussian war with a scenario condensing the action of the novel into one set, and completed the play fairly rapidly. Not having yet attained the celebrity which would have gained a sympathetic reading for his play at the major theaters, he took it to the *Renaissance*, which was willing to gamble on this daring play by a comparative unknown, particularly since the celebrated actress, Marie Laurent, wanted to play the role of Madame Raquin. During rehearsals, the play was reduced from five acts to four, and a scene was inserted showing the drowning of the husband in the Seine. This scene was withdrawn before the opening, and Zola's original conception restored, except that the play remained in four acts. The critics were generally antipathetic to the work, finding it morbid and depressing (3). It closed after nine performances.

Like *Madeleine*, *Thérèse Raquin* resolves itself into a drama where the guilty are haunted and eventually driven to suicide by memories of the past ; but the past is much more terrible in the later play. Whereas Madeleine was suffering from the romantic notion that her first lover had marked her for life (a notion which at the time Zola believed " scientific "), Thérèse and Laurent, her lover, are haunted by their murder of Camille, Thérèse's sickly husband. The murder is planned in the first

(1) Letter to C. MONTROSIER, 13 February 1872, in LES ŒUVRES COMPLÈTES, *Correspondance (1872-1902)*, p. 404. ZOLA is referring to the failure of a play by Daudet, presumably *Lise Tavernier*.
(2) ALEXIS, *ibid.*, pp. 132-136.
(3) For extracts from the critics reviews, see LES ŒUVRES COMPLÈTES, *Théâtre II*, pp. 685-692.

act, and carried out, in the interval between the first and second
acts, so as to appear a simple boating accident on the Seine.
The second act opens a year later. No suspicion has attached
to the lovers, who, in fear of discovery, have suspended their
relationship until such time as they may marry in security.
They have so well carried out their deception that the question
of re-marriage is first broached by Camille's mother and the
family friends ; the lovers, concealing their eagerness, acquiesce
with apparent reluctance. In the third act, they are at last
together on their wedding night, and it is here that the author's
intention becomes clear. Zola is not primarily interested in the
fact of murder, which he disdains to show on the stage. Nor
is he interested in its detection, although near the end of the play,
he has resorted to unabashed melodrama in a scene where the
mother, Madame Raquin, stricken with paralysis and unable to
speak, has recovered the use of her hands sufficiently to spell
out the beginning of an incriminating message in the presence of
the family friends. But the message is not completed, and the
lovers are not brought before a tribunal. It is they who judge
and execute themselves, in a double suicide.

Zola's intention is not to tell the story of a crime and its
detection, but to dissect the mentality of the participants and their
eventual disintegration. His preface, written a few days after
the play had closed, reveals the inspiration which he drew from his
conception of the writer as a sort of scientist (italics are mine) :

Certes, je n'ai point l'ambition de planter mon drame comme un
drapeau. Il a de gros défauts, et je suis plus sévère pour lui que personne ;
si j'en faisais la critique, il ne resterait qu'une chose debout, la volonté
bien nette d'aider au théâtre le *large mouvement de vérité et de science
expérimentale*, qui, depuis le siècle dernier, se propage et grandit dans
tous les actes de l'intelligence humaine. Le branle a été donné par *les
nouvelles méthodes scientifiques*. De là, le naturalisme a renouvelé la
critique et l'histoire, en soumettant l'homme et ses œuvres à une analyse
exacte, soucieuse des circonstances, des milieux, des cas organiques.
Puis, les arts et les lettres ont subi à leur tour l'influence de ce grand
courant... C'est pourquoi je suis absolument convaincu de voir prochai-
nement *le mouvement naturaliste* s'imposer au théâtre, et y apporter la
puissance de la réalité, la vie nouvelle de l'art moderne.
... J'ai la conviction profonde... que *l'esprit expérimental et scientifique
du siècle* va gagner le théâtre, et que là est le seul renouvellement
possible de notre scène...
Ou le drame mourra, ou le drame sera moderne et réel (1).

(1) LES ŒUVRES COMPLÈTES, *Théâtre I, Thérèse Raquin*, Préface, pp. II-III.
I have italicized certain expressions referring to science and experimen-

Actually, science has no role in the play : it served Zola only as inspiration. But the inspiration was important in leading him to place greater emphasis upon character analysis than upon complexity of plot. As he says in his preface :

J'allais pouvoir faire une étude purement humaine, dégagée de tout intérêt étranger, allant droit à son but ; l'action n'était plus dans une histoire quelconque, mais dans les combats intérieurs des personnages ; il n'y avait plus une logique de faits, mais une logique de sensations et de sentiments ; et le dénouement devenait un résultat arithmétique du problème posé (1).

By accurate analysis, human conduct could be forecast with mathematical certainty. The scientific inspiration also led Zola to place his characters in situations approximating those of daily life as closely as possible, in the same way that a scientist controls his experiments so as to draw accurate conclusions. Quoting further from his preface :

Alors, j'ai suivi le roman pas à pas ; j'ai enfermé le drame dans la même chambre, humide et noire, afin de ne rien lui ôter de son relief, ni de sa fatalité ; j'ai choisi des comparses sots et inutiles, pour mettre, sous les angoisses atroces de mes héros, la banalité de la vie de tous les jours ; j'ai tenté de ramener continuellement la mise en scène aux occupations ordinaires de mes personnages, de façon à ce qu'ils ne « jouent » pas, mais à ce qu'ils « vivent » devant le public (2).

The conclusion which Zola reaches in his " experimental " tragedy is that two unstable minds so diseased as to plot and execute a murder cannot find happiness even when it appears to be within their reach. In the scene of the wedding night which terminates the third act, it is inevitable that Thérèse has lost her capacity to love, and that Laurent is impotent to awaken it. " Ne fais pas le brave ", she warns him. " Nous ne sommes pas des mariés comme les autres. " They try to hide their anguish under a veneer of idle conversation :

THÉRÈSE

Assieds-toi. Causons. Il a fait beaucoup de vent aujourd'hui.

LAURENT

Un vent très froid. Il s'est un peu calmé, l'après-midi.

tation. Some years later, Zola made use of Claude BERNARD's *Introduction à la médecine expérimentale* to expand and elaborate this analogy between the methods of science and those of literature. (See *infra*, Chapter III.)

(1) *Ibid.*, p. III.
(2) *Ibid.*, p. III.

THÉRÈSE

Oui, il y avait des toilettes sur les boulevards... N'importe, les abricotiers feront bien de ne pas se presser de fleurir.

LAURENT

Les coups de gelée, en mars, sont très mauvais pour les arbres fruitiers.

. . . .

THÉRÈSE

C'est étonnant, la nuit est longue... Est-ce que tu es comme moi ? je n'aime guère aller en fiacre. Rien n'est plus stupide que de rouler pendant des heures. Ça m'endort... Je déteste aussi manger au restaurant.

LAURENT

On n'y est jamais aussi bien que chez soi.

THÉRÈSE

A la campagne, je ne dis pas.

LAURENT

On mange d'excellentes choses, à la campagne...

(Act III, scene III.)

This might be a tea-table conversation, but in the mouths of the two murderers trying, on their wedding-night, to suppress the spectre of the dead husband, it has the ring of truth.

In the fourth act, Zola analyzes the final disintegration of the couple. They now hate each other and their life has become a nightmare of recriminations.

THÉRÈSE

Camille était bon, entends-tu, et je voudrais que tu fusses à sa place dans la terre.

LAURENT

Tais-toi !

THÉRÈSE

Tiens, tu ne connais pas le cœur des femmes. Comment veux-tu que je ne te haïsse pas, maintenant que te voilà couvert du sang de Camille ?

LAURENT

Te tairas-tu !... J'entends des coups de marteau dans ma tête. Elle me brisera le crâne... Quelle est encore cette infernale invention, d'avoir des remords, maintenant, et de pleurer l'autre tout haut ! Je vis éternellement avec l'autre, à cette heure. Il faisait ceci, il faisait cela, i était bon, il était généreux. Ah ! misère, je deviens fou... L'autre habite avec nous. Il s'assoit sur ma chaise, se met à table près de moi, se sert

des meubles. Il a mangé dans mon assiette, il y mange encore... Je ne
sais plus, je suis lui, je suis Camille... J'ai sa femme, j'ai son couvert,
j'ai ses draps, je suis Camille, Camille, Camille...

(Act IV, scene VI.)

The final moments of the play descend quite unrestrainedly
into the realm of melodrama. Zola has contrived to have the
guilty pair attempt to murder each other at precisely the same
moment — one with a poisoned drink, the other with a knife —
while the paralysed Madame Raquin gloats over the spectacle,
finding their mutual hatred and remorse sufficient punishment
for the murder of her son. She recovers her speech at the end,
and pronounces a final malediction before the double suicide
which brings the tragedy to a close. Despite some over-
theatrical effects, the play remains a character study and an
artistically successful attempt to treat a morbid subject in terms
of reality.

Although *Thérèse Raquin* was a financial failure at the time
of its first presentation in Paris, it has been played successfully
throughout Europe and has been revived a number of times in
France (1). An American adaptation was played for nearly
100 performances at the Biltmore Theater in New York during
October-December 1945 (2).

« Les Héritiers Rabourdin »

Zola's next play was a comedy — more precisely, a satirical
farce — which, interpreted by a group of young, inexperienced
actors at the third-rate *Théâtre Cluny*, received only 17 performances. " C'est navrant, pour un homme de valeur, d'être
interprété dans une telle salle ", was the comment of Edmond
de Goncourt, whom Zola had invited to one of the rehearsals (3).

(1) The Rondel theatrical collection in the Bibliothèque de l'Arsenal,
Paris, contains theater programs and newspaper clippings relating to the
following revivals (collection Rondel, RF 49078) : in 1905, at the Ba-ta-clan ;
in May 1910, at the Odéon ; " Tournées Ch. Baret " during the season 1912-1913 ;
in August 1916, at the Moncey ; in 1920, at the Belleville ; in August 1920,
at the Empire ; in August 1928, at the Folies-Dramatiques ; in May 1929,
at the Royal ; and in July 1932, at the Casino Montparnasse.
(2) " *Thérèse*, a Tragedy in two Acts, by Thomas JOB (from Emile ZOLA's
Thérèse Raquin) ", published by Samuel French. According to Burns Mantle,
Best Plays 1945-1946, the adaptation ran for 96 performances. The American author follows, in general, the structure of the Zola play, with the principal
difference that Madame Raquin dies at the end, leaving Thérèse and Laurent
to be arrested by the police.
(3) *Journal des Goncourt*, année 1874, 1er novembre.

Zola, however, defended his actors and placed blame for the failure squarely upon the critics. In his savage and somewhat incoherent preface to the play (written, like that of *Thérèse Raquin*, a few days after it had closed), he accuses the critics of bad faith and of failing to allow credit for his good intentions, which he sums up as follows :

> J'avoue que mon intention très arrêtée a été d'écrire un pastiche ; j'entends un pastiche particulier, et fait dans un certain but d'expériences. J'ai voulu, en un mot, remonter aux sources de notre théâtre, ressusciter la vieille farce littéraire, telle que nos auteurs du xviie siècle l'ont empruntée aux Italiens. Afin que nul n'en ignore, j'ai pris à Molière des tournures de phrases, des coupes de scènes... Il n'est pas une scène dans la pièce, je le répète, qui n'aurait dû ouvrir les yeux de la critique et lui inspirer le soupçon qu'elle avait devant elle une protestation contre la façon dont nos auteurs comiques gaspillent l'héritage de Molière. Qu'a-t-on fait de ce beau rire, si simple, si profond dans sa franchise, de ce rire vivant où il y a des sanglots (1) ?

A true naturalist comedy, he admits, would not be a mere imitation of the XVIIth Century :

> Il ne s'agit point d'un décalque. Il s'agit simplement de retourner à la source même du génie comique en France. Ce qu'il est bon de ressusciter, ce sont ces peintures larges de caractères, dans lesquelles les maîtres de notre scène ont mis l'intérêt dominant de leurs œuvres. Ayons leur beau dédain pour les histoires ingénieuses ; tâchons de créer, comme eux, des hommes vivants, des types éternels de vérité. Et restons dans la réalité contemporaine, avec nos mœurs, nos vêtements, notre milieu. Il y a certainement là une formule à trouver. Ce serait, à mon avis, cette formule naturaliste que j'indiquais dans ma préface de *Thérèse Raquin* (2).

Zola confesses that his play is a simple transposition of XVIIth Century themes and that it remains therefore outside of the naturalist formula which he is seeking. He explains that he attempted the play as an experiment, in the hope that the inspiration of the masters (notably Molière) would place him on the right path. Zola gives a further clue to his intentions in declaring that his initial idea of the comedy came from Ben Jonson's *Volpone* (3), which he admires for its " crudité splen-

---

(1) Les Œuvres complètes, *les Héritiers Rabourdin*, Préface, p. v.
(2) *Ibid.*, p. vi.
(3) Stated on the title page of the 1616 Folio to have been acted in the year 1605.

dide ", its " violence continue dans le vrai ", its " rage admirable de satire ", its " rire terrible " (1).

Unfortunately, he selects for emulation the bitter and satiric values in Molière and Ben Jonson, and gives too little importance to their wit and comic inventiveness.

Les Héritiers Rabourdin is a satire of greed, specifically the greed of prospective heirs waiting for an old man to die. As in *le Malade imaginaire*, *Volpone*, and Regnard's *le Légataire universel*, the climax revolves about the apparent death and resuscitation of the testator. Zola's debt to Ben Jonson is limited to the first act of *Volpone*, from which he has taken the idea of a healthy man feigning to be at the point of death in order to induce gifts from prospective heirs who hope to be named in his will. He has also taken from Jonson's satire a few other plot elements, such as the idea of deceiving several individual heirs with the belief that each is the sole legatee. Here is a short passage — one of Zola's best — inspired directly from Act I, scene 4 of *Volpone*. Chapuzot, a prospective heir and an old man himself, is hearing the welcome news that Rabourdin is at the point of death. Charlotte is Rabourdin's ward, and plays the counterpart of the intriguing XVIIth Century servant :

CHARLOTTE

Alors, il est devenu tout pâle.

CHAPUZOT

Bien !

CHARLOTTE

Il avait les yeux retournés...

CHAPUZOT

Bien !

CHARLOTTE

Les joues glacées, la langue pendante.

CHAPUZOT

Bien ! bien !

CHARLOTTE

Et il ressemblait à un vrai noyé, sauf votre respect.

CHAPUZOT

Très bien !... Mais est-ce qu'il n'a pas craché le sang ?

(1) Preface to *les Héritiers Rabourdin*, p. VII.

CHARLOTTE

Le sang, bon Dieu ! J'ai craint qu'il ne se vidât comme une cruche...
Il ne serait pas capable maintenant de remuer le petit doigt.

CHAPUZOT

Parfait ! *(Après un coup d'œil sur Rabourdin.)* Et la voix ? Comment
a-t-il la voix ? Très faible, n'est-ce pas ?

CHARLOTTE

Hélas ! mon bon monsieur, il n'a plus parlé.

CHAPUZOT, *ravi, très haut*

Dis-tu vrai ?... *(Baissant le ton.)* J'ai le verbe si haut, que je
l'incommode peut-être.

CHARLOTTE

Non, ne vous gênez pas. Il a perdu l'ouïe et la vue.

CHAPUZOT, *s'approchant de Rabourdin*

Il n'entend plus, il ne voit plus ! Ah ! le digne ami, l'excellent ami !...

(Les Héritiers Rabourdin, Act II, scene IV.)

The play contains some scattered comic lines, but Zola has
not succeeded in building a single sustained scene. Situations
which might be comic if they were more thoroughly pursued
are permitted to lapse before the laughter is extracted, and give
way to new situations, or to a repetition of old ones, which in
turn flicker out before a climax is reached. Zola's own particular
invention was to make Rabourdin's wealth an illusion in the
minds of his prospective heirs, whereas in fact he was impove-
rished. The discovery of the truth should have yielded a scene
of really comic proportions, but Zola failed to build it. Nor
was he able to create a comic scene from the final twist in the
play when the relatives, in order to maintain their credit in the
community, are obliged to continue the pretence of Rabourdin's
wealth.

In his preface, Zola considers one by one the three principal
reproaches which the critics made of his play : " Ma comédie
manque de gaieté ; on n'y rencontre aucun personnage sympathique ; la situation reste la même pendant les trois actes. "
He acknowledges that for a conventional comedy, these would
be serious defects indeed, but on the authority of Molière, he
denies that they are defects in the type of comedy which he
wanted to write. Replying to the objection that his play is
lacking in gaiety, he states :

Je nie que dans Molière, il y ait de la gaieté, j'entends de la gaieté
telle qu'on en demande aujourd'hui. Dandin à genoux devant sa femme

fait saigner le cœur ; Arnolphe aux petits soins pour Agnès mouille les yeux de pitié ; Alceste inquiète et Scapin donne peur. Sous le rire, il y a des gouffres (1).

This, of course, is true. But Molière served an apprenticeship of many years before writing his great comedies. Zola attempted to imitate Molière's profundity without the master's skill in constructing a comic scene. Zola relied again upon Molière in replying to the objection that his play had no sympathetic character :

Je nie que Molière se soit jamais inquiété de tempérer ses cruautés d'analyse, en peuplant ses pièces de personnages sympathiques ; à part son éternel couple d'amoureux, qui est une concession à la mode du temps, tous les types qu'il a créés sont humains, c'est-à-dire plutôt mauvais que bons (2).

As this passage clearly indicates, the want of sympathy in the play is not owing to the inherent nature of the characters, but to the author's own lack of sympathy for them. Here, perhaps, Zola felt that he was following Molière's cold, dispassionate analysis of human nature, but whereas Molière's theater is peopled with logical and memorable characters, Zola's Rabourdin emerges as an incredible hodge-podge of absurdity. The fault of Zola's characters is not that they are unsympathetic, but that the author has failed to endow them with the breath of life.

To the third criticism, that the situation of his play remains unchanged during three acts, Zola replies :

Enfin, je nie que Molière ait jamais soupçonné le besoin de compliquer une comédie pour la rendre plus intéressante ; son théâtre est d'une nudité magistrale ; une intrigue unique s'y développe largement, logiquement, en épuisant le long du chemin toutes les vérités humaines qu'elle rencontre (3).

Zola's preface, put forward as a defense, is in fact a self-incriminating document. In renouncing gayety, sympathetic characters and a progressing plot, he voluntarily deprived himself of the three basic resources of a comic dramatist. Zola was insensitive to the boisterous sweep of Jonson's *Volpone* and failed to perceive the dreadful emasculation which he performed

(1) *Ibid.*, p. vi.
(2) *Ibid.*, p. vi.
(3) *Ibid.*, p. vi.

in restricting this Elizabethan comedy to the mold of French classicism. His attempted emulation of Molière was equally woeful. The satiric purpose with which *les Héritiers Rabourdin* was undertaken far exceeded Zola's theatrical skill. He tried rashly to reach in one bound the summit which had taken so great a genius as Molière many years to scale (1).

« Le Bouton de Rose »

By the time Zola's next play was produced, in May of 1878, *l'Assommoir* had made him a celebrity. This novel, published in 1876, marked a stage in his career comparable to that of *le Cid* in the career of Corneille. Zola was no longer considered as one of a group of moderately-talented writers, but as the leader of the naturalist school of literature. He had, moreover, acquired notoriety from his weekly articles on the current theater, begun in *le Bien public* in 1876 (2). For these two reasons, the announcement of a new play by Zola aroused the anticipations of critics and public alike, who, believing that they were to witness a new form of dramatic art, were unprepared for a commonplace domestic farce. *Le Bouton de Rose* closed after seven performances at the *Palais-Royal*.

The play contains no trace of satire or of social purpose. Zola wrote it to divert himself as well as the audience. As he states in a letter to Flaubert more than a year before the play was performed :

> En ce moment, je me délasse, j'écris une farce en trois actes, un cocuage pour le Palais-Royal, dont le directeur est venu me demander une pièce (3).

And in his preface to the play he confesses :

> Mon espoir était que le public de la première représentation comprendrait qu'une pareille farce avait été, pour moi, une simple récréation, prise entre deux travaux d'importance (4).

---

(1) According to an article by Eileen E. PRYME, '' Zola's Plays in England, 1870-1900 '', in *French Studies*, vol. 13 (1959), pp. 28-38, at pp. 36-37, this play was successfully presented in Holland and Germany, but failed in London in 1894.

(2) To be examined in the following chapter.

(3) Letter dated 3 January 1877, in LES ŒUVRES COMPLÈTES, *Correspondance (1872-1902)*, p. 464.

(4) LES ŒUVRES COMPLÈTES, *Le Bouton de Rose*, Préface, p. III.

But the critics, awaiting a work of far greater originality from the master of naturalism, were unwilling to be diverted by Zola's intentions, and it is probable, as Zola claims in his preface, that they judged the play more severely coming from him than they would have done if it had been the work of a less celebrated author. He was accused even of having slighted the French army because of a drinking scene in which army officers participated. While essentially inoffensive, the scene wounded feelings of national pride, which were particularly strong as an aftermath of the Franco-Prussian war. From this point in the second act to the end of the play, the hooting of the first-night audience was such that the lines could scarcely be heard (1).

The idea of the play, as Zola reveals in his preface, was suggested to him by *le Frère d'armes*, one of Balzac's *Contes drolatiques*. The story concerns the trust of a married woman's chastity to the best friend of the husband during the latter's absence from the home. The lady, insulted by her husband's want of confidence, seeks to teach him that wives are the best guardians of their own virtue. Zola drew also upon Molière's Agnès of *l'École des femmes* in the creation of his heroine, who conceals her cunning behind an appearance of innocent ignorance. Zola's heroine allows both men to think she has been seduced, but, through a contrivance in the plot, another woman has been substituted in her place, so that even the supposed seducer is deceived. The truth is learned in time to avert a duel, and the husband has presumably learned his lesson.

Zola himself had grave doubts as to the merits of this play. " Quant au *Bouton de Rose* ", he wrote to Flaubert seven months before the opening, " je crois fort que je vais le mettre sous clef, dans un tiroir. Décidément, ce n'est pas trop bon " (2). And some weeks later, he wrote to the manager of the Palais-Royal requesting postponement of the play on the grounds that it was commonplace and lacking in originality (3).

---

(1) See *ibid.*, p. v.
(2) Letter dated 12 October 1877, in LES ŒUVRES COMPLÈTES, *Correspondance (1872-1902)*, p. 497.
(3) This letter of 2 December 1877 to Dormeuil, manager of the Palais-Royal, has not been published. It is referred to in a letter from Henry Céard to Zola dated 13 June 1884, in which Céard informs Zola that two letters written by Zola to Dormeuil concerning *le Bouton de Rose* are being offered for sale at an auction. Céard writes concerning these letters : " La première du 2 décembre 1877 lui propose d'ajourner la représentation de votre pièce que vous trouvez " peu crâne, ordinaire, sans cette originalité que le public exigera sans doute " ; la seconde du 8 mai 1878 compte sur sa bonne amitié " pour amortir un peu ce désastre qui m'a beaucoup secoué ". " (Céard's manus-

As a theatrical trifle, *le Bouton de Rose* is diverting enough. But coming from Zola, with his high aims of reforming the theater, it was a tactical blunder incompatible with his doctrines.

« Renée »

Zola was proud enough of his three failures to publish them, in 1878, under the title *Théâtre*, with a short, defiant preface predicting many more plays from his pen :

> ... je publie mes pièces sifflées et j'attends. Elles sont trois, les trois premiers soldats d'une armée. Lorsqu'il y en aura une vingtaine, elles sauront se faire respecter. Ce que j'attends, c'est une évolution dans notre littérature dramatique, c'est un apaisement du public et de la critique à mon égard, c'est une appréciation plus nette et plus juste de ce que je suis et de ce que je veux (1).

Actually, he was to produce, as sole author, only one more naturalist play, although he was to collaborate on a number of adaptations of his novels.   If any excuse be sought for his failure to live up to the promise of this preface, it is sufficient to recall that Zola, the most diligent and prolific writer of his generation, was throughout this period publishing a new novel of the *Rougon-Macquart* in almost every year.

That he was chastened, but not disheartened, by the failures of *Thérèse Raquin* and *Les Héritiers Rabourdin* is evident from his letter to Léon Hennique of 29 June 1877 :

> Travaillez bien et songez au théâtre... Ce serait une grande affaire pour nous tous, si un de nous conquérait les planches. Je crois qu'il faudrait être pratique, sans rien abandonner des tendances nouvelles (2).

cript letter is in the Bibliothèque Nationale, Paris, " Nouvelles acquisitions françaises 24516, *Correspondance Emile Zola*, t. VII, feuillets 204-205 ". Céard suggests that Zola is entitled to take legal action to stop sale of these letters. Zola replied 14 June 1884 that he would permit them to be sold, saying : " ... je ne suis pas fâché qu'elles viennent appuyer l'histoire vraie du *Bouton de Rose*, déjà contée par moi. — Je n'ai pas de secrets, les clefs sont sur les armoires... " (LES ŒUVRES COMPLÈTES, *Correspondance (1872-1902)*, pp. 167-168).

(1) This preface appears also in *le Voltaire*, 7 September 1878 (in which Zola was conducting a weekly column of theatrical and literary criticism), and is reprinted in LES ŒUVRES COMPLÈTES, *Théâtre II*, pp. 675-676.

(2) LES ŒUVRES COMPLÈTES, *Correspondance (1872-1902)*, p. 474.

Doubt as to his own fitness to write for the stage is expressed in a letter to Huysmans :

... le théâtre continue à me terrifier. Je sens la nécessité de l'aborder, et je ne sais vraiment par quel point commencer l'assaut (1).

And in another letter to Hennique, he insists upon the urgency of bringing naturalism to the theater :

... il faudra bien que nous nous occupions du théâtre ; c'est là que nous devrons un jour frapper le coup décisif (2).

In 1882, his intimate friend, Paul Alexis, published an invaluable contemporary biography, *Émile Zola, Notes d'un ami*, in which he summarizes Zola's theatrical ambitions as of this time :

Après ses pièces de première jeunesse, après ses trois œuvres jouées et, toutes, sifflées ou étouffées — ne comptant que trente-trois représentations à elles trois — après les adaptations théâtrales de ses romans, auxquelles il prend plus ou moins part, il n'a nullement renoncé à faire du théâtre tout seul, malgré *le Bouton de Rose* et à le faire en poursuivant la réalisation de certaines idées.

Quelles idées ? — Quiconque a suivi sa campagne de critique dramatique pendant quatre ans, au *Bien public* et au *Voltaire*, les connaît. On peut les résumer, je crois, en une phrase : Zola voudrait porter au théâtre l'évolution qui s'est produite dans le roman avec Stendhal, Balzac et Flaubert. Son rêve serait évidemment de réaliser lui-même cette évolution, que, selon lui, Alexandre Dumas fils, Émile Augier, Sardou, Meilhac et Halévy, n'ont fait qu'ébaucher. Mais il se sent tellement enfoncé dans le roman, les *Rougon-Macquart* à terminer sont une si lourde besogne, qu'il recule toujours ses nouvelles tentatives, et qu'il doit désespérer jusqu'à un certain point, aujourd'hui, d'avoir jamais le temps.

Cependant, il reste plein de projets. Certains jours, il se sent pris de la tristesse de n'avoir pas fait et d'envies terribles de faire. Ces jours-là, il se met à *Renée*, une sorte de *Phèdre* contemporaine. Actuellement, sa situation est nette au théâtre. Lorsqu'il donnera de nouveau une pièce signée de son nom seul, il faut que ce soit une mémorable bataille : la première d'*Hernani* pour le naturalisme (3) !

Renée fell short of these expectations. Written during 1880-1881, the play was refused successively by the *Théâtre-Français*,

---

(1) 3 August 1877, *ibid.*, p. 479.
(2) 2 September 1877, *ibid.*, p. 493.
(3) ALEXIS, *ibid.*, pp. 144-145.

by Sarah Bernhardt (for whom it had originally been written),
by the *Gymnase* and by the *Odéon*, and finally opened in
April 1887 at the *Vaudeville*, where it had a moderate run of
38 performances (1). For this play, in which he hoped to give
theatrical expression to the principles of naturalism, Zola went
back to his novel *la Curée*, second of the *Rougon-Macquart*
series (2). The play cannot be considered a thorough-going
adaptation of the novel. The novel is a pungent satire of the
speculative hunt for wealth and of the vices and perversions of
Parisian society, as Zola conceived them to be in the years
following the *Coup d'État* of 1852. For the play, Zola extracted
the triangle situation which existed between a husband (Aristide
Saccard), his second wife (Renée) and his son by a former
marriage (Maxime). The situation at its outset is similar to
that treated in Euripides' *Hippolytus*, Seneca's *Phaedra*, and
Racine's *Phèdre*. It will be recalled that in none of these classic
plays was there consummation of an illicit relationship between
step-mother and step-son : Hippolytus was the innocent victim
of a false accusation. Racine even sought to moderate the
situation by changing the accusation against Hippolyte to an
accusation of intent, rather than of actual commission of the
crime (3). Zola, on the contrary, rendered the classic situation
harsher and more brutal in his novel, where the incestuous (or
pseudo-incestuous) adultery is accomplished (4).

While *la Curée* was being published serially in *la Cloche*, it
attracted the hostility of the censorhip, and it was feared that
proceedings would be instituted against the newspaper unless the
novel were withdrawn. Zola acquiesced in the decision to
suspend publication of the novel. He expressed his views in a
friendly letter to Louis Ulbach, the publisher, in which appears

(1) Zola gives the history of the play in his preface, LES ŒUVRES COMPLÈTES,
Théâtre II, Renée, Préface, pp. I-VII.
  (2) Publication of *la Curée* was begun serially in ULBACH's, *la Cloche*,
in September 1871, and suspended under the threat of censorship (see ZOLA's
letter to Louis ULBACH, 6 November 1871, in LES ŒUVRES COMPLÈTES, *Correspondance, I*, pp. 382-386). The novel was published by Lacroix in 1872.
(This was the last of Zola's works to be published by Lacroix. Thereafter,
his publisher was Georges Charpentier.)
  (3) RACINE states in his preface to *Phèdre* : " Hippolyte est accusé, dans
Euripide et dans Sénèque, d'avoir en effet violé sa belle-mère : *Vim corpus
tulit.* Mais il n'est accusé ici que d'en avoir eu le dessein. J'ai voulu épargner
à Thésée une confusion qui l'aurait pu rendre moins agréable aux spectateurs. "
  (4) It is unnecessary here to ascertain whether an illicit relation between
a step-mother and step-son is legal incest, in other words, whether, in the
event of the husband's death, they could legally marry. ZOLA, in his preface
to *Renée*, considered the relationship to be incestuous.

the following particularly informative passage concerning his intentions in re-writing the *Phèdre* story :

Il faut bien que je le dise, puisqu'on ne m'a pas compris, et puisque je ne puis achever ma pensée : *la Curée*, c'est la plus malsaine poussée sur le fumier impérial, c'est l'inceste grandi dans le terreau des millions. J'ai voulu, dans cette nouvelle *Phèdre* montrer à quel effroyable écroulement on en arrive, que les mœurs sont pourries et que les liens de la famille n'existent plus. Ma Renée, c'est la Parisienne affolée, jetée au crime par le luxe et la vie à outrance ; mon Maxime, c'est le produit d'une société épuisée, l'homme-femme, la chair inerte qui accepte les dernières infamies ; mon Aristide, c'est le spéculateur né des bouleversements de Paris, l'enrichi impudent, qui joue à la Bourse avec tout ce qui lui tombe sous la main, femmes, enfants, honneur, pavés, conscience. Et j'ai essayé, avec ces trois monstruosités sociales, de donner une idée de l'effroyable bourbier dans lequel la France se noyait (1).

In this same letter, Zola describes himself as an " écrivain consciencieux qui fait œuvre d'art et de science ", and justifies his work on the grounds of its " côté scientifique " (2).

One may readily perceive the several reasons which led Zola, searching for a subject that would project naturalism on the stage, to choose this particular material. First, it could be treated " scientifically " by analysing the characters from the point of view of their heredity and environment. It had been successfully handled by illustrious predecessors — Euripides, Seneca, Racine. It was the sort of daring subject which, in prose fiction, had come to be associated in the minds of public and critics alike with the naturalist movement. And finally, the great Sarah Bernhardt was begging Zola to adapt *la Curée* so that she might play the rôle of Renée (3).

However, Zola was sufficiently chastened by his three failures to realize that concessions were sometimes necessary in the theater. When he began work on the adaptation, Sarah was still associated with the *Comédie-Française* (4), where Zola felt it would have been impossible to present the subject of incest. How was he to preserve the vice, which was essential to his story,

---

(1) Letter dated 6 November 1871, in LES ŒUVRES COMPLÈTES, *Correspondance (1858-1871)*, p. 384.
(2) *Ibid.*, p. 383 and 385.
(3) See ZOLA's preface to *Renée*, p. i.
(4) Following a quarrel with the *Comédie-Française* she resigned her position in 1880, and made a tour in America. Zola submitted the play to her on her return, but, needing to re-establish her position in France, she felt that she could not afford to compromise her popularity by undertaking a questionable rôle.

and yet remove the incestuous taint ? He conceived the extraordinary device of an unconsummated marriage between Renée
and Aristide Saccard, so that, when the latter's son, Maxime,
yields to his father's wife, there is, according to Zola, no real
incest. Zola relates how he was seized of this inspiration during
a visit with Sarah Bernhardt :

... et dans une visite que je lui fis, comme je lui démontrais l'inutilité
de la tentative, l'impossibilité du sujet, si l'inceste était consommé,
nous trouvâmes, dans la discussion, l'expédient, la tricherie, pour dire
le mot, qui esquive l'inceste réel, en établissant que Saccard n'est que
de nom le mari de Renée... Mon tort, si tort il y a, est d'avoir voulu être
pratique (1).

It will be recalled that in the novel, *la Curée*, the widower
Aristide, a penniless adventurer in Paris, has the opportunity
of making a wealthy second marriage with a young woman of
good family (Renée), who has been seduced by the husband
of one of her friends, and stands in need of a husband to repair
her " fault ". The need is more imaginary than real, since no
pregnancy resulted from the seduction. This notion of feminine
honor is a curious survival of romanticism in Zola, who shows
himself here less modern than his contemporaries. Even so
conservative and traditional a critic as Francisque Sarcey points
out that Renée was under no obligation to marry, since her fault
had no visible consequences and might have lain hidden
forever (2). The marriage is consummated in the novel, but
when Zola began work on his adaptation, he remembered his
short story *Nantas* (3), which dealt romantically with a similar
situation, and in which the parties agree that their marriage
shall remain sexless. In writing *Renée*, Zola took this story
element from *Nantas*, and also the character Mademoiselle Chuin,
Renée's governess who procures Aristide as a husband for her.
(In the novel, the intermediary is Aristide's sister, Sidonie.)
Of the five acts of the play, the first serves as a prologue
which sets forth the bargain between Renée and Aristide. The
other four acts take place ten years later. In the second, we see
the affection which Renée bears for her step-son, Maxime,

(1) Preface to *Renée*, p. i.
(2) Francisque SARCEY, *Quarante ans de théâtre* (Paris, 1902), vol. VII,
pp. 69-70.
(3) *Nantas* was first published, in a Russian translation, in *Viestnik Evropy*
(" Messenger of Europe "), a St. Petersburg journal to which Zola contributed
short stories and articles of literary and theatrical criticism from 1875 to 1880.

although neither is yet aware of the strength of her feeling. In the third act, she discovers with horror the extent of her passion, and here, for a moment, Zola's play runs parallel to the scene of Phèdre's confession to Œnone in the first act of Racine's tragedy. Unlike Phèdre, who has a clear insight into her own mind from the beginning, Renée is slow in learning of her love for Maxime, and becomes aware of it only after she has fainted at the news of his engagement to be married, and subsequently recovered upon hearing that the engagement has been broken. Zola's nearest approach to Racine is at the moment in which Renée becomes aware of her passion. She is speaking to her father :

RENÉE

Ce qu'il s'est passé ? Attendez, il faut que je m'interroge, car ma mémoire se brouille... Voyons, que s'est-il donc passé ? Voilà que la peur me prend de me souvenir... Il s'est passé que j'ai beaucoup souffert pendant ce dîner, oui ! de choses qu'on faisait devant moi et qui me déchiraient le cœur. Ensuite, je me suis évanouie, je vous ai rêvé, mon père : vous m'emportiez d'ici, vous me couchiez dans la terre, où je voulais mourir... Oh ! j'étais triste, j'étais triste !... Et puis, on m'a annoncé une nouvelle, qui, brusquement, m'a inondée de bonheur... Attendez ! il faut que je voie... *(Elle recule devant ce qu'elle voit, hagarde.)* Oui, je vois, c'est bien cela... Il m'échappait, et il m'a été rendu, tout mon sang en a brûlé d'allégresse... Grand Dieu ! voilà le crime, je n'y songeais pas, et il était là, qui nous enveloppait. Ah ! misérable ! Ah ! c'est infâme !... *(Elle se jette dans les bras de son père.)* O mon père, prenez-moi, gardez-moi, sauvez-moi !

BÉRAUD

De qui parles-tu ? Qui aimes-tu ?... Achève.

RENÉE

Non, non, une abomination, un cauchemar, quelque chose qui ne peut pas être. L'horreur en glacerait mes lèvres... Je n'aime personne, personne, entendez-vous !

(Act III, scene VII.)

From here, Zola departs from Racine. Renée, for the moment, conceals her love from all but Maxime, into whose arms she throws herself at the end of the act.

In the fourth act, Zola reaches the paradoxical, yet logical, conclusion of his premise of an unconsummated marriage. Aristide, having lived for ten years apart from his wife, has fallen in love with her and now seeks to begin a normal married life. But it is too late. Because his son by a former marriage has preceded him to the nuptial bed, Aristide, the legal husband,

cannot exercise his rights, or fulfill his obligations, without
himself committing incest. In Zola's paradoxical view, the
marital relationship has become more criminal than the adulterous one, and Renée, forced to choose between incest and
adultery, adopts the lesser evil in rejecting her husband and
continuing relations with his son. A number of subsidiary
complications — Aristide's financial trickery, Mlle Chuin's
betrayal of Renée, Maxime's vain effort to make over his life
by marrying a wholesome Swedish girl — intervene before the
final curtain in the fifth act, which falls on Renée's inevitable
suicide.

The characters are well conceived, and rise above the artifi-
cialities of the plot. In re-writing the Phèdre story in naturalist
terms, Zola has sought to supplant the Greek sense of fate with
the modern conception of heredity and environnement. As
he states in his preface ; " ... j'ai détruit le symbole de la fatalité
antique, en mettant scientifiquement Renée sous la double
influence de l'hérédité et des milieux " (1). Zola's inexperience
as a playwright prevented him from wholly successful accomplishment of his purpose, but this statement could well serve as a
model for modern realism.

With *Renée*, Zola sought also to bring to the stage protagonists who were not models of virtue, and who, incorporating
a mixture of good and evil qualities, were closer to reality than
the conventional stage heroes and heroines. It is in this respect,
as he explains in his preface, that the novel is so far in advance
of the stage :

Pourquoi, avec Balzac, avec Flaubert, avec les Goncourt, la vie,
toute la vie, est-elle entrée si largement dans le roman ? C'est qu'ils
ont pu s'affranchir des idées faites sur la jeune fille, la mère, l'amant,
toutes ces perfections dont le poncif passait de main en main. Ils se sont
risqués à montrer que rien n'est absolu chez l'homme, que la vertu
ne va pas sans vice, ni le vice sans vertu, que tout se mélange et se
complique, que la grandeur est même là, dans ces luttes de l'être pour
l'existence. Dès lors, le roman a compté des personnages réels, agissant
et respirant comme nous, tandis que le théâtre gardait son personnel de
marionnettes, taillés dans l'idéal comme dans du bois... Tant que le
public exigera des personnages sympathiques, je veux dire des poupées
ornées conventionnellement de toutes les vertus, l'évolution naturaliste
est impossible au théâtre (2).

(1) Preface to *Renée*, p. IX.
(2) *Ibid.*, pp. X-XI.

Finally, Zola admits that *Renée* is " incomplète ", having been debased (" abâtardie ") to fit the particular needs of Sarah Bernhardt and of the *Comédie-Française*, for whom it had originally been written (1). This explanation can hardly have satisfied those of his admirers who were hoping to find in *Renée* the *Hernani* of naturalism. Neither Sarah Bernhardt nor the *Comédie-Française* were concerned in the production at the *Vaudeville*, and can scarcely be held accountable for defects in a play in which they were no longer interested. If Zola considered *Renée* inadequate as an expression of his ideas, he was at liberty to re-write it. A better explanation for the comparative failure of this play is to be found in Zola's impatience with the theater. Devoting, quite understandably, his major effort to his novels, he was unwilling to lavish upon his theatrical work the care and thought which would have been needed to create a stage masterpiece. Although *Renée* shows traces of dramaturgical talent, it comes far short of Zola's aspirations.

Conclusions

Thérèse Raquin is generally considered to be Zola's best play. In 1927, on the occasion of the 25th anniversary of his death, a movement was launched by a number of critics, foremost among whom were Gustave Kahn and Antoine, to persuade the *Comédie-Française* to include it in its repertory (2). To be sure, the play has deteriorated with time. Much of its dialogue and some of its situations appear stilted and artificial to modern tastes, so that it is enveloped today in an atmosphere of melodrama which is injurious to its survival as a character study. Nevertheless, the play remains exciting, and it has acquired the additional value of historical interest. The very fact that it was attacked so bitterly by the critics as too stark and sordid a subject for the stage indicates the extent of Zola's innovation.

Zola's plays do not, of course, measure up to his great panoramic novels — *l'Assommoir, Germinal, la Terre, la Débâcle*. The reasons for this comparative failure are quite apparent. None of the plays of his naturalist period were products of his

---

(1) *Ibid.*, p. XI.
(2) See LES ŒUVRES COMPLÈTES, *Théâtre II*, " Notes et commentaires ", p. 685. Articles by Antoine and Kahn are given at pp. 691-692.

maturity ; the latest in composition, *Renée*, was derived principally from an early novel. He was impatient with the stage,
and, as one may see particularly in the case of *Renée*, resorted
to short-cuts to bring about desired situations without regard
to plausibility, with the result that his tragedies tend to degenerate into melodrama, and his comedies into farce. His greatest
novels are panoramic in scope, and Zola — as was the case with
every other dramatist of his generation — was unable to bring
this quality to the stage. Although his lesser novels deal with
various levels of bourgeois society, his greatest and most celebrated naturalist works are studies of manual workers, with a
detailed presentation of their speech, habits, environment and
morality ; but, excluding his collaborations and lyric dramas, no
manual worker appears in his theater. Finally, and perhaps
most important, Zola's characters are exceptional cases placed
in exceptional circumstances, with the result that their action
on the stage is limited to the stage, instead of embracing the
real life which lies beyond it. In planning the series of *Rougon-
Macquart* novels at the outset of his career, Zola realized that
he would have to choose between the creation of normal characters and the creation of exceptional ones. Because the *Rougon-
Macquart* were based upon the " scientific " analysis of hereditary
and environmental factors, he was obliged to choose the latter
course. Thus he writes in his " Notes générales sur la nature de
l'œuvre " (the *Rougon-Macquart*) :

Comprendre chaque roman ainsi : poser d'abord un cas humain
(physiologique) ; mettre en présence deux, trois puissances (tempéraments) ; établir une lutte entre ces puissances ; puis mener les personnages au dénouement par la logique de leur être particulier, une puissance
absorbant l'autre ou les autres (1).

Although Taine advises : " Faites fort et général ", Zola
concludes that as to himself : " Faire général ne m'est pas
permis par la constitution même de mes livres. " He then
considers the arguments for and against the two types of characters — the normal and the exceptional — and concludes in
favor of the latter :

Il y a deux genres de personnages : Emma et Germinie, la créature
vraie observée par Flaubert et la créature grandie créée par les de
Goncourt. Dans l'une, l'analyse est faite à froid, le type se généralise.

_____

(1) LES ŒUVRES COMPLÈTES, *la Fortune des Rougon*, " Notes et variantes ",
p. 355.

Dans l'autre, il semble que les auteurs aient torturé la vérité, le type devient exceptionnel. Ma Thérèse et ma Madeleine sont exceptionnelles. Dans les études que je veux faire, je ne puis guère sortir de l'exception. Ces créations particulières sont, d'ailleurs, plus d'un artiste, ce mot étant pris dans le sens moderne. Il semble aussi qu'en sortant du général, l'œuvre devient supérieure (Julien Sorel) ; il y a création d'homme, effort d'artiste. *L'œuvre gagne en intérêt humain ce qu'elle perd en réalité courante.* [Italics ours.] Il faudrait donc faire exceptionnel comme Stendhal, éviter les trop grandes monstruosités, mais prendre des cas particuliers de cerveau et de chair. Quand Taine conseille de faire général et qu'il approuve Flaubert de faire général, il est l'homme de sa théorie des milieux ; d'ailleurs, il a dit de Stendhal qu'il était « un homme supérieur », et Stendhal a pourtant créé des êtres exceptionnels, résumant une époque ou un pays, si l'on veut, mais à coup sûr, hors de la foule (1).

The greater scope of the novel allowed Zola to balance the eccentricities of his characters (where such eccentricities exist) with life-like descriptions of their environment, and with explanations of their behavior, so that the novel as a whole emerged as a work of observed reality. Working with abnormal characters in the restricted medium of the theater, he was unable to bring to the stage that quality of observed reality of which he was a master in the novel.

(1) *Ibid.*, pp. 355-356.

CHAPTER III

ZOLA'S DRAMATIC CRITICISM

Introduction. — Origins of naturalism. — Emergence of naturalism. — Naturalism in the theater. — Sardou, Dumas *fils*, Augier. — Laughter and fantasy. — Appraisal of Zola's naturalism.

Introduction

Zola's greatest impact in the theater was provided by the series of weekly articles which he wrote in the Paris press during 1876-1881 (successively in *le Bien public, le Voltaire* and *le Figaro*), augmented by articles contributed during 1875-1880 to the St. Petersburg journal *Viestnik Evropy* (" Messenger of Europe "), where they appeared in Russian translation. Zola collected and published most of these articles, classified according to subject, in six volumes during 1880-1882 ; in 1880, *le Roman expérimental* ; in 1881, *le Naturalisme au théâtre, Nos auteurs dramatiques, les Romanciers naturalistes*, and *Documents littéraires* ; and in 1882, *Une campagne.* As he states in the prefaces to these collections, two of the volumes (*les Romanciers naturalistes* and *Documents littéraires*) are made up of articles which appeared in *Viestnick Evropy* (1) ; three (*le Naturalisme au théâtre, Nos auteurs dramatiques* and *Une campagne*) contain articles which appeared in his weekly Paris column ; and the remaining volume *(le Roman expérimental)* contains articles from both sources (2).

(1) These volumes contain also a few added sections which appeared in *le Voltaire.*

(2) For a recent summary and analysis of these contributions to newspapers, see two articles by F. W. J. HEMMINGS, " Zola, le Bien public and le Voltaire ", in *The Romanic Review*, vol. 47 (April 1956), pp. 103-116 ; and Zola, Manet, and the impressionists (1875-1880) ", in *PMLA*, vol. 73 (Sept. 1958), pp. 407-417. At p. 116 of the former article, HEMMINGS gives a list of those articles in *le Bien public* and *le Voltaire* which Zola did not include in the volumes published during 1880-1882. Zola's press articles of this period are discussed also at pages 248-249 of HEMMINGS' valuable work, *Emile Zola.*

For a list and analysis of Zolas's Russian articles, see Jean TRIOMPHE, " Zola collaborateur du Messager de l'Europe ", in *Revue de Littérature comparée*, XVII (1957), pp. 754-765. And see *Zola journaliste*, by Henri MITTERAND.

Zola's contributions to *le Bien public* beginning in 1876 have
sometimes been considered to be his first articles as a dramatic
critic regularly assigned to cover theatrical openings. Actually,
his first experience as a regularly-assigned dramatic critic was
some years earlier. During nearly four months of 1873, he
served as dramatic critic for the Paris journal *l'Avenir national*,
to which he contributed more than twenty articles under the
heading " Causerie dramatique et littéraire ", " Causerie dramatique " or " Causerie littéraire ". Of particular interest is the
first articles of the series, in the issue of 25 February 1873, where
Zola speaks for perhaps the first time of " experimental "
literature. Writing on the agonizing illness of the theater, Zola
proposes :

... il me plaît de constater qu'un même mouvement depuis le commen-
cement du siècle se manifeste dans toutes les productions de l'esprit
humain. C'est le mouvement scientifique, le mouvement de l'analyse
exacte. Après avoir transformé la science, il s'est accentué parallèlement
dans les lettres et dans les arts. L'histoire a reçu un souffle nouveau, la
critique s'est créée, la littérature est devenue tout expérimentale. Dans
le roman surtout, Balzac est né, apportant une méthode chirurgicale,
s'appuyant sur la science, aidant la science. Il semble ainsi que tout ce
siècle marche d'un bloc à la découverte de la vérité. C'est comme une
caravane de l'humanité créatrice partant pour la solution du grand
problème. Je crois dès lors impossible que le théâtre n'entre pas, à un
moment donné, dans ce large entraînement des intelligences. Il doit
subir à son tour l'action immédiate de l'esprit scientifique de l'époque...
Lorsque Lavoisier, reprenant l'alchimie à sa source, s'imagina de
décomposer l'air, cet air banal que les savants de tant de siècles avaient
respiré sans le connaître, il créa la chimie. En art, nous en sommes à
ce point, à cette nécessité de décomposer les faits les plus simples, si
nous voulons ouvrir un champ nouveau. C'est ce que j'appelais plus
haut la littérature expérimentale, la littérature d'un siècle de science.

Were these words, written in 1873, inspired by Claude
Bernard's *Introduction à la Médecine expérimentale*, which was
published in 1865 ? Lavoisier, but not Bernard, is mentioned in
the article, and, as will be seen later in this chapter, it is generally
agreed that Zola did not read Bernard's work until 1876-1878.
If this belief is correct, it would seem that Zola was inspired by
his general interest in science, rather than by the work of any
one scientific scholar, in drawing an analogy between the
methods of science and literature and in arriving at his idea of
" experimentation " in literature. Not until some years later,
in his article " Le Roman expérimental ", did Zola use Bernard's

celebrated work to buttress and amplify his theory of experimental literature and give it an aura of scientific respectability. As was the case during his first years in Paris, Zola had recourse to newspaper articles as a means of livelihood during the years between the Franco-Prussian war and the publication of *l'Assommoir* (1). His first novels of the *Rougon-Macquart* *(la Fortune des Rougon, la Curée, le Ventre de Paris, la Conquête de Plassans)* were not selling well. His plays *(Thérèse Raquin, les Héritiers Rabourdin)* were failures. The intransigeance of his political outlook caused him to be looked upon with suspicion : one of his articles, on the unemployment crisis late in 1872, led to the suspension for two months of a Paris newspaper (2). Only a few intimate friends recognized Zola's talent, but among these were the most important writers of the new school : Flaubert, de Goncourt, Daudet. These novelists had a particular bond in common with Zola in the fact that they too had failed in the theater. Flaubert, after the withdrawal of his *le Candidat* in 1874, organized a " dîner des auteurs sifflés ", for which these authors, together with Zola and the Russian novelist Tourgueneff, assembled at monthly intervals (3). His assignments to write in 1875 for *Viestnik Evropy* (to which Tourgueneff introduced him) and in 1876 for the *Bien public* yielded a welcome and necessary increment to his meager income. Fame and fortune were not long in coming. In one momentous week appeared his first " Revue dramatique " in *le Bien public* of 10 April 1876, and, in the same journal of 13 April, the first instalment of *l'Assommoir* (4).

Zola's column appeared in the *Bien public* at weekly intervals from 10 April 1876 until the end of June 1878, when the news-

(1) A list of periodicals to which Zola contributed is given in LES ŒUVRES COMPLÈTES, *Mélanges, Préfaces et Discours,* " Notes et commentaires ", p. 387. A review of Zola's critical works appears in DOUCET, *l'Esthétique d'Emile Zola et son application à la critique,* pp. 231-243.
(2) " Le lendemain de la crise ", in *le Corsaire,* 22 December 1872. Zola compares the miseries of the unemployed with the luxurious life (as he imagined it) of a group of royalists waiting to seize power when starvation has brought about the fall of the Republic.
(3) Zola's account of these dinners appears in LES ŒUVRES COMPLÈTES, *les Romanciers naturalistes,* " Gustave Flaubert, l'Homme, II ", p. 151.
(4) Because of protests by readers of *le Bien public,* publication of *l'Assommoir* was suspended after the termination of Part I in the issue of 7 June 1876. The remainder of the novel was published in *la République des Lettres,* from July 1876 to January 1877. Suspension of the novel did not affect the cordial relations which existed between ZOLA and the *Bien public.* The *Bien public* published coupons entitling its readers to receive *la République des Lettres* free of charge as long as *l'Assommoir* was being published in the latter journal.

paper itself went out of existence, stating to its readers that they would be served almost immediately by " un autre journal, également républicain ". Le Voltaire began publication 5 July 1878, promising to be " le Figaro des républicains ". Zola's first column in the new journal appeared a few days later in the issue of 9 July, and his column continued to appear, with few exceptions, at weekly intervals until a quarrel between Zola and the editor terminated the relationship on 31 August 1880. From 20 September 1880 to 22 September 1881, he contributed weekly articles to le Figaro. For many years thereafter, he gave up regular contributions to the press, although he submitted occasional articles from time to time. Between December 1895 and 13 June 1896, he contributed a further series of articles to le Figaro, which he published in volume in 1897 under the title Nouvelle campagne (1).

During the first year and more of Zola's contributions to the Bien public, his column was entitled " Revue dramatique ". Beginning with the issue of 4 June 1877, the title was changed to " Revue dramatique et littéraire ", the words " et littéraire " in smaller capitals on the second line. The column continued under this title in the Bien public and throughout its existence in the Voltaire. In the Figaro, each article bore its individual title without a comprehensive name for the column. As the change in title indicates, Zola deviated more and more from his original intention of devoting his column to purely theatrical matters. His phenomenal rise to success, which began with l'Assommoir, entitled him to far greater freedom in the use of his column than would have been accorded to a less celebrated writer. He came to feel that his duties as a critic did not oblige him to report on every play which opened in Paris, but only on those which raised questions of importance. Edmond Lepelletier, his colleague in charge of the daily theatrical news column in the Bien public, recalls that Zola frequently asked him to report in the back pages of the newspaper upon plays which Zola disdained to discuss in his first-page column :

... assez fréquemment il lui arrivait de développer des théories sur l'art dramatique et sur le roman expérimental plutôt que de gaspiller l'espace dont il disposait, au rez-de-chaussée du journal, les dimanches soir, au profit d'une revue insipide ou d'un drame baroque. Zola me

(1) Unlike his other collections of critical articles, all of ZOLA's articles of this last series are published in Nouvelle campagne. The volume also contains an article, " les Droits du critique ", which was rejected by the Figaro.

priait alors de « corser » mon courrier théâtral quotidien, et d'y insérer un aperçu de la pièce nouvelle, suffisant pour renseigner le public et tenir lieu de compte rendu (1).

A similar service was performed by Zola's intimate friend, Henry Céard, who frequently sat in Zola's orchestra seat and sent notes on certain plays to Zola (then residing at his country home in Médan) — notes of which Zola made use in writing his theatrical column (2).

Zola himself explained his point of view in a column of the *Voltaire* :

Il est vrai, peut-être, que je comprends le journal d'une façon qui m'est personnelle. Peu importe qu'une pièce soit absolument nulle, le public veut quand même être renseigné, et vous, journaliste, avez pour devoir de le renseigner. Sans doute, tel devrait être strictement mon rôle. Eh bien ! dans ce cas, je suis un triste journaliste, car je me refuse à cette besogne de greffier. Si je vaux quelque chose, c'est par ma passion, et je me sens tout à fait mauvais, quand je ne suis pas pris pour ou contre ; à plus forte raison, je deviens absurde, si certaines considérations, auxquelles personne n'échappe, me forcent à mentir. Donc le mieux est de laisser aux reporteurs leur besogne et de compter seulement sur moi, lorsque la littérature est en jeu et que je me passionne (3).

When one considers that Zola's labors in creative literature continued unabated throughout this period, it is understandable that his weekly column was sometimes a burden and that he employed considerable ingenuity in filling it. For example, during the summer of 1877, he was in the south of France, engaged in writing the novel, *Une page d'amour*, and in corresponding with William Busnach concerning the stage adaptation of *l'Assommoir*. " Heureusement ", he writes to Huysmans, " que je me débarrasse du *Bien public*, en reproduisant des fragments de mes articles de Russie " (4). Reproduction of his

(1) Edmond LEPELLETIER, *Emile Zola, sa vie, son œuvre* (Paris, 1908), p. 185. See also pp. 14-15.
(2) I am in debted to C.-A. BURNS for this information, which is given in his preface (p. 23) to his recent publication, *Henry Céard, Lettres inédites à Emile Zola.*
(3) *Le Voltaire*, 30 December 1879. Not reprinted.
(4) Letter dated 3 August 1877, LES ŒUVRES COMPLÈTES, *Correspondance (1872-1902)*, p. 480. Zola published not only occasional fragments of his Russian essays in his weekly column, but also many of the complete essays in separate articles (outside of his weekly column) prior to their publication in book form in 1880-1881.

Russian articles was not the only device employed to fill the column. In his " Revue dramatique et littéraire " of 6 August 1877, he wrote :

Voici quelque temps que je médite de prendre une récréation d'été, dans ce feuilleton, si grave l'hiver. Je vais donc parler de tout autre chose que de théâtre et de littérature. L'idée m'est venue d'étudier l'influence des prêtres en France — vous voyez que je suis loin de mes sujets habituels — mais d'étudier cette influence en observateur plus qu'en moraliste. Je publierai donc cinq courtes scènes, cinq nouvelles de quelques pages, qui me semblent devoir résumer la matière. Et voici, aujourd'hui, la première de ces nouvelles. Elle ne saurait arriver plus à propos, elle est d'actualité.

This column, and the four following, are accordingly given up to five short stories concerning priests (1). The next three are reminiscences of his early days at Aix and in Paris, with apparently some elements of fiction (2), and it is not until October that his strictly critical articles are resumed.

More serious than these summer-time lapses from critical duties is the charge that Zola used his column to further his own interests — specifically, to promote the sale of his novels. Insofar as the charge relates to publicity, there is some truth in it. Zola had always been conscious of the value of publicity, particularly when it accrued from denunciations and attacks from which he might emerge as a martyr to the cause of truth. Commenting on the benevolent reception accorded to his first book, *Contes à Ninon*, he wrote to Valabrègue : " J'aurais préféré un véritable éreintement (3). " Writing again to Valabrègue about the possibility of police action against his forthcoming *Thérèse Raquin* (the novel), he confessed : " Il est vrai que quelques mois de prison ne me font pas peur (4). " When,

---

(1) *Le Bien public*, 1877, 6, 13, 20 and 27 August and 3 September. Not reprinted.
For a résumé of these stories, see the article by F. W. J. HEMMINGS, in *The Romanic Review*, vol. 47 (April 1956), p. 106 et seq.
A commentary on the various priests which appear in the *Rougon-Macquart* is to be found at pages 69-72 of Henri GUILLEMIN's, *Zola, légende ou vérité* ?
(2) *Ibid.*, 10, 17 and 24 September. Not reprinted.
(3) Letter dated 6 February 1865, LES ŒUVRES COMPLÈTES, *Correspondance (1858-1871)*, p. 266. (This edition of Zola's correspondance gives the reading " véritablement ". The correct reading, " véritable " is given by the earlier Fasquelle edition, Emile ZOLA, *Correspondance, les lettres et les arts* (Paris, 1908), p. 28).
(4) Letter dated 29 May 1867, LES ŒUVRES COMPLÈTES, *ibid.*, p. 305. Zola's fears — or hopes — of police action did not materialize in this case.

therefore, he came into possession of a weekly, front-page column in the Paris press, he occasionally availed himself of the opportunity to publicize works in which he had a personal interest. Two columns in *le Voltaire* are devoted to the stage adaptation of *l'Assommoir* (1). Another, a defense of his novel *Nana*, begins with the frank statement, " J'ai un journal et j'en use " (2). Later, in *le Figaro*, he devoted several columns to the stage adaptation of *Nana* (3), and two other articles were perhaps written to stimulate interest in his novel *Pot-Bouille*, although this work is not mentioned (4).

Zola sought to promote and protect not only his own work but that of all writers whom he deemed to be exponents of naturalism. He was generally lavish in praise of Flaubert, de Goncourt and Daudet, and used his column to advertise the work of his favorite disciples : Maupassant, Hennique, Huysmans, Céard, Alexis (5).

Zola could afford to ignore the charge that he was publicity-conscious, but he protested vigorously against accusations that his entire system of naturalism had been devised *après coup* to justify and advertise his novels. Many of his defenses against this accusation — his disclaimer of responsibility for naturalism, his plea that the highest morality is the truth — will be examined

---

(1) 1) *Le Voltaire*, 28 January 1879. This was Part I of Zola's preface to the published play : William BUSNACH et Octave GASTINEAU, *l'Assommoir, drame en cinq actes et neuf tableaux, avec une préface d'Emile Zola et un dessin de Georges Clairin* (Paris, 1880). This preface, appears in LES ŒUVRES COMPLÈTES, *Mélanges, Préfaces et Discours*, pp. 203-227.
2) *Le Voltaire*, 2 September 1879. With some omissions, this is Part III of ZOLA's preface to *l'Assommoir* (the play). Reprinted as noted above.
(2) *Le Voltaire*, 28 October 1879. Not reprinted.
(3) *Le Figaro*, 12 January, 7 February and 21 February 1881, reprinted in LES ŒUVRES COMPLÈTES, *Une campagne*, under the titles, respectively, of " la Fille au théâtre ", " Nana ", and " Comment elles poussent ".
(4) *Le Figaro*, 28 February and 18 April 1881, reprinted in *Une campagne* under the titles, respectively, of " l'Adultère dans la bourgeoisie " and " Femmes honnêtes ".
(5) The extent of Zola's enthusiasm to be of service to his friends is illustrated by a hoax which he practised upon the public early in 1869. In order to help launch his compatriot, Paul Alexis, on a literary career, he published a poem by ALEXIS, *les Lits*, in his column, " Livres d'aujourd'hui et de demain " (*le Gaulois*, 10 January 1869) *as a poem of Baudelaire*, intending to reveal the true author after the poem had received the attention which an undiscovered poem of Baudelaire would naturally evoke. The fraud was soon discovered, and a retraction made by ZOLA in *le Gaulois* of 19 January 1869. It is a credit to Zola that he had nothing whatever to gain personally from the imposture. Details of the conspiracy are revealed in Zola's letter to Marius Roux, published, with an explanatory footnote, in LES ŒUVRES COMPLÈTES, *Correspondance (1858-1871)*, pp. 329-330. The date of the letter is given as 9 January 1868, and must be in error, inasmuch as ZOLA published *les Lits* in 1869.

below. As to the charge that he had but recently discovered naturalism, and that his discovery was motivated by the hope of personal gain, he pointed out that there had been no essential variation in his theories, and that his present views (as of the late 1870s) were simply elaborations of opinions which he had held before beginning the *Rougon-Macquart*. In support of his claim, he reprinted in his column an article on Victor Hugo's *les Chansons des rues et des bois* which he had published years earlier in *Mes haines* (1), with the following prefatory note :

Voici quelques pages que j'ai écrites il y a quatorze ans, et qui viennent de reparaître dans une nouvelle édition de *Mes haines*. Je les donne, pour répondre à ceux qui m'accusent d'obéir dans ma critique à des intérêts immédiats et personnels. La vérité est que mes idées d'aujourd'hui sont les mêmes que mes idées d'il y a quatorze ans. J'ai dit alors de Victor Hugo ce que j'en ai dit dans ces temps derniers. Depuis le premier jour de mes débuts, je n'ai fait que développer la formule naturaliste. Nous voilà loin du fameux plan qu'on prête à mon orgueil, de vouloir immoler sur l'autel de *l'Assommoir* les plus illustres de mes confrères. Toute la campagne que je fais aujourd'hui est déjà commencée dans *Mes haines*, ouvrage publié en 1866 (2).

Zola's defense appears well-founded. There was no essential variation in his ideas (3), although in two respects, his opinions of the 1870s had a slightly different coloration than those expressed a decade earlier. He settled on the term " naturalism ", used only sparingly in his earlier articles, as the slogan of the highest good in all human endeavor — science, history, literature, the arts, and even politics. And he expanded his theory by the concept of " experimental " literature, analogous to scientific experimentation as described by the physiologist, Claude Bernard (4).

In his articles of 1876-1880, Zola re-iterates his early definition of a work of art, substituting, without change of meaning,

(1) LES ŒUVRES COMPLÈTES, *Mes haines*.
(2) *Le Voltaire*, 2 July 1879. Not reprinted.
(3) Some modern scholars may disagree with this statement. F. W. J. HEMMINGS writes (p. 123 of *Emile Zola*) : " In *le Roman expérimental*... the importance attributed to the originality of the artist has noticeably dwindled and, if *Mes haines* is taken as the starting-point, it can be seen that Zola's attitude to this question has undergone a complete reversal. "
On the other hand, Guy ROBERT (p. 44 of his *Emile Zola, principes et caractères généraux de son œuvre*) writes that Zola's ideas have varied little since his formative years.
(4) Claude BERNARD, *Introduction à l'étude de la médecine expérimentale* (Paris, 1865).

the word " nature " for " création ". " Il est certain ", he
writes, " qu'une œuvre ne sera jamais qu'un coin de la nature vu
à travers un tempérament " (1). He continues to recognize the
importance of the artist's personality :

Certes, si la vérité seule comptait dans une œuvre, l'art progresserait
avec les sciences, les œuvres deviendraient d'autant plus grandes qu'elles
seraient plus vraies. Seulement, il faut introduire la personnalité de
l'artiste, et aussitôt la vérité n'est plus qu'un des deux membres de la
formule (2).

Truth in literature cannot, therefore, be mathematical. The
only possible way of measuring the truth of a work of art is to
compare it with nature, but this should be only a preliminary
operation, because the exact reproduction of nature is mere
photography. The human element must be introduced, and
after this is done, the possibilities of art become as varied as the
differing minds of humanity. The critical process must include
both parts of the formula ; Zola describes its operation in this
way :

Quand on a une œuvre en face de soi, il suffit d'abord de chercher
quelle somme de réalité elle contient ; puis, sans la juger encore, on
passe à l'étude du tempérament qui a pu amener l'œuvre les
déviations du vrai qu'on y constate. Peu importe alors le plus ou le
moins d'exactitude. Il faut simplement que le spectacle de l'écrivain
aux prises avec la nature reste grand ; l'intensité avec laquelle il la voit,
la façon puissante dont il la déforme pour la faire entrer dans son
moule, l'empreinte enfin qu'il laisse sur tout ce qu'il touche, telle est la
véritable création humaine, la véritable signature du génie (3).

As to the word " naturalisme ", Zola correctly insists that he
did not invent it, but he acknowledges his paternity of its present
use to designate the growth of methodical observation and
experimentation in science, letters and the arts (4) :

... je constate la grande évolution d'observation et d'expérimentation
qui caractérise notre siècle, et j'appelle naturalisme la formule littéraire

---

(1) *Le Roman expérimental*, " le Naturalisme au théâtre, I ", p. 92. Page
numbers in the remainder of this chapter refer, unless otherwise stated, to
the pagination of LES ŒUVRES COMPLÈTES.
(2) *Documents littéraires*, " Victor Hugo, II ", p. 45.
(3) *Ibid.*, " Réception de M. Dumas fils à l'Académie française ",
pp. 203-304.
(4) *Le Naturalisme au théâtre*, " Polémique, II ", p. 147. Reprinted from
le Voltaire, 5 November 1878. See also *le Roman expérimental*, " Lettre à la
jeunesse, IV ", pp. 76-78.

amenée par cette évolution. Les écrivains naturalistes sont donc ceux dont la méthode d'étude serre la nature et l'humanité du plus près possible, tout en laissant, bien entendu, le tempérament particulier de l'observateur libre de se manifester ensuite dans les œuvres comme bon lui semble (1).

He chose " naturalisme " in preference to the slogan " réalisme ", current thirty years previously, because " le réalisme d'alors était une chapelle et rétrécissait l'horizon littéraire et artistique. Il m'a semblé que le mot naturalisme élargissait au contraire le domaine de l'observation. D'ailleurs, que ce mot soit bien ou mal choisi, peu importe. Il finira par avoir le sens que nous lui donnerons " (2).

Zola's theory of experimentation in literature is fully set forth in his article " Le Roman expérimental " (3). As he states, he has taken the program for experimental medicine given by Claude Bernard in his *Introduction à l'étude de la médecine expérimentale* and applied it to the novelist. Bernard demonstrated that the experimental method in use in chemistry and physics could also be applied to the study of living bodies in physiology and in medicine. Zola argues that the experimental method can be carried still further into the study of emotional and intellectual life. If the method can be extended from physics and chemistry into physiology, it can also be extended from physiology to anthropology and sociology (p. 12). The purpose of the experimental method is to find the relation which links the phenomenon to its proximate cause. The method does not undertake to explain the *why* of matters, but only the *how* (p. 13) (4). Experimentation is an induced observation (pp. 12, 15). The experimental novelist proceeds as follows :

... le romancier est fait d'un observateur et d'un expérimentateur. L'observateur chez lui donne les faits tels qu'il les a observés, pose le

(1) *Le Naturalisme au théâtre,* " Polémique, II ", p. 149.
(2) *Ibid.,* p. 147.
(3) In the volume *le Roman expérimental,* pp. 11-50. This is one of the articles published in *Viestnik Evropy.* It also appeared in *le Voltaire,* 16, 17, 18, 19 and 20 October 1879.
(4) The method is basically that of Comte's *état positif,* but Zola fails to mention Comte in his article. Compare, too, this statement by Bernard, quoted by Zola (p. 34), with Comte's *état théologique, métaphysique* and *scientifique* : " L'esprit humain, dit-il, aux diverses périodes de son évolution, a passé successivement par le sentiment, la raison et l'expérience. D'abord, le sentiment seul s'imposant à la raison créa les vérités de foi, c'est-à-dire la théologie. La raison ou la philosophie devenant ensuite la maîtresse, enfanta la scolastique. Enfin l'expérience, c'est-à-dire l'étude des phénomènes naturels apprit à l'homme que les vérités du monde extérieur ne se trouvent formulées, de prime abord, ni dans le sentiment ni dans la raison. "

point de départ, établit le terrain solide sur lequel vont marcher les personnages et se développer les phénomènes. Puis, l'expérimentateur paraît et institue l'expérience, je veux dire fait mouvoir les personnages dans une histoire particulière, pour y montrer que la succession des faits y sera telle que l'exige le déterminisme des phénomènes mis à l'étude (p. 16).

By " determinism ", Bernard means proximate cause (" cause prochaine "). Bernard, and Zola with him, distinguishes fatalism from determinism :

Il faut préciser : nous ne sommes pas fatalistes, nous sommes déterministes, ce qui n'est point la même chose. Claude Bernard explique très bien les deux termes : « Nous avons donné le nom de déterminisme à la cause prochaine ou déterminante des phénomènes. Nous n'agissons jamais sur l'essence des phénomènes de la nature, mais seulement sur leur déterminisme, et par cela seul que nous agissons sur lui, le déterminisme diffère du fatalisme sur lequel on ne saurait agir. Le fatalisme suppose la manifestation nécessaire d'un phénomène indépendant de ses conditions, tandis que le déterminisme est la condition nécessaire d'un phénomène dont la manifestation n'est pas forcée... » (p. 31).

The experimenter must start with something akin to the Cartesian doubt :

Tout le raisonnement expérimental est basé sur le doute, car l'expérimentateur doit n'avoir aucune idée préconçue devant la nature et garder toujours sa liberté d'esprit. Il accepte simplement les phénomènes qui se produisent, lorsqu'ils sont prouvés (p. 12).

This doubt is the great scientific lever, starting from which an experimental writer may hope to arrive at absolute knowledge (p. 19). Cartesian, too, is the purpose, or ethics, of the experimental method : " se rendre maître de la vie pour la diriger " (p. 28) (1).

Zola takes issue with Bernard only in respect to the latter's view of the arts and letters as personal and spontaneous creations having nothing to do with the observation of natural phenomena. The personal feeling of the artist, Zola points out, must always remain subject to the control of truth (pp. 46-47).

This valiant effort by Zola to equate the process of literary creation with that of scientific experimentation has been condemned by scholars as producing a theory of literature which

(1) The comparison to Descartes is mine. Zola does not mention him.

is patently false (1). Certainly a pronouncement such as this
from le Roman expérimental is hardly valid :

Souvent j'ai dit que nous n'avions pas à tirer une conclusion de nos
œuvres, et cela signifie que nos œuvres portent leur conclusion en elles.
Un expérimentateur n'a pas à conclure, parce que, justement, l'expérience conclut pour lui (2).

However, the facts of literature do not, like those of science,
speak for themselves. They speak for the author, who, having
chosen and arranged his facts in such a way as to lead to a
foreseeable conclusion, can hardly disclaim responsibility for a
result preordained by himself. Zola's pretension to scientific
objectivity is an abuse of his doctrine. One may concede his
right to find an analogy between science and literature, provided
that it remain an analogy and not be confused with an equation.
The author may proceed like the scientist only within certain
limits. He may, like the scientist, choose the subject of his
" experiment " and resolve to observe it as accurately as possible.
From this point his method necessarily departs from that of the
scientist. Whereas a true experiment proceeds independently
of the will of the experimenter, every thought and every action
of a character in a novel or play is dependent upon the will of
the author. An objective writer will, to be sure, reproduce life
with the utmost fidelity of which he is capable, but his manner of
observing, arranging and recording the facts is necessarily colored
by his own purposes and prejudices. The writer cannot reach
the perfect objectivity of the scientist although he may, if he
choose, increase up to a point short of perfection the degree of
objectivity with which he observes and comments on the world
about him.

It is generally agreed that Zola did not read Claude Bernard's

---

(1) See, for example, F. W. J. HEMMINGS, Emile Zola, pp. 109, 121 ;
Guy ROBERT, Emile Zola, principes et caractères généraux de son œuvre,
pp. 38, 45-46 ; Angus WILSON, Emile Zola, an Introductory Study of his Novels,
pp. 25, 30, 84-85 ; Reino VIRTANEN, Claude Bernard and his Place in the
History of Ideas, p. 122.
    In a recently published volume : Henry CÉARD, Lettres inédites à Emile Zola,
publiées et annotées par C.-A. Burns avec une préface de René Dumesnil, Letter
No. 34 (pp. 107-108) contains a vigorous protest to Zola by his young disciple,
Céard, against " un sophisme capital " in Zola's study of the experimental
novel. As Céard puts it, the difference between the scientist and the novelist
is this : " Claude Bernard avec son système expérimente et peut conclure ; le
romancier, avec vos théories, expérimente aussi, mais c'est le public qui
fatalement conclut à sa place, car lui est dans l'impossibilité scientifique
d'imposer ses résultats. D'où le sophisme. " Céard's objection appears to
have had no effect on Zola's thinking.
(2) Le Roman expérimental, " le Roman expérimental, III ", p. 32.

Introduction à la médecine expérimentale (published in 1865) until 1876-1878. Zola himself, having perhaps forgotten the exact sequence of events, stated in an interview in 1880 that he had read Claude Bernard prior to conceiving the *Rougon-Macquart* (1). On the other hand, a modern scholar, Lote, points out that Zola's projects of 1868 for the *Rougon-Macquart* make no mention of experimentation, and suggests that Zola may have developed this aspect of his naturalistic principles at a later date in order to lend justification and support to his novels (2). Maurice Le Blond, Zola's son-in-law and editor of LES ŒUVRES COMPLÈTES, is also of the opinion that Zola became acquainted with the work of Claude Bernard after beginning the *Rougon-Macquart* (3). F. W. J. Hemmings and Guy Robert are of the same opinion. Hemmings, on the basis of a letter written by Zola's friend, Henry Céard, gives 1876 as the earliest probable date of Zola's first contact with the work of Bernard ; Robert gives 1878 as the earliest probable date (4). However this may be, the principle of " experimentation " appears in no way to be a significant change or reversal of Zola's early theories, but rather a further development of them — a development which, to be sure, was at times carried to a rather fanciful extreme, as in the case of *le Roman expérimental*.

It is of course very clear that Zola invoked science as a defense against accusations of indecency and that he stood to gain more than any other contemporary writer from his own championship of the naturalist cause. But it is also clear that his principle of scientific observation was the initial inspiration for his early naturalist novels (*Thérèse Raquin* and *Madeleine Férat*) and for the entire series of the *Rougon-Macquart*, although it is probable that he did not speak of experimentation in literature until 1873, in his first article for *l'Avenir national* and

(1) Fernand XAU, *Emile Zola* (Paris, 1880). This booklet of 68 pages is an account of a long interview of Zola by Xau. The interview is dated 15 April 1880, and is said to have taken 2 1/2 hours. Zola is reported to have said : " Dès 1868, c'est-à-dire avant la chute de l'Empire, tout le plan des Rougon-Macquart était préparé, arrêté. Dans *Madeleine Férat*, vous pourrez trouver l'idée que j'avais déjà de faire la physiologie d'une famille. A cette époque, j'avais lu *l'Hérédité naturelle* du Dr LUCAS et les ouvrages de physiologie de Claude BERNARD " (p. 45).
(2) G. LOTE, " la Doctrine et la méthode naturalistes d'après Emile Zola ", in *Zeitschrift für französische Sprache und Literatur*, vol. 51 (1928), pp. 193-224 and 389-418, at p. 209.
(3) LES ŒUVRES COMPLÈTES, *le Roman expérimental*, " Notes et commentaires ", p. 341.
(4) F. W. J. HEMMINGS, *Emile Zola*, p. 121 ; Guy ROBERT, *Emile Zola* p. 37 ; and see Reino VIRTANEN, *Claude Bernard*, p. 121.

in the preface to *Thérèse Raquin* (the play). He appears justified, therefore, in contending that his principles ante-dated his
work and that they remained constant except for logical enlar-
gement and development. Granting that he frequently used
naturalism as a defense against charges of indecency, it must
surely be considered legitimate for an author to defend his
work by the principle which inspired it.

Naturalism was of course far more than a personal defense.
It was the principle by which Zola hoped to free literature and
the drama from the shackles of convention, and to enable writers
to present a greater measure of truth.

Origins of naturalism

Zola considered naturalism as the end-result of both an
evolutionary and revolutionary process. As an evolution, the
movement culminating in naturalism was motivated by the
gradual substitution of physiological for metaphysical man.

Toute l'histoire de notre théâtre est dans ce triomphe de l'homme
physiologique apparaissant davantage à chaque époque, sous le manne-
quin de l'idéalisme religieux et philosophique. Corneille, Molière, Racine,
Voltaire, Beaumarchais, et de nos jours, Victor Hugo, Émile Augier,
Alexandre Dumas fils, Sardou lui-même, n'ont eu qu'une besogne,
même lorsqu'ils ne s'en sont pas nettement rendu compte : augmenter
la réalité de l'œuvre dramatique, progresser dans la vérité, dégager de
plus en plus l'homme naturel et l'imposer au public. Et, fatalement,
l'évolution ne s'arrête pas avec eux, elle continue, elle continuera
toujours. L'humanité est très jeune (1).

Zola is here looking at several centuries of dramatic history
from a very distant perspective indeed. Frequently he adopted
the view, which has come to be traditional, that naturalism was
the result of successive revolutions — of romanticism against
classicism and, in his time, of naturalism against romanticism.

Zola points out that the seeds of both romanticism and
naturalism were sown in the Eighteenth Century. Rousseau

---

(1) *Le Naturalisme au théâtre,* " le Costume, I ", p. 93. Reprinted from
le Voltaire, 16 December 1879.

    I have stated that Zola considered naturalism an " end-result ". This
does not conflict with his opinion that the evolution " continuera toujours ",
since in his view naturalism was itself an evolving process — but a process
which would evolve by ever-increasing reliance upon scientific method. He
dit not foresee — at least at this time — that there would be an idealist reaction to naturalism.

was the father of the romantics, while Diderot was the veritable forefather of the positivists and naturalists, since he gave birth to methods of observation and experimentation in literature and was the first to advocate the exact truth on the stage and in the novel (1). Because Diderot's suggested reform in the direction of greater truth has not yet penetrated to the stage, Zola is continuing the campaign (2). Perhaps Zola's best single article on naturalism is the essay " Le naturalisme au théâtre " reprinted in the volume *le Roman expérimental* (3). He begins by denying that he invented either the word or the system. He simply applied the word, already in use, to the current evolution taking place in French literature. The system itself is " une école littéraire vieille comme le monde... Mon opinion personnelle est que le naturalisme date de la première ligne qu'un homme a écrite. Dès ce jour-là, la question de la vérité était posée " (4). More specifically, naturalism was born in the Eighteenth Century — " ce merveilleux épanouissement d'intelligence ", " ce mouvement prodigieux ", in which the salient fact was the creation of a method based on observation and analysis (5). Rousseau and his followers opened literature to nature. Diderot, the great figure of the century, had a perception of truth which was in advance of his epoch, and made constant war on the wormy structure of conventions and rules. Zola here defines naturalism :

... c'est cette évolution que j'ai appelée naturalisme, et j'estime qu'on ne pouvait employer un mot plus juste. Le naturalisme, c'est le retour à la nature, c'est cette opération que les savants ont faite le jour où ils se sont avisés de partir de l'étude des corps et des phénomènes, de se baser sur l'expérience, de procéder par l'analyse. Le naturalisme, dans les lettres, c'est également le retour à la nature et à l'homme, l'observation directe, l'anatomie exacte, l'acceptation et la peinture de ce qui est (6).

(1) *Une campagne,* " le Naturalisme ", p. 102. Reprinted from *le Figaro,* 17 January 1881.
(2) *Le Naturalisme au théâtre,* " Polémique, IV ", p. 154. Reprinted from *le Bien public,* 18 March 1878.
(3) This article is not to be confused with the volume bearing the same title. The volume *le Naturalisme au théâtre* is compiled of his weekly press articles. The essay in question was one of Zola's Russian articles, and appeared in France as the preface to Edouard NoëL and Edmond STOULLIG's, *les Annales du théâtre et de la musique, précédées du Naturalisme au théâtre par M. Emile Zola, quatrième année, 1878* (Paris, 1879). Subsequently it was reprinted in *le Roman expérimental,* pp. 91-126.
(4) *Le Roman expérimental,* " le Naturalisme du théâtre, I ", pp. 91 and 93.
(5) *Ibid.,* pp. 93, 94.
(6) *Ibid.,* p. 95.

One sees clearly in this passage the double source of Zola's naturalism, which derives both from Rousseau's return to nature and from the spirit of inquiry of the Age of Enlightenment. Although naturalism is a reaction against romanticism, this particular romantic element — a return to nature — has survived, and, more than surviving, forms a necessary link between classicism and naturalism. With the growth of the natural sciences, classicism was doomed, although it had enough latent strength to survive even the French Revolution. The question was whether naturalism would triumph immediately or whether it would have to lie dormant until a later evolution. Unfortunately for the theater, neither Diderot nor Mercier (1), who laid the basis for naturalism in the theater, was able to write a play important enough to inaugurate a naturalist trend in the drama (2). Rousseau and his followers carried literature into romanticism, and the naturalist ideas of Diderot had to await the abatement of the romantic frenzy before they could be heard again.

Zola sometimes considered romanticism as a halt, or even as a retreat, in the inevitable progress of French literature (3), but more frequently he considered it a link between classicism and naturalism :

... le drame romantique est un premier pas vers le drame naturaliste auquel nous marchons. Le drame romantique a déblayé le terrain, proclamé la liberté de l'art (4).
... il est bien visible que le romantisme n'a été que le chaînon nécessaire qui devait attacher la littérature classique à la littérature naturaliste (5).
... le romantisme, en un mot, est la période initiale et troublée du naturalisme (6).

Although Zola consistently denounced the rhetorical falseness of the romantics (7), he recognized, as an affirmative contri-

---

(1) Louis-Sebastien Mercier, 1740-1814.
(2) *Le Roman expérimental,* " le Naturalisme au théâtre, III ", pp. 106-107.
(3) *Documents littéraires,* " Théophile Gautier, III ", p. 126. Part of a Russian article reprinted in *le Voltaire,* 29 July 1879.
(4) *Le Naturalisme au théâtre,* " le Naturalisme, I ", p. 15.
(5) *Ibid.,* " le Naturalisme, II ", p. 20. Reprinted from *le Bien public,* 18 March 1878.
(6) *Le Roman expérimental,* " les Chroniques parisiennes de Sainte-Beuve ", p. 257. Reprinted from *le Voltaire,* 26 August 1879.
(7) See, among many examples which might be chosen, *le Naturalisme au théâtre,* " le Naturalisme, II ", pp. 19-20 ; *Nos auteurs dramatiques,* " Théâtre classique, IV ", p. 27.

bution to literature, the rebellion against outworn conventions :

Ils apportent la rébellion de la couleur, de la passion, de la fantaisie, parlant de briser violemment les règles, et renouvelant la langue par un flot de poésie lyrique, éclatante et superbe. En outre, la vérité les a touchés, ils exigent la couleur locale, ils croient ressusciter les âges morts. Tout le romantisme est là. C'est une réaction violente contre la littérature classique ; c'est le premier usage insurrectionnel que les écrivains font de la liberté littéraire reconquise (1).

Romanticism achieved liberty in literature, and was a necessary insurrection (2). This attainment of freedom is the only quality of romanticism worth surviving (3). Zola recognized the great force of Victor Hugo as a lyric poet, as the liberator of literature from the conventions of classicism. But Hugo and his followers had become just as outmoded as, in their time, the classic tradition which they had replaced. The Preface to *Cromwell* is a " piétinement sur place ", and Hugo's romanticism, based on the Christian dualism of body and soul (the *grotesque* and the *sublime*), should now be replaced by naturalism, the literature based on positivism (4). Hernani acts like a ten-year old child (5). *Ruy Blas*, despite the noble declamations of the characters, is basically immoral, and wholly unreal, although as a lyric poem, it is one of the glories of French literature (6). Hugo's lyricism, rhetorical as it must now be judged, served nevertheless to expand the language and to create a large, supple and brilliant instrument of expression. Notwithstanding Zola's deep-rooted antagonism to Hugo's method, he gave the great poet credit for his enrichment of the language :

Il faut donc saluer dans Victor Hugo l'ouvrier puissant de cette langue. Si, en lui, l'auteur dramatique, le romancier, le critique, le philosophe sont discutables, si le lyricisme, le coup de démence sublime arrive toujours à détraquer à un moment ses jugements et ses concep-tions, il a été quand même et partout le rhétoricien de génie que je viens

(1) *Le Roman expérimental,* " le Naturalisme au théâtre, I ", p. 96.
(2) *Le Naturalisme au théâtre,* " les Reprises, II ", p. 309.
(3) *Nos auteurs dramatiques,* " Théâtre classique, IV ", p. 28, reprinted from *le Bien public,* 21 May 1877 ; *ibid.,* " Victor Hugo I ", p. 45, reprinted from *le Bien public,* 26 November 1877.
(4) *Ibid.,* " Victor Hugo, IV ", p. 64, and " Victor Hugo, V ", p. 69. Reprinted from *le Voltaire,* 3 and 10 June 1879.
(5) *Ibid.,* " Victor Hugo, I ", p. 41. Reprinted from *le Voltaire,* 26 November 1877.
(6) *Ibid.,* " Victor Hugo, II ", pp. 45-52, reprinted from *le Voltaire,* 8 April 1879 ; *le Roman expérimental,* " Lettre à la jeunesse, I ", pp. 56-62, reprinted from *le Voltaire,* 17 May 1879.

d'étudier. Elle est la raison de la souveraineté qu'il a exercée et qu'il exerce encore. Il a créé une langue, il tient le siècle, non par les idées, mais par les mots ; les idées du siècle, celles qui le conduisent, ce sont la méthode scientifique, l'analyse expérimentale, le naturalisme... Victor Hugo reste un grand poète, le plus grand des poètes lyriques. Mais le siècle s'est dégagé de lui, l'idée scientifique s'impose (1).

A revival of de Vigny's *Chatterton* evoked reflections upon the moribund state of the romantic movement. The lamentations of the romantic poets were a pose. It was fashionable to be disgusted with life, to despise money, and to inveigh against society, but in point of fact, the best of them accommodated themselves very well to money, society and long life (2). Musset is an exception among the romantics.

More human than Hugo (3), Musset is " l'auteur le plus original et le plus exquis qu'on puisse voir ". Zola especially admires *Lorenzaccio*, which he calls worthy of Shakespeare, and regrets that it has not yet been staged (4).

Both the classic and romantic formulas are based on the arrangement and systematic amputation of the truth (5). Both are outmoded ; both contain false elements. Of the two, Zola believes the classic formula more serviceable to naturalism. " Mensonge pour mensonge, je n'hésite plus entre cette formule qui se déroule si noblement, toute à l'analyse et à la peinture des personnages, et cette autre formule qui fait danser à des pantins peinturlurés une danse épileptique et sans excuse (6). " The spirit of analysis, the simplicity and the grandeur of the classics are the qualities which the naturalists should emulate, substituting, however, the type generalization of the classics with individualization based on observation and analysis. If this be done, French classicism is a useful guide :

Aujourd'hui, nos classiques si dédaignés sont la seule source où l'on doit remonter, si l'on veut tenter une renaissance dramatique. Je le répète, il faut leur prendre leur esprit, et non leur formule. Il faut voir le théâtre comme ils l'ont vu, comme un cadre où l'homme importe avant tout, où les faits ne sont déterminés que par les actes, où l'éternel sujet reste uniquement la création de figures originales se heurtant sous le fouet des passions. La seule différence, à mon sens, serait celle-ci : la

(1) *Le Roman expérimental*, " Lettre à la jeunesse, I ", pp. 61-62.
(2) *Le Naturalisme au théâtre*, " les Reprises, I ", pp. 302-306. Reprinted from *le Bien public*, 12 February 1877.
(3) *Nos auteurs dramatiques*, " Victor Hugo, VI ", pp. 73-74.
(4) *Documents littéraires*, " Alfred de Musset, V ", pp. 99 and 103.
(5) *Le Naturalisme au théâtre*, " le Naturalisme, IV ", p. 22.
(6) *Le Bien public*, 31 December 1877. Not reprinted.

tragédie généralisait, aboutissait à des types et à des abstractions, tandis que le drame naturaliste moderne devrait individualiser, descendre à l'analyse expérimentale et à l'étude anatomique de chaque être (1).

The characters of French classicism were true without being real (2). The naturalist method would bring to the stage the reality lacking in classicism. Zola repeats these ideas in his important article on stage naturalism :

Ma conviction est que la formule naturaliste ne sera que le développement de cette formule classique, élargie et adaptée à notre milieu...
On trouve précisément dans les tragédies de Corneille, dans les comédies de Molière, cette analyse continue des personnages que je demande ; l'intrigue est au second plan, l'œuvre est une longue dissertation dialoguée sur l'homme. Seulement, au lieu d'abstraire l'homme, je voudrais qu'on le replaçât dans la nature, dans son milieu propre, en étendant l'analyse à toutes les causes physiques et sociales qui le déterminent. En un mot, la formule classique me paraît bonne, à la condition qu'on y emploiera la méthode scientifique pour étudier la société actuelle, comme la chimie étudie les corps et leurs propriétés (3).

To be sure, our language, and our notions of man and of art, are no longer those of the Seventeenth Century (4). Nor is it desirable to follow the plot construction of the classic masters. Nevertheless, " Il n'en faut pas moins revenir à eux, si nous voulons nous tirer de la comédie d'intrigue, et ne voir dans une œuvre dramatique qu'une analyse des personnages, placés dans de certains faits et soumis à l'influence des milieux (5). "

Emergence of naturalism

In Zola's opinion naturalism in the creative arts first emerged in the novel, and reached its greatest development in that form. Its nineteenth century founder was Balzac, who fulfilled the requirements of *race*, *milieu* and *moment* by appearing at

(1) *Nos auteurs dramatiques*, " le Théâtre classique, VI ", pp. 36-37. Reprinted from *le Bien public*, 12 June 1876.
(2) *Le Naturalisme au théâtre*, " les Décors et les accessoires, I ", p. 77, reprinted from *le Bien public*, 28 January 1878.
(3) *Le Roman expérimental*, " le Naturalisme au théâtre, III, V ", pp. 112 and 122.
(4) ZOLA's criticism of *Mithridate*, *le Voltaire*, 11 February 1879. Not reprinted.
(5) *Re. Britannicus*, *le Voltaire*, 23 March 1880. Not reprinted.

precisely that moment in history when classic literature was dying and new methods of science were encouraging the substitution of analysis for unbridled imagination.

Dès lors, le premier, il était appelé à employer puissamment ces outils nouveaux. Il créa le roman naturaliste, l'étude exacte de la société, et du coup, par une audace du génie, il osa faire vivre dans sa vaste fresque toute une société copiée sur celle qui posait devant lui. C'était l'affirmation la plus éclatante de l'évolution moderne. Il tuait les mensonges des anciens genres, il commençait l'avenir (1).

The romantic movement, then at its peak, prevented contemporary recognition of Balzac's achievement, but his influence increased as Hugo's declined, and now he stood as the leader of the literary movement which would surely be that of the Twentieth Century (2).

Stendhal, Zola finds, was a transition between the metaphysical idea of the Eighteenth Century and the scientific idea of the present. He has not arrived at a concept of physiological man, but his metaphysics is no longer that of Racine, nor even that of Voltaire. Zola perceives the influence of Condillac and the first stirrings of positivism (3). However, a gulf separates him from Balzac. Stendhal is not an observer who arrives logically at the truth, but a logician who often reaches the truth without benefit of observation (4).

Champfleury and Duranty, who adopted the slogan of " realism " for the purpose of attacking the romantic school, foreshadowed the naturalist movement. But one of their greatest faults was to restrict the rôle of literature to a limited class of society.

Il faut admettre la peinture de toutes les classes. Je ne vois nulle part qu'ils conseillent d'appliquer la méthode naturaliste à tous les personnages, princes ou bergers, grandes dames ou gardeuses de vaches. On dira que cela va de soi. Nullement. Le réalisme de 1856 était exclusivement bourgeois. Par ses théories, par ses œuvres, il ne sortait pas d'un certain cercle limité. Il n'avait pas la largeur qui s'impose (5).

Another weakness of these early realists was their failure to assess Balzac and Stendhal at their true value, and particularly

(1) *Les Romanciers naturalistes,* " Balzac, VI ", p. 52.
(2) *Ibid.,* p. 53.
(3) *Ibid.,* " Stendhal, II ", p. 80.
(4) *Ibid.,* p. 75.
(5) *Le Roman expérimental,* " le Réalisme ", p. 250. Reprinted from *le Bien public,* 22 April 1878.

their unjust appraisal of *Madame Bovary*. They were bold enough to attack contemporary literature, but lacked the talent to fill the vacuum which they sought to create (1).

Flaubert, de Goncourt and Daudet — all three personal friends of Zola — were the contemporary novelists whose work (aside from his own) he considered to be the best fulfillment of the naturalist movement up to that time. Zola lists three characteristics of the naturalist novel as exemplified by *Madame Bovary* : first, an exact reproduction of life, avoiding all roma- nesque elements ; second, the creation of human characters, rather than of heroic puppets ; third, the author's self-effacement from his story. Zola stressed the last point in particular :

C'est même cet apparent désintéressement qui est le trait le plus distinctif. On chercherait en vain une conclusion, une moralité, une leçon quelconque tirée des faits. Il n'y a d'étalés, de mis en lumière, uniquement que les faits, louables ou condamnables. L'auteur n'est pas un moraliste, mais un anatomiste qui se contente de dire ce qu'il trouve dans le cadavre humain. Les lecteurs concluront, s'ils le veulent, chercheront la vraie moralité, tâcheront de tirer une leçon du livre (2).

In this last respect, Flaubert differs from Balzac, who conti- nually intervenes to explain the lesson to be drawn from his stories. The evolution of the novel accomplished by Flaubert is summed up as follows :

... il l'a assujetti à des règles fixes d'observation, l'a débarrassé de l'enflure fausse des personnages, l'a changé en une œuvre d'art harmo- nique, impersonnelle, vivant de sa beauté propre, ainsi qu'un beau marbre (3).

Of the novels by the de Goncourt brothers, Zola particularly admires *Germinie Lacerteux*, both as an early study of the lower walks of life, and as a surgical dissection which reveals a sore of humanity. The authors' powers of analysis are greatly enhanced moreover, by their rich and distinctive style (4).

Daudet is the most seductive of the naturalist writers, " chargé de toucher les cœurs, d'ouvrir les portes à la troupe des romanciers plus farouches qui viennent derrière lui " (5).

(1) *Ibid.*, pp. 247-252. *Les Romanciers naturalistes*, " les Romanciers contemporains, I, II ", pp. 274-279.
(2) *Les Romanciers naturalistes*, " Gustave Flaubert, l'écrivain, I ", p. 110.
(3) *Ibid.*, pp. 110-111.
(4) *Ibid.*, " Edmond et Jules de Goncourt, III, V ", pp. 201, 206-208.
(5) *Ibid.*, " Alphonse Daudet, VII ", pp. 242-243.

Commenting on the success of Daudet's *Nabab*, Zola attributes the present high state of the novel to the methods of observation introduced by Balzac, enriched by the language innovations of Hugo :

> Évidemment, le roman est entré chez nous dans une période de triomphe qu'il n'avait jamais connue, même du temps de Balzac. On peut dire que les deux grands courants du siècle, le courant d'observation, partant de Balzac, et le courant de rhétorique savante, partant d'Hugo, se sont réunis, et que nos romanciers actuels se trouvent à ce confluent, à la naissance de cet unique fleuve du naturalisme pratiqué par des stylistes, qui semble désormais vouloir couler à pleins bords... Aujourd'hui, le roman est devenu l'outil du siècle, la grande enquête sur l'homme et sur la nature (1).

In other fields — music, painting, poetry, criticism, and even politics — naturalism emerged in varying degrees, but in no case to as full an extent as in the novel. In music, Zola credited to science the increase in instruments and the new methods of orchestration which enabled Beethoven, Meyerbeer and Wagner to create more powerful works than their predecessors (2).

In painting, " le naturalisme, l'impressionnisme, la modernité, comme on voudra l'appeler, est aujourd'hui maître des Salons officiels " (3). The impressionists are on the road to naturalism when they seek out nature at its source, and, through observation and analysis, add to their knowledge of light :

> D'ailleurs, remarquez que l'évolution est la même en peinture que dans les lettres, comme je l'indiquais tout à l'heure. Depuis le commencement du siècle, les peintres vont à la nature, et par des étapes très sensibles. Aujourd'hui, nos jeunes artistes ont fait un nouveau pas vers le vrai, en voulant que les sujets baignassent dans la lumière réelle du soleil, et non dans le jour faux de l'atelier ; c'est comme le chimiste, comme le physicien qui retournent aux sources, en se plaçant dans les conditions mêmes des phénomènes. Du moment qu'on veut faire de la vie, il faut bien prendre la vie avec son mécanisme complet. De là, en peinture, la nécessité du plein air, de la lumière étudiée dans ses causes et dans ses effets... Voilà donc ce qu'apportent les peintres impressionnistes : une recherche plus exacte des causes et des effets de la lumière, influant aussi bien sur le dessin que sur la couleur (4).

(1) *Ibid.*, p. 268.
(2) *Une campagne*, " Adieux ", pp. 323-324. Reprinted from *le Figaro*, 22 September 1881.
(3) " Le Naturalisme au salon ", published in four sections in *le Voltaire*, 18, 19, 21 and 22 June 1880, published by F. W. J. HEMMINGS and Robert J. NIESS, in *Salons* (1959).
(4) *Ibid.*, Section II.

The impressionists, however, are only fore-runners of naturalism ; the man of genius has yet to appear (1).

François Coppée was the contemporary poet whom Zola
most admired, preferring his simple verses of humble life to the
vulgarities of Jean Richepin, of whom he wrote : " On prend trop
souvent l'audace pour la vérité (2)." Coppée's *le Petit Épicier*
remains " le drapeau du naturalisme en poésie ; en la lisant, on
est loin de *la Charogne*, de Baudelaire, et des vers bibliques de
M. Leconte de Lisle. C'est là une note nouvelle, un écho du
roman contemporain " (3). But Coppée lacks force, and Zola
concludes that no creative poet has arisen since Lamartine, Hugo
and Musset, upon whom all modern poets without exception
draw for sustenance (4).

" Quand une génération ne trouve pas son critique ", wrote
Zola, " c'est un grand malheur pour elle. La lutte est beaucoup
plus longue, et la victoire manque d'éclat " (5). Naturalism had
not yet found a great supporting critic. Sainte-Beuve was
merely a transitional figure between pedagogical and scientific
criticism — a precursor of Taine (6). Taine, however, had
disappointed the naturalists by cloistering himself in studies of
history and philosophy, instead of interesting himself in the
struggles of his contemporaries (7). As to critics of the drama,
Sarcey is deservedly the voice heard with the greatest attention.
He has the merit of conscientious observation and of expressing
exactly what he thinks in terms understandable to the average
theater-goer. Unfortunately, his criterion of a good play is one
which provides a good evening in the theater — a standard which
favors mediocrity and penalizes genius. Zola's objections to
Sarcey betray the chagrin of a novelist frustrated in the theater :

Parmi ses opinions les plus entêtées, je citerai les suivantes. Il fait

(1) *Ibid.* See also " Après une promenade au salon ", *le Figaro*,
23 May 1881.
    Zola's final views on impressionism are to be found in *Nouvelle campagne*,
" Peinture ", pp. 91-98, reprinted from *le Figaro*, 2 May 1896. Zola expresses
his stupefaction at the results of the movement.
    (2) *Documents littéraires*, " les Poètes contemporains, V ", p. 148.
    (3) *Ibid.*, Section IV, p. 145.
    (4) *Ibid.*, Section VI, p. 152.
    (5) *Ibid.*, " la Critique contemporaine, I ", p. 257.
    (6) *Ibid.*, " Sainte-Beuve, II ", pp. 219, 221.
    (7) *Documents littéraires*, " la Critique contemporaine, I ", pp. 259-260,
reprinted from *le Bien public*, 19 February 1877.
    Le Roman expérimental, " la Formule critique appliquée au roman ",
p. 180, reprinted from *le Voltaire*, 27 May 1879.
    ZOLA's article on the reception of Taine into the French Academy, in
le Voltaire, 23 January 1880, not reprinted.

du théâtre un domaine à part, où les hommes doués d'une façon provi-dentielle peuvent seuls se hasarder. Tout le monde est capable d'écrire un roman, mais tout le monde n'est pas capable d'écrire un drame. Le théâtre est un sanctuaire où l'on pénètre avec des mots de passe. Il dit carrément : « Ceci est du théâtre, cela n'est pas du théâtre », et il ne reste plus qu'à s'incliner. Peu importe le mérite littéraire de l'œuvre ; un vaudeville idiot peut être du théâtre, tandis qu'un drame superbe peut n'être pas du théâtre. Tout se résume à une machine particulière, fonctionnant d'une certaine façon, une machine-type, de la fabrication de laquelle il ne faut pas s'écarter, sous peine de n'obtenir qu'une patraque. Même il pose sa machine comme la machine par excellence, qui contient l'unique vérité, l'absolu, dans les temps et dans l'espace. Il n'y a pas pour lui des théâtres, il y a le théâtre. Cela coupe court aux fantaisies des poètes et aux écarts du génie (1).

Zola's standard of criticism prohibited the contemplation of a work of art in and of itself, and required that it be studied in relation to the individual and social forces which brought it into being. Novelist and critic should have the same starting point — the exact environment and documentation of life — and proceed by identical methods to the understanding and expla-nation of their respective subject matter, which, in the case of the critic, is the work written by a specific individual, and, in the case of the novelist, the action of a character — both the written work and the action being considered as products of a human machine subjected to environmental influences. Zola concludes accordingly : " Il est évident qu'un romancier natura-liste est un excellent critique (2). " Since no critic having the stature of a Sainte-Beuve or a Taine had risen to the defense of naturalism, Zola felt justified in undertaking the task himself, and considered himself fully qualified to do so.

Naturalism extended even to politics. In a letter to the director of the *Bien public*, Zola defends himself against the accusation that he, a republican (in the French sense), has mali-gned the common people in *l'Assommoir*. He argues that facts are necessary to good government, and gives the following definition of political naturalism :

J'appelle politique naturaliste la politique qui entend d'abord pro-

---

(1) *Documents littéraires*, " la Critique contemporaine, V ", pp. 274-280, at p. 278 ; this article appears in *le Bien public*, 2 July 1877.
See also *le Naturalisme au théâtre*, " Polémique, I ", pp. 139-145, reprinted from *le Voltaire*, 29 October 1878.
(2) *Le Roman expérimental*, " la Formule critique appliquée au roman ", p. 182.

céder par l'expérience, qui est basée sur des faits, qui soigne en un mot une nation d'après ses besoins (1).

His striking observation, " La république sera naturaliste ou elle ne sera pas ", appears in his article " La république et la littérature " (2). Apparently this observation aroused some amusement, and Zola felt called upon to explain it in a later article :

Cela parut d'un comique extraordinaire. Voyez-vous cet auteur imbécile de vanité qui prétend faire une république à l'image de l'*Assommoir*, et qui déclare carrément que la république ne sera pas, si la république ne parle pas la langue de Coupeau ! Voilà l'esprit en France. La méthode dont je parlais était évidemment la méthode expérimentale, et j'avais écrit « la république sera naturaliste », comme j'aurais écrit « la république sera scientifique », car les deux mots se valaient dans mon esprit et représentaient la même idée. Je n'avais forcé un peu le sens de « naturaliste » que pour montrer l'unité de l'évolution du siècle dans les sciences, dans les lettres et dans la politique (3).

Zola conceived naturalism as a vast and inevitable movement embracing all fields of human endeavor. Given this postulate, it was easy to conclude that the theater, having failed as yet to respond to the call of naturalism, was behind the times and ready for change.

Naturalism in the theater

Whereas naturalism had reached a high level of development in the novel, its progress on the stage had been very slight. There were, indeed, two literatures — one for the novel, growing constantly stronger and more vital because it was in harmony with the scientific spirit of the century ; the other for the stage, in danger of perishing because it refused to progress with the times and remained, instead, the last fortress of withered conven-

---

(1) Letter dated 10 February 1877 which appeared in *le Bien public,* 13 February 1877. Published in LES ŒUVRES COMPLÈTES, *Correspondance (1872-1902)* under date of 13 February 1877. The quotation is at p. 465.
(2) In *le Roman expérimental,* p. 301.
(3) *Le Voltaire,* 20 July 1880. Not reprinted. For some further views on politics, see the articles in *Une campagne* under the titles : " la République en Russie " (written shortly after the assassination of Czar Alexander II), " la Politique expérimentale ", and " la Démocratie ".

tions (1). " Le théâtre devient de plus en plus un cadre bâtard qui décourage le génie ; le roman ouvre, au contraire, son cadre libre, son cadre universel, aussi large que les connaissances humaines, et appelle à lui tous les créateurs (2). " The following passage may be taken as a fairly complete single expression of Zola's program for the theater :

J'attends qu'on plante debout au théâtre des hommes en chair et en os, pris dans la réalité et analysés scientifiquement, sans un mensonge. J'attends qu'on nous débarrasse des personnages fictifs, de ces symboles convenus de la vertu et du vice qui n'ont aucune valeur comme documents humains. J'attends que les milieux déterminent les personnages et que les personnages agissent d'après la logique des faits combinée avec la logique de leur propre tempérament. J'attends qu'il n'y ait plus d'escamotage d'aucune sorte, plus de coups de baguette magique, changeant d'une minute à l'autre les choses et les êtres. J'attends qu'on ne nous conte plus des histoires inacceptables, qu'on ne gâte plus des observations justes par des incidents romanesques, dont l'effet est de détruire même les bonnes parties d'une pièce. J'attends qu'on abandonne les recettes connues, les formules lasses de servir, les larmes, les rires faciles. J'attends qu'une œuvre dramatique, débarrassée des déclamations, tirée des grands mots et des grands sentiments, ait la haute moralité du vrai, soit la leçon terrible d'une enquête sincère. J'attends enfin que l'évolution faite dans le roman s'achève au théâtre, que l'on y revienne à la source même de la science et de l'art moderne, à l'étude de la nature, à l'anatomie de l'homme, à la peinture de la vie, dans un procès-verbal exact, d'autant plus original et puissant, que personne encore n'a osé le risquer sur les planches (3).

And a few pages later, he solemnly affirms : " Ou le théâtre sera naturaliste, ou il ne sera pas, telle est la conclusion formelle (4). "

Although naturalism had failed to develop to any considerable extent in the current theater, Zola pointed out a number of steps which had been taken in that direction. Conspicuous among these were efforts to escape from the " well-made play " formula of Scribe into comparatively formless plays, where plot devices were subordinated to scenes of every-day life. Zola admired this quality particularly in the plays of Meilhac and

(1) *Le Naturalisme au théâtre*, " la Comédie, III ", pp. 245-246, reprinted from *le Bien public*, 25 December 1876.
Le Roman expérimental, " le Naturalisme au théâtre, II ", pp. 98-99.
(2) *Nos auteurs dramatiques*, " Victorien Sardou, III ", p. 170, in *le Bien public*, 11 March 1878.
(3) *Le Roman expérimental*, " le Naturalisme au théâtre, IV ", p. 116.
(4) *Ibid.*, p. 119.

Halévy, " des peintres très souples de la vie moderne " (1).
Reviewing their *Mari de la débutante*, he congratulates them for
continuing to remain free of the theatrical conventions and for
presenting loosely-knit scenes taken from life, instead of a
contrived and symmetrically-balanced plot. He admires, too,
their introduction of characters for the sake of representing life,
rather than of satisfying the exigencies of a plot.

... il y a là une nouvelle application, heureuse et applaudie, des idées
que je défends. Une fois de plus, il est prouvé que le sujet n'importe pas,
que l'intrigue peut manquer, que les personnages n'ont pas même besoin
d'avoir un lien quelconque avec l'action ; il suffit que les tableaux offerts
au public soient vivants et qu'ils le fassent rire ou pleurer (2).

Characters are more important than situations. " Dans toute
œuvre littéraire de talent, les faits tendent à se simplifier, l'étude
de l'homme remplace les complications de l'intrigue (3). "

In some other works, too, Zola found a welcome departure
from Sribe's " well-made play " formula in favor of scenes of
daily life. Such were Edmond Gondinet's *le Club* and his *les
Tapageurs*, Édouard Pailleron's *l'Age ingrat*, Theodore Barrière's
les Faux Bonshommes, Erckmann and Chatrian's *l'Ami Fritz*,
Louis Davyl's *Monsieur Chéribois*, Albert Delpit's *le Fils de
Coralie*, and the stage adaptation of Daudet's *le Nabab* (4).
Conventional-minded critics, attached to Scribe's formula, denied
that loosely-constructed, episodical works should be classified as
" plays " at all. Reviewing the stage adaptation of *le Nabab*,
Zola ridicules this point of view, and goes on to explain the
progress towards naturalism which such plays have brought to
the theater :

... examinons donc cette question des pièces où il n'y a pas de pièce.
Il me semble que ces pièces-là ne se portent pas mal. Tout le répertoire
de MM. Meilhac et Halévy est dans ce cas. M. Sardou lui-même réussit
beaucoup plus par les tableaux que par le drame... Maintenant, voici
le *Nabab* : la salle a applaudi tout le temps, les spectateurs sont restés

(1) *Nos auteurs dramatiques*, " Meilhac et Halévy, I ", p. 213.
(2) *Ibid.*, " Meilhac et Halévy, III ", p. 222. Reprinted from *le Voltaire*,
11 February 1879.
(3) *Le Naturalisme au théâtre*, " le Drame, VI ", pp. 193-194. Reprinted
from *le Voltaire*, 13 April 1880.
(4) *Nos auteurs dramatiques*, " Edmond Gondinet, I, II ", pp. 237-245 :
" Edouard Pailleron, I ", pp. 255-259 ; " Théodore Barrière ", pp. 277-283 ;
" Erckmann-Chatrian, I, II ", pp. 323-333.
Le Naturalisme au théâtre, " la Comédie, VI ", pp. 254-258 (Louis Davyl);
" la Comédie, VII ", pp. 258-263 (Albert Delpit).

jusqu'à une heure du matin, tous intéressés, amusés, empoignés ; et l'on vient nous dire : « Il n'y a pas de pièce ! » d'un air de dédain. Ah ! ça, se moque-t-on de nous ?... Aujourd'hui, un fait tend à se généraliser : les œuvres à situations tombent, tandis que les œuvres à tableaux réussissent. Telle est la stricte vérité. Dès lors, la conclusion devrait être facile à tirer. Nous nous trouvons ici en face du triomphe certain du naturalisme. Le mouvement s'est d'abord opéré dans le roman. Aux romans d'aventures, aux romans romantiques, ont succédé les romans d'observation dont la victoire aujourd'hui est absolue et incontestable. Eh bien ! c'est ce mouvement qui s'est communiqué au théâtre et qui s'y accentue de plus en plus. Le succès du *Nabab*, après le succès du *Club*, de M. Gondinet, de *l'Ami Fritz*, d'Erckmann-Chatrian, et du répertoire entier de MM. Meilhac et Halévy, arrive comme un argument décisif. On ira plus loin, on élargira encore la formule. Mais, dès aujourd'hui, les gens d'ignorance et de mauvaise foi seuls peuvent se refuser à reconnaître l'accueil de plus en plus empressé du public pour les œuvres dramatiques où il retrouve la vie analysée en larges tableaux (1).

Zola pleaded, too, for a closer resemblance to life in scenery, costumes and the art of acting, and found that some progress towards naturalism was already being made in these respects. Scenery serves the same purpose in a play as description in a novel (2), which Zola defines as " un état du milieu qui détermine et complète l'homme " (3). Scenery should not be merely picturesque ; it should be comparable to a description of Balzac, so that, when the curtain is raised, the audience will receive a first impression of the character and habits of the people in the play (4). There has been a constant progression towards reality, from the neutral scenery of the classical period, when abstract man was analyzed apart from his environment, though the increasing use of scenery by Voltaire, the large fantasies of the romantic period, the background dances of Scribe, up to contemporary scenes where the greatest possible reality is presented on the stage, even to the extent, in *l'Ami Fritz*, of exhibiting a live cherry tree and a fountain with real water. It is not the novelty of real-life sets which Zola applauds, but the opportunity which they give for the enactment of scenes of ordinary life (5). Costumes, too, have participated in the naturalist

(1) *Le Voltaire*, 3 February 1880. Not reprinted.
(2) *Le Roman expérimental*, " le Naturalisme au théâtre, V ", p. 123.
(3) *Ibid.*, " De la description ", p. 187.
(4) *Le Naturalisme au théâtre*, " le Costume, III ", p. 105.
(5) *Ibid.*, " les Décors et les accessoires, I, II, III ", pp. 73-88. *Nos auteurs dramatiques*, " Erckmann-Chatrian, I ", pp. 323-329.

evolution by acquiring ever-closer resemblance to those of real life (1).

As to acting, " il faut aimer voir les acteurs vivre la pièce, au lieu de les voir la jouer " (2). Zola condemns as ridiculous the conventions which require an actor to make unnaturally emphatic entrances and exists, to cross the stage without motivation, to speak facing the audience regardless of the position of the fellow-actor to whom the speech is addressed. " Les exagérations de gestes, les passades, les coups de talon, les temps solennels pris entre deux phrases, les effets obtenus par un grossissement de la charge, ne sont en aucune façon nécessaires à la pompe de la représentation. D'ailleurs, la pompe est inutile, la vérité suffirait (3). " Zola praises the Italian actor, Salvini, for demonstrating that a natural style of acting is possible on the stage (4).

The progress which naturalism has so far made, while giving grounds for hope, is still far from adequate to assure the survival of the theater. Zola is still awaiting the genius who, as Balzac in the novel, will consummate the naturalist evolution on the stage (5). The novelists themselves have been unsuccessful in the theater. Balzac, Zola believes, might have been a great playwright. His last play, *Mercadet*, was his best, but death cut short his career at a time when, freed from debt, he was preparing to write for the theater (6). Flaubert's *le Candidat* " nous consterna " (7). The de Goncourts and Daudet, on the other hand, had written good plays which had been unjustly neglected. The de Goncourts' *Henriette Maréchal* had failed in 1865 because of a political cabal (8). Their *la Patrie en danger* (based on the French Revolution) was " le modèle du genre historique nouveau " (9), and it was deplorable that no theater manager had as yet seen fit to present it on a stage. Speaking of the authors' accomplishment in the field of historical drama, Zola wrote :

... ils ont créé là le véritable drame historique, non plus l'histoire arrangée en grand opéra comme le romantisme l'accommodait vers 1830,

(1) *Le Naturalisme au théâtre*, " le Costume, I, II, III ", pp. 89-107.
(2) *Ibid.*, " les Décors et les accessoires, I ", p. 77.
(3) *Ibid.*, " les Comédiens, II ", p. 114.
(4) *Ibid.*, " les Comédiens, III ", pp. 116-121.
(5) *Ibid.*, " Polémique, I ", p. 140.
(6) *Les Romanciers naturalistes*, " Balzac, IV ", pp. 35-36.
(7) *Ibid.*, " Gustave Flaubert, l'Homme, IV ", p. 168.
(8) See *ibid.*, " Edmond et Jules de Goncourt, II ", pp. 195-196.
(9) *Le Naturalisme au théâtre*, " le Drame patriotique, II ", p. 217.

mais l'histoire ramenée à sa stricte vérité dans des scènes typiques, où tout se trouve rétabli : le langage, les mœurs, jusqu'aux modes et aux airs de figure (1).

La Patrie en danger was a departure from the usual sort of historical play, which ordinarily lacked any serious effort to reconstruct the life of the past. " Le domaine de l'histoire ", as Zola wrote complainingly of another historical play, " paraît au contraire n'avoir été choisi jusqu'ici par les dramaturges que pour y mentir plus à l'aise " (2).

Daudet's *l'Arlésienne*, too, had failed to receive the recognition it deserved. The structure of this dramatic idyl was too unconventional, the personal note of its language too poetic for the backward taste of the public (3). However, the success of the stage adaptation of Daudet's *le Nabab* was an indication that naturalism was gaining ground in the theater. Zola felt that as a rule the adaptation of a novel was of a lower order of merit than a work written directly for the stage. " Le drame doit avoir sa vie propre. " But in the present transitional stage of the theater, the naturalist novel adapted to the stage was a valuable battering-ram in the war on theatrical conventions (4).

Zola was confident that, in the course of time, a great dramatist would emerge to consummate the naturalist evolution in the theater, as had already been done in the novel. The very survival of the theater was at stake :

... nous aurons toute la vie au théâtre comme nous l'avons déjà dans le roman... A la place d'un théâtre de fabrication, nous aurons un théâtre d'observation. Comment l'évolution s'achèvera-t-elle ? C'est ce que demain nous dira. J'ai essayé de prévoir, mais je laisse au génie le soin de réaliser. J'ai déjà donné ma conclusion : notre théâtre sera naturaliste ou il ne sera pas (5).

Sardou, Dumas fils, Augier

Of the three leading dramatists of the period, Zola found the least merit in Sardou. His plays, continuing the tradition of Scribe, are ingenious fabrications in which puppets are moved

---

(1) *Le Bien public*, 5 June 1876. Not reprinted.
(2) *Le Voltaire*, 1 April 1879. Not reprinted.
(3) *Nos auteurs dramatiques*, " Alphonse Daudet ", pp. 317-321. *Les Romanciers naturalistes*, " Alphonse Daudet, VI ", pp. 237-240.
(4) *Nos auteurs dramatiques*, " Meilhac et Halévy, VI ", pp. 232-237, reprinted from *le Voltaire*, 9 March 1880. As will be seen in our Chapter IV, some of Zola's own novels were currently being adapted to the stage.
(5) *Le Roman expérimental*, " le Naturalisme au théâtre, V ", p. 126.

about in the interest of action and excitement, not of life. The formula is enormously successful, but its success constitutes a danger to the theater. Zola is somewhat inconsistent in his criticism of Sardou, reproaching him in one instance with sacrificing his talent to popular success (1), and later, when the popular playwright did make a serious effort to raise the literary stature of his work, advising him never to try it again (2).

Qu'il retourne à ses marionnettes !
Chacun doit rester à sa place. M. Sardou est simplement un amuseur. Il a beaucoup de verve, beaucoup de mouvement, le flair du théâtre et de l'actualité, un esprit de petit journaliste lâché à travers les ridicules contemporains. Mais il ne pense pas, mais il n'écrit pas, mais il est incapable de rien créer de solide et de vivant (3).

Nevertheless, he served the cause of naturalism in his own special way, by developing the public taste for life-like settings and bringing to the stage at least the physical representation of reality. " Pour moi, sa raison d'être est surtout là. Il est venu à son heure, il a donné au public le goût de la vie et des tableaux taillés dans la réalité (4). "

Dumas *fils* and Augier are on a much higher literary level — indeed, on the highest level of the contemporary French theater. Expressing his admiration for an Italian play, *la Mort civile*, Zola states that among French dramatists only Dumas and Augier would have been able to write so fine a work (5).

Dumas is " un des ouvriers les plus puissants du naturalisme ", but for three main reasons, he has failed to bring the movement to its consummation : first, he has yielded to a lamentable desire to preach and convert ; second, he has destroyed the truth of his dialogue by an excess of witty lines, which he places indiscriminately in the mouths of all his characters ; third, he leaps from observed truth to baroque inventions for the sake of

---

(1) Review of *les Bourgeois de Pont-Arcy*, in *Nos auteurs dramatiques*, " Victorien Sardou, III ", pp. 169-174, at p. 172. Reprinted from *le Bien public*, 11 March 1878.
(2) Review of *Daniel Rochat, ibid., ,,* Victorien Sardou, IV ", pp. 175-180.
(3) *Ibid.*, p. 179.
(4) *Le Roman expérimental*, " le Naturalisme au théâtre, III ", p. 110.
(5) *Le Voltaire*, 3 December 1878. Not reprinted. (This is ZOLA's review of *Conrad*, an adaptation in French by August VITU of GIACOMMETTI's, *Mort civile*. ZOLA's review of this play in Italian appears in *le Naturalisme au théâtre*, " les Comédiens, III ", pp. 116-121, reprinted from *le Bien public*, 14 January 1878.)

theatrical effect (1).　Applying his definition of a work of art as being a corner of nature seen through the eyes of a certain individual temperament, Zola finds less reality in the work of Dumas than appears at first sight.　Dumas writes of a restricted world where the characters lack the traits of real humanity. His women are all good or all bad ; the husbands strain self-sacrifice to the point of folly, and vengeance to the point of madness ; the children speak like adults ; and all are caught willy-nilly in a world of logic and argumentation in which they have no life of their own.　Zola concludes :

> Ce n'est point un coin de la vie ordinaire que M. Dumas nous repré-sente ; c'est un carnaval philosophique dans lequel on voit sauter vingt, trente, cinquante petits Dumas, déguisés en hommes, en femmes, en enfants, avec des perruques selon les âges et selon les conditions (2).

Zola's most-repeated objection to Dumas is that the latter is intent on preaching and proving a thesis.　The following is typical of many passages which might be cited :

> En somme, Balzac veut peindre et M. Dumas veut prouver. Tout est là. M. Dumas est de l'école idéaliste de Georges Sand. Le monde tel qu'il le voit, lui semble mal bâti, et son continuel besoin est de le rebâtir. Dans la préface du *Fils naturel*, il déclare très nettement qu'il entend jouer un rôle de moraliste et de législateur.

Whereas Zola's creed, as he goes on to say, is quite the contrary :

> J'ai d'autres idées ; je crois que, dans notre siècle d'expérience scientifique, nous ne devons pas vouloir marcher plus vite que la science. Lorsque nos savants en sont revenus à la simple étude des phénomènes, à l'analyse exacte du monde, nous ne pouvons avoir d'autre besogne, nous autres observateurs des faits humains, que de faire un travail parallèle, de nous en tenir à l'analyse exacte de l'homme. Connaissons d'abord l'homme réel, apportons le plus possible de documents humains ; ensuite, si les législateurs sont sages, ils aviseront.
> Telle est ma foi littéraire. Toutes les grandes œuvres posent les thèses sociales, mais ne les discutent ni ne les résolvent (3).

Dumas' " preaching " violated the principle of naturalism requiring the self-effacement of the author.　" L'auteur n'est

---

(1) *Le Roman expérimental,* " le Naturalisme au théâtre, III ", pp. 110-111.
(2) *Documents littéraires,* " Réception de M. Dumas fils à l'Académie française ", pp. 205-206.
(3) *Nos auteurs dramatiques,* " Alexandre Dumas fils, V ", p. 133.

pas un moraliste ", Zola wrote of Flaubert, " mais un anatomiste qui se contente de dire ce qu'il trouve dans le cadavre humain. Les lecteurs concluront, s'ils le veulent, chercheront la vraie moralité, tâcheront de tirer une leçon du livre " (1). And again, reviewing the Goncourts' *Germinie Lacerteux*, Zola wrote :

... il ne s'agit pas d'une histoire plus ou moins intéressante, mais d'une véritable leçon d'anatomie morale et physique... Il arrive que cette dissection est un spectacle poignant, plein d'une haute moralité. Les gens honnêtes, qui ont jeté tant de boue à Germinie, n'ont rien compris à la leçon (2).

There is, thus, a latent moral or lesson in a naturalist work, but the author should not intervene to draw it. To be sure, Zola frequently alleged, in defense of his work, that he was motivated by a purpose of social reform. He objected to Dumas' ' preaching ' not because Dumas was a reformer, but because his method was inartistic. As he said in reviewing a one-act play by his friend, Paul Alexis, a good play should contain a thesis :

Il y a toujours une thèse dans une pièce écrite par un homme de talent, je veux dire qu'il y a une idée générale dominant l'ensemble, une pensée supérieure qui sert de pivot (3).

But the idea of the play should be developed by the facts, not by moral homilies :

Ce qui est fâcheux, c'est le plaidoyer direct, les personnages raides en arguments, la dispute philosophique étalée en tirades devant le trou du souffleur. Heureusement, M. Alexis est resté dans le drame pur, et ce sont simplement des faits qu'il nous donne.

This was the esthetic method of the naturalists — a method which survived on the stage long after Zola's voice was stilled. Dumas' method of sermonizing, on the contrary, disappeared. Zola was extremely perspicacious in pointing out the glaring defect which caused Dumas' plays to fall into disfavor, and in advocating what came to be, for at least a good part of the twentieth century, the accepted method of dramatizing a basic idea or thesis.

(1) *Les Romanciers naturalistes*, " Gustave Flaubert, l'écrivain, I ", p. 110.
(2) *Ibid.*, " Edmond et Jules de Goncourt, III ", p. 201.
(3) *Le Voltaire*, 16 September 1879. Not reprinted.

The contemporary dramatist whom Zola preferred to all others was Émile Augier, " le maître actuel de notre scène française ". *Les Lionnes pauvres, le Mariage d'Olympe, Maître Guérin, le Gendre de M. Poirier, les Effrontés,* and *le Fils de Giboyer* are " des œuvres très remarquables, qui toutes, plus ou moins, dans quelques scènes, réalisent le théâtre nouveau, le théâtre de notre siècle " (1). Augier is more human than Dumas, and it is this human quality which places him ahead of his contemporaries. Then why, Zola enquires, has he not been the awaited genius destined to enfranchise the theater and to accomplish the naturalist evolution ? Zola attributes Augier's failure to fill this rôle to his predilection for sympathetic characters and moral homilies :

C'est à mon sens, qu'il n'a pas su se dégager assez des conventions, des clichés, des personnages tout faits. Son théâtre est continuellement diminué par des poncifs, des figures exécutées de chic, comme on dit familièrement dans les ateliers de peintre. Ainsi, il est rare de ne pas trouver, dans ses comédies, la jeune fille immaculée, très riche, et qui ne veut pas se marier, parce qu'elle s'indigne d'être épousée pour son argent. Les jeunes hommes sont également des héros d'honneur et de loyauté, sanglotant lorsqu'ils apprennent que leurs pères ont fait une fortune peu scrupuleuse. En un mot, le personnage sympathique triomphe, j'entends le type idéal des bons et beaux sentiments, toujours coulé dans le même moule, véritable symbole, personnification hiératique en dehors de toute observation vraie. C'est le commandant Guérin, ce modèle des militaires, dont l'uniforme aide au dénouement ; c'est le fils de Giboyer, cet archange de délicatesse, né d'un homme taré, et c'est Giboyer lui-même, si tendre dans sa bassesse ; c'est Henri, le fils de Charrier, des *Effrontés,* qui s'engage, parce que son père a tripoté dans une affaire louche, et qui l'amène à rembourser les gens qu'il a trompés. Tout cela est très beau, très touchant ; seulement, comme documents humains, tout cela est très contestable. La nature n'a pas ces raideurs dans le bien ni dans le mal. On ne peut accepter ces personnages sympathiques que comme une opposition et une consolation (2).

Zola can praise Augier's *les Fourchambault* as " supérieurs à tout ce que nous avons vu jouer cet hiver ", but he dislikes the excessive " theatrical honesty " of the play. " Il est si bon, au théâtre ", he comments, " d'applaudir les actes dont on serait incapable dans la vie " (3) ! In *Paul Forestier,* he admires those

---

(1) *Le Roman expérimental,* " le Naturalisme au théâtre, III ", p. 112.
(2) *Ibid.,* p. 113.
(3) *Nos auteurs dramatiques,* " Emile Augier, I ", pp. 77-83, at p. 79.
Reprinted from *le Bien public,* 15 April 1878.

moments of the play which were denounced by other critics as salacious — " ... comme la santé, hélas ! n'est pas l'état chronique de l'humanité, il faut bien permettre aux écrivains d'étudier et de peindre les maladies " (1) — but deplores the happy ending, which he considers false and unworthy of Augier's talent. And despite the admirable creation of the character Pommeau in *les Lionnes pauvres*, Zola condemns Augier's concession to public taste in surrounding his work with an aura of morality. This play furnished Zola with an occasion to denounce the falsity of theatrical virtue :

Notre comédie moderne meurt d'honnêteté. Ce n'est point un paradoxe que je soutiens ici, et il faut me bien comprendre. Cette rage que nous avons de vouloir faire à la misère humaine la plus petite part possible, de ne risquer sur les planches une figure de chair et d'os qu'à la condition de la masquer derrière la convention d'un pantin vertueux, est à coup sûr la raison de notre médiocrité dramatique. Je ne nie point les personnages honnêtes ; seulement, je leur demande d'être humains, d'apporter le mélange du bon et du mauvais qui est dans toute créature humaine. Ce que je demande plus énergiquement encore, c'est que, lorsqu'on veut clouer un vice à la scène, on l'y cloue carrément, fortement, sans l'enguirlander de tous les poncifs connus des vertus consolantes...
... il n'y a que notre époque qui se soit senti le besoin de paraître honnête. Nous avons inventé l'honnêteté d'étalage, celle qu'il faut absolument mettre dans la vitrine, si l'on veut achalander la maison. Je ne sais quel mauvais vent de protestantisme a soufflé sur nous. Nous ne sommes plus les hardis esprits qui ne s'effrayaient guère des mots, qui voulaient regarder les choses en face. Eh bien ! je le répète, cette honnêteté de pure parade, ce besoin de voiler le personnage vrai derrière une demi-douzaine de personnages faux, découragent les esprits les plus vigoureux et les poussent aux œuvres médiocres. Pas d'œuvres grandes sans une grande vérité (2).

The problem of uprooting conventional stage morality was of the utmost importance : " C'est sur ce point surtout que se livre la bataille du naturalisme (3). " Because they failed to abide by the conventional standards of literary morality, the naturalist writers were accused of speculating in vice. Zola turned the argument against his opponents and accused them of

(1) *Ibid.*, " Emile Augier, II ", p. 84. Reprinted from *le Bien public*, 6 November 1876.
(2) *Ibid.*, " Emile Augier, III ", pp. 90-91. Reprinted from *le Voltaire*, 2 December 1879.
(3) *Le Roman expérimental*, " le Naturalisme au théâtre, V ", p. 125.

speculating in virtue (1). He denied emphatically that this latter form of speculation, inasmuch as it taught worthy lessons, was in the public welfare. " Le mensonge, si noble qu'il soit ", he declared, " a toujours des conséquences désastreuses " (2). " Tout mensonge, même noble ", he wrote in another article, " ne peut que pervertir " (3). Stage morality and the morality of real life seem to come from two separate worlds, whose inhabitants have radically different laws, customs, feelings and languages (4). The works of the naturalists are more highly moral than those of George Sand (5), written with a scientific detachment and a social purpose wholly lacking in the Marquis de Sade (6). " Nous ne cherchons pas ce qui est répugnant, nous le trouvons ; et si nous voulons le cacher, il faut mentir, ou tout au moins rester incomplet (7). "

Augier had not dared to liberate the stage of truth-veiling concessions to public taste, and had therefore failed to consummate the naturalist evolution in the theater.

Laughter and fantasy

Zola regretted having called Eugène Labiche, in one of his articles, " un rieur, rien de plus " (8). A month later, feeling that his judgment of Labiche had been too harsh, he undertook to explain his views of laughter. " Ne rit pas qui veut, au théâtre surtout ", he observed, remembering, in all probability, the failure two months earlier of his own farce, le Bouton de Rose.

The comic writer is an analyst, just as his more serious colleague. Both have difficulty in taking man seriously, but according to their respective temperaments, " les uns se fâchent, tandis que les autres s'amusent ". Here Zola distinguishes between the two ways of exhibiting the comic spirit : " En bon enfant, comme M. Labiche, ou en esprit amer et cruel, comme les

---

(1) *Documents littéraires*, " De la moralité dans la littérature, IV ", pp. 312-319.
(2) *Ibid.*, p. 317.
(3) *Le Naturalisme au théâtre*, " les Deux morales ", p. 47.
(4) *Ibid.*, p. 43.
(5) *Documents littéraires*, " George Sand, VI ", pp. 183-184.
(6) *Ibid.*, " De la moralité dans la littérature, III ", pp. 311-312.
Zola's article, " le Marquis de Sade ", in *le Figaro*, 24 January 1881. Not reprinted.
(7) *Le Roman expérimental*, " les Frères Zemganno, I ", p. 219.
(8) *Nos auteurs dramatiques*, " Eugène Labiche, I ", p. 205. Reprinted from *le Bien public*, 17 June 1878.

grands satiriques (1). " It will be recalled that Zola himself had experimented with both types of comic play — the satirical, in *les Héritiers Rabourdin*, and the good-natured, in *le Bouton de Rose* — and failed in both attempts.

There is little in Zola's collected articles to indicate his capacity for enjoying farce or the lighter sorts of comedy. This capacity was very real, however, and manifested itself occasionally in articles which have not been reprinted in volume. For example, reviewing Jules Verne's *un Neveu d'Amérique, ou les deux Frontignac*, he wrote :

> Que le rire est bon... Je suis ravi pour ma part, que la comédie de M. Verne ne soit qu'un vaudeville, qu'une farce heureuse et sans prétention. J'avais peur d'une pièce honnête et médiocre. Aussi quelle joie de pouvoir se mettre à son aise et de s'amuser comme un grand enfant !... Que voulez-vous, on ne rit pas tous les jours. Les temps sont tristes. Celui-là est le bienvenu, qui nous apporte de la gaieté, et nous serions des sots de le disputer sur la qualité de son rire (2).

And in a later article, he said :

> On ignore quelle force toute-puissante est la gaieté. Rire est si bon, j'entends rire pour rire, sans arrière-pensée satirique, sans aucune méchanceté sournoise contre l'humanité. *Bébé* n'a justement pas de grandes prétentions ; ce n'est ni une farce littéraire, ni une comédie de mœurs ; c'est une pièce pleine de bonne humeur, pas davantage. Je m'étonne que, dans les foyers des théâtres on n'ait pas encore élevé de statues allégoriques à la bonne humeur, car elle devrait être la reine charmante du petit monde dramatique. Un coup de baguette, et les rires sonnent de l'orchestre au cintre (3).

These views are, to be sure, somewhat exceptional in Zola. And in any case, they apply only to the lower orders of the comic spirit, where there is no pretense of portraying or commenting upon real life. The highest comedy, he believed, was bitter and close to tears, having the effect of a scourge. Thus he finds in *le Misanthrope* " des amertumes qui en font par moments la haute figure de la tristesse humaine " (4). *George Dandin* is

---

(1) *Ibid.*, " Eugène Labiche, II ", p. 206.
(2) *L'Avenir national*, 24 April 1873. Not reprinted.
(3) *Le Bien public*, 19 March 1877. A large part of this article is reprinted in *le Naturalisme au théâtre*, " le Vaudeville, II ", pp. 273-276, but the first two paragraphs of the newspaper article, including the quoted passage, have been omitted. The article refers to *Bébé*, by NAJAC and HENNEQUIN.
(4) *Nos auteurs dramatiques*, " Théâtre classique, I ", p. 12. Reprinted from *le Bien public*, 21 January 1878.

" une farce dont le génie a fait une des pages les plus amères et les plus cruellement humaines que je connaisse. Jamais le mépris de l'homme n'a été poussé plus loin, jamais la société n'a reçu un soufflet si rude. Il faut chercher dans la littérature anglaise et lire le *Volpone* de Ben Jonson pour trouver une telle satire " (1). And as to Molière's *Amphitrion*, he writes : " Jamais notre grand comique n'a caché l'amertume de sa satire sous un éclat de rire plus fin (2). " Beaumarchais scourges, too, but Zola is dissatisfied with his method. " *Le Mariage de Figaro* est beaucoup plus une satire dialoguée qu'une véritable œuvre dramatique ; car la leçon n'est jamais dans les faits, mais toujours dans les tirades. " And he concludes : " Le cri humain de Molière nous remue toujours aussi profondément, tandis que souvent nous ne sentons qu'à fleur de peau le cinglement spirituel de Beaumarchais (3). "

Fantasy (" la féerie ") was the only theatrical form in which Zola conceded that truth might be neglected, and he confessed to a particular liking for this type of play : " Avec ses rois grotesques, ses princesses belles comme le jour, ses amoureux qui peuvent tout et qui gagnent leurs amoureuses après des exploits plus nombreux que ceux de Don Quichotte. Je m'y amuse comme un enfant (4). " Inasmuch as a fantasy is presented with no pretense of portraying the truth, no fraud is committed upon the public. Here alone, theatrical conventions are permissible (5). Here lyric poetry may, and should, enter the theater. Zola dreams of how such an " adorable école buissonnière de l'imagination" might be constructed, given the co-operation — highly improbable — of the best talent in all of the arts :

Je veux dire quelle serait la féerie que je souhaite. Le plus grand de nos poètes lyriques en aurait écrit les vers; le plus illustre de nos musiciens en composerait la musique. Je confierais les décors aux peintres qui font la gloire de notre école, et j'appellerais les premiers d'entre nos sculpteurs pour indiquer des groupes et veiller à la perfection de la plastique. Ce n'est pas tout, il faudrait, pour jouer ce chef-d'œuvre, des femmes belles, des hommes forts, des acteurs célèbres dans le drame et dans la comédie.

---

(1) *Ibid.*, " Théâtre classique, II ", p. 15. Reprinted from *le Bien public*, 13 November 1876. (Instead of " une telle satire ", the newspaper reads " une satire aussi abominable ".)
(2) *Le Bien public*, 9 April 1877. Not reprinted.
(3) *Le Voltaire*, 25 November 1879. Not reprinted.
(4) *Le Bien public*, 27 May 1878. Not reprinted. See also *le Naturalisme au théâtre*, " la Féerie et l'Opérette, II ", p. 287.
(5) *Ibid.*, pp. 289-290. See also *Nos auteurs dramatiques*, " Théodore de Banville, II ", pp. 304-305.

Ainsi, l'art humain tout entier, la poésie, la musique, la peinture, la sculpture, le génie dramatique, et encore la beauté et la force, se joindraient, s'emploieraient à une unique merveille, à un spectacle qui prendrait la foule par tous les sens et lui donnerait le plaisir aigu d'une jouissance décuplée (1).

Lyricism may be harnessed to unbridled imagination, provided there be no pretense of reality :

Pas d'œuvres bâtardes et hypocrites, voilà tout. Pas de mélange inacceptable, pas de monstres moitié réels et moitié fabuleux ; pas de prétention à conclure sur des mensonges, dans une pensée morale et patriotique. Ou vous êtes un observateur qui rassemblez des documents humains, ou vous êtes un poète qui me contez vos rêves, et je ne vous demande que du génie pour vous admirer. J'ajoute que l'évolution contemporaine s'opère évidemment en faveur de l'observateur, du romancier naturaliste, et je m'explique cela par des raisons sociales et scientifiques. Mais j'accepte tout, je suis heureux de tout, parce que j'aime la vie en savant qui la note au jour le jour (2).

Appraisal of Zola's naturalism

Surely Zola, in undertaking to forge an alliance between the methods of science and those of literature and drama, was seeking to vanquish the idealists, whom he recognized as the arch-enemies of naturalism, meaning by " naturalism " the whole complex of ideas which represented to Zola his own philosophy and justification in life. Zola's faith in the ability of science to bring humanity ever closer to a utopian world bore his imagination to giddy heights, from which he might look down upon the idealists mired in superstition. He describes them as :

... les écrivains qui sortent de l'observation et de l'expérience pour baser leurs œuvres sur le surnaturel et l'irrationnel, qui admettent en un mot des forces mystérieuses, au-dehors du déterminisme des phénomènes... les romanciers idéalistes restent de parti pris dans l'inconnu, par toutes sortes de préjugés religieux et philosophiques, sous le prétexte stupéfiant que l'inconnu est plus noble et plus beau que le connu (3).

The naturalists have an ideal : " Nous sommes tous idéalistes, si l'on entend par là que nous nous occupons tous de l'idéal (4). "

(1) *Le Naturalisme au théâtre,* " la Féerie et l'Opérette, I ", p. 287.
(2) *Le Roman expérimental,* " les Documents humains ", pp. 213-214.
(3) *Ibid.,* " le Roman expérimental, III ", p. 29.
(4) *Ibid.,* " le Roman expérimental, IV ", p. 36.

Their ideal, however, is not an end in itself, but an incentive to
spur them to still further conquest of the unknown by scientific
means :

Ce qu'il faut accepter seulement, c'est ce que je nommerai l'aiguillon
de l'idéal. Certes, notre science est bien petite encore, à côté de la masse
énorme de choses que nous ignorons. Cet inconnu immense qui nous
entoure ne doit nous inspirer que le désir de le percer, de l'expliquer,
grâce aux méthodes scientifiques (1).

The idealists were perhaps stunned by the impact of naturalism, but by no means vanquished. Within a decade after
these lines were written, an idealist reaction set in against the
scientific basis of Zola's doctrine, which had become an excuse
for extremes of vulgarity. The reaction was aided by the
rashness of Zola's pretentions. Zola did not conceive of naturalism as a school or method of literature which might coexist
with other methods, but as an inevitable, all-embracing movement to which every writer must subscribe or perish. The
rigorous application of his doctrine would have resulted in the
absolute exclusion of spiritual values from literature and the
theater — a restriction which would of course have been into-
lerable. The doctrine, moreover, necessarily weakened, as it
became evident with the passing years that scientific progress
was not so well able to remedy the ills of humanity as had been
supposed earlier in the century.

On the credit side, naturalism was as effective a movement of
enfranchisement as romanticism had been a generation earlier.
Whereas the romantics had rebelled against the stereotyped
mold of classicism, the naturalists rebelled against stereotyped
formulas of morality and rhetoric which frustrated efforts to
bring a greater measure of truth to literature and the drama.
Zola's dramatic criticism attacked those conventions which
restricted the scope of the stage. He opened the eyes of theatrical workers to the possibilities of new forms and new subjects.
His recommendations in behalf of more life-like scenery, costumes
and methods of acting were prophetic of future stage productions. His scorn of sympathetic characters and of happy
endings widened the horizons of the theater, and created an
atmosphere in which the plays of Becque and the *Théâtre-Libre*
of Antoine were able to survive. His strong advocacy of scenes
taken from every-day life, presented by actors " living " rather

(1) *Ibid.*, p. 37.

than " playing " their rôles, was reflected a decade later in Jean Jullien's celebrated pronouncement :

UNE PIÈCE EST UNE TRANCHE DE LA VIE MISE SUR LA SCÈNE AVEC ART...

... *Ce n'est donc qu'une tranche de la vie* que nous pouvons mettre en scène, l'exposition en sera faite par l'action même et le dénouement ne sera qu'un arrêt facultatif de l'action qui laissera par-delà la pièce le champ libre aux réflexions du spectateur ; car notre but n'est pas de prêter à rire, mais surtout de donner à penser (1).

Jullien's " slice of life " formula, inspired by Zola and by the liberalization of the theater which followed Zola's campaign, survives to this day. Zola's doctrine, dependent upon the alliance of science and literature, was in a sense merely a primitive expression of modern naturalism, which has discarded his scientific pretensions. Yet the alliance was necessary in its time. The scientific spirit was needed to regenerate literature and the drama and to free them of conventions and taboos. To Zola belongs the credit for this temporary, yet fertile, mating.

(1) Preface (dated 1 August 1890) to *l'Echéance* (produced in 1889). The quotation is in Jean JULLIEN, *le Théâtre vivant, essai théorique et pratique* (Paris, 1892), pp. 11, 13. Jullien's slice of life formula is a restrictive one — i. e., a play should consist entirely of action, without exposition or contrived ending ; it should be *only* a slice of life.

CHAPTER IV

STAGE ADAPTATIONS
AND COLLABORATIONS
(Excluding plays with music)

Introduction

Soon after publication of *l'Assommoir*, Zola became associated with the minor playwright, William Busnach (1), in the stage adaptation of this novel. The success of the production led Zola to continue the relationship, and during the next decade, Busnach, with the real but seldom acknowledged collaboration of the novelist, undertook adaptations of *Nana, Pot-Bouille, Germinal,* and *le Ventre de Paris.* A sixth novel, *la Bête humaine,* was adapted by Busnach, but not produced. For *l'Assommoir,* Busnach had the collaboration also of Octave Gastineau, who died, however, before the play opened.

Zola's name did not appear as co-author in the theatrical programs of these plays, and he persistently refused to acknowledge publicly the extent of his collaboration. For example, he wrote in *le Voltaire* a few days after the opening of *l'Assommoir* :

Je suis bien à l'aise pour parler de *l'Assommoir*, le drame que MM. Busnach et Gastineau ont tiré de mon roman ; car je ne les ai

(1) William-Bertrand Busnach, 1832-1907. Recently published is an article by Martin KANES, " Zola and Busnach : The Temptation of the Stage ", in *PLMA*, LXXVII, No. 1 (March 1962), pp. 109-115. For biographical data concerning Busnach, see this article and also Léon DEFFOUX, *la Publication de l'Assommoir*, p. 116.

autorisés à faire cette adaptation qu'à la condition absolue de n'avoir à m'occuper en rien de la pièce. Elle m'est donc étrangère, je puis la juger avec une entière liberté d'appréciation (1).

And he wrote a similar denial the following September, when the play re-opened after the customary summer vacation :

... je m'étonne de la persistance que certains critiques mettent à m'attribuer la paternité de ce drame. Il me semble que ma déclaration aurait dû suffire. Je répète que j'ai simplement donné à deux auteurs dramatiques de talent, MM. Busnach et Gastineau, l'autorisation de tirer un drame de mon roman, imitant d'ailleurs en cela d'illustres exemples. Il est donc d'une mauvaise foi absolue de discuter l'œuvre comme étant de moi, d'y chercher mes idées, de me combattre avec les arguments qu'on peut y trouver. Il s'agit ici uniquement d'une adaptation faite par des hommes de théâtre, gens d'esprit et d'habileté, qui ont eu naturellement en vue le succès, et qui, ce me semble, ont parfaitement atteint le but qu'ils se proposaient (2).

The fact that these denials are at variance with the record displayed in Zola's published correspondence has sometimes been noted (3). Zola's two published letters to Busnach (which will be discussed more fully below) show that he gave his collaborator detailed advice and instructions concerning the scenario of *l'Assommoir* (4). He admits to working on the play in a letter to Hennique, to whom he writes :

Vous savez qu'on tire un drame en cinq actes et douze tableaux de *l'Assommoir*. J'ai travaillé fortement au plan ; mais n'en dites rien, je ne veux pas que cela se sache (5).

As well as in two letters to Flaubert :

J'ai autorisé deux braves garçons à tirer un drame de *l'Assommoir*. Puis, je me suis laissé emballer, j'ai travaillé moi-même au scénario ; mais il est bien entendu que je ne serai pas nommé.

Ce sont deux braves garçons, Busnach et Gastineau, qui signeront *l'Assommoir* au théâtre. Mais entre nous, je dois vous dire que j'ai

---

(1) *Le Voltaire*, 28 January 1879. Reprinted in Part I of ZOLA's preface to the play *l'Assommoir*. This preface is in LES ŒUVRES COMPLÈTES, *Mélanges, Préface et Discours*, pp. 203-227.
(2) *Le Voltaire*, 2 September 1879. Most of this article is reprinted as Part III of Zola's preface, but the portion quoted here was omitted.
(3) See, for example, Werner SCHILDBACH, *Die Dramatisierung des naturalistischen Romans bei Emile Zola* (Halle, 1937), pp. 79-81.
(4) Letters dated 19 August and 23 August 1877, in LES ŒUVRES COMPLÈTES, *Correspondance (1872-1902)*, pp. 480-487 and 490-492.
(5) *Ibid.*, p. 493. Letter dated 2 September 1877.

beaucoup travaillé à la pièce, bien que j'aie mis comme condition formelle que je resterai dans la coulisse (1).

Zola's refusal to recognize his part in Busnach's adaptations acquired, in his own family, the force of tradition. Even after Zola's death, his widow protested to Adolphe Brisson, dramatic critic of *le Temps*, concerning the latter's review of a revival of *Nana*. Brisson reproduces the pertinent part of Madame Zola's letter, together with his justification for considering the adaptation of *Nana* as being in part Zola's work :

Mme Émile Zola m'a fait la grâce de m'adresser une lettre au sujet de mon dernier feuilleton. « Je crois devoir vous rappeler me dit-elle, qu'aucun des drames tirés des romans d'Émile Zola n'a été signé de lui. Si vous aviez tenu compte de ce fait, vous auriez dirigé vos critiques sur l'auteur de la pièce et non sur celui du livre, puisque ce dernier n'est pas en cause. » Je n'ignorais pas que William Busnach a été l'unique signataire de l'adaptation de *Nana*, comme de *l'Assommoir* et de *Pot-Bouille*. Mais je n'ai pas cru téméraire de supposer que Zola l'avait aidé de ses conseils, influencé, guidé, approuvé. Je ne m'abusais pas. Des confidences jadis recueillies de la bouche du célèbre romancier par notre confrère, Ange Galdemar, nous renseignent. « Nous établissions le plan complet de la pièce en causant, dit Zola ; les actes, les tableaux, les épisodes, les personnages arrêtés et définis. Busnach écrivait le dialogue qu'il me soumettait et que je modifiais ou que je développais à mon gré. Les pages du manuscrit de Busnach avaient une grande marge, destinée à recevoir mes observations. » Il n'en faut pas davantage pour constituer les éléments d'une collaboration véritable. Nous connaissons des collaborateurs plus paresseux que l'auteur de *Nana* et qui se donnent moins de peine. D'ailleurs pourquoi la piété de Mme Zola s'alarmerait-elle de la révélation d'un accord, qui, s'il n'a pas produit des chefs-d'œuvre, n'ôte rien à la gloire de son illustre mari (2) ?

The most conclusive proof of Zola's active collaboration in these dramas is to be found in the *Bibliothèque Nationale's* collection of manuscript letters written to Zola, *Correspondance Émile Zola, Tomes I-XV. Nouvelles acquisitions françaises 24510-24524*. Only two letters written by Zola to Busnach have been published in Zola's LES ŒUVRES COMPLÈTES ; certainly many other letters were written by Zola which have either been lost or remain in private hands. On the other hand, Busnach's manuscript letters to Zola, preserved in the *Bibliothèque Natio-*

---

(1) *Ibid.*, pp. 496 and 497. Letters dated 17 September and 12 October 1877.
(2) Adolphe BRISSON, " Chronique théâtrale ", in *le Temps*, 30 September 1912.

nale, number several hundred and occupy two volumes and part
of a third of this 15-volume manuscript collection (1). These
letters, portions of which will be quoted below, reveal beyond
dispute that Zola was an active collaborator with Busnach in all
the plays which the latter adapted from Zola's novels, with the
exception of *la Bête humaine*.

Zola's disavowal of his part in the collaboration was quite
natural in the circumstances. It will be recalled that his first
article on the theater, published in *Mes haines*, dealt with the
quarrel between Dumas *fils* and Émile de Girardin over *le
Supplice d'une femme*, which they had written in collaboration
and which neither Dumas nor de Girardin chose to acknowledge.
This early lesson in the ethics of authorship remained with Zola
all his life. It was the privilege of a collaborator to acknowledge
the joint work or not, as he saw fit. Moreover — unlike the case
of *le Supplice d'une femme* — the failure of one author to acknowledge a joint work did not imply a quarrel with his collaborator.
The question of admitting authorship lay in the unrestricted
discretion of the writer.

In Zola's collaboration with Busnach, the authors were in
complete agreement by the time the plays went into production.
Zola, it seems probable, withheld his name because these adaptations were not intended to be examples of naturalism in the
theater. They did not meet, nor were they intended to meet,
the standards for the theater which he had been proclaiming
in his capacity of dramatic critic. Publicly, he merely hinted
at the reasons which disposed him to withhold his name, and
appears to have considered efforts to penetrate his motive as an
invasion of his privacy. He writes, for example, in his preface
to the adaptation of *Nana* :

> Reste la grosse question de savoir si j'ai collaboré à la pièce et dans
> quelle mesure. En vérité, MM. Dumas fils et Sardou ne sont-ils pas
> dix fois restés dans la coulisse, sans qu'on leur en ait fait un crime.

(1) *Correspondance Emile Zola*, t. IV (710 feuillets), t. V (750 feuillets),
t. VI (feuillets 1-292) (*Nouvelles acquisitions françaises*, 24513, 24514, 24515).
    The word " feuillet " designates a separate sheet or page. Most of Bus-
nach's letters consist of more than one *feuillet*. The letters are arranged
chronologically in several categories, according to the relative completeness
of their dates ; i. e., the first group of letters are " Lettres datées " (by day,
month and year), and are in t. IV, feuillets 1-400 ; the next group are " Lettres
datées du jour et du mois ", from t. IV, f. 401 to t. V, f. 148 ; the next group,
" Lettres datées du jour ", from t. V, f. 149 to t. VI, f. 235; and a final group,
" Lettres non datées ", in t. VI, f. 236-292.
    The collection as a whole comprises letters to Zola from more than 350 cor-
respondents, of which Busnach's letters are by far the largest single group.

J'estime que je n'ai pas à répondre. On ne m'a pas nommé, cela doit
suffire. Cherchez les causes, dites que j'ai juré de ne jamais rien signer
en collaboration, ajoutez que *Nana* pourrait bien être une expérience et
un acheminement, imaginez encore que je veux un autre terrain. Et
il y a de grandes chances pour que vous soyez dans la vérité. Mais ce
sont là des suppositions. Un fait seul demeure : on ne m'a pas nommé,
je ne suis pas de la pièce.
     N'ai-je donc pas le droit de mener ma vie littéraire comme je
l'entends ? Soyez tranquilles, le jour où un drame sera de moi, vraiment
de moi, je le signerai, et tous les sifflets du monde ne m'y feront pas
changer un mot (1).

     Busnach's adaptations were intended to be popular dramas,
benefiting from such concessions to public taste as the authors
saw fit to introduce in the interests of success. There is no
reason to question Zola's right to disavow his part in the collaboration. However, it is necessary to rebut the belief, sometimes
expressed, that Busnach, rather than Zola, was responsible for
the decision to adapt these novels in terms of conventional
theater. For example, Denise Le Blond-Zola writes in her
biography :

     Busnach n'apportait à la scène aucun des soucis littéraires de Zola.
Homme de théâtre habile, il ne reculait pas devant de faciles effets,
comme l'introduction du personnage classique du traître, Virginie,
dans *l'Assommoir*. Si Zola avait écrit le drame lui-même, jamais il
n'aurait fait une pareille concession au goût du public (2).

     The fact is, as we shall see, that this alteration in the rôle of
Virginie was Zola's own idea. Zola was the leader of the collaboration. His wishes prevailed. Busnach's adaptations were
tailored as much as possible to the public taste because Zola
himself so desired it.
     None of the plays to be discussed in this chapter are published
in LES ŒUVRES COMPLÈTES, which are limited to Zola's work as
sole author. Of Busnach's six adaptations, only three (*l'Assommoir*, *Nana* and *Pot-Bouille*) have been published (3), but Zola's
prefaces to these plays appear in LES ŒUVRES COMPLÈTES, in

(1) LES ŒUVRES COMPLÈTES, *Une campagne*, " Nana ". In speaking of a
play which he intended to sign, as his own work, ZOLA is thinking of *Renée*,
discussed in our Chapter II.
     (2) Denise LE BLOND-ZOLA, *Emile Zola raconté par sa fille* (Paris, 1931),
p. 180.
     (3) William BUSNACH et Octave GASTINEAU, *l'Assommoir, drame en cinq
actes et neuf tableaux avec une préface d'Emile Zola* (Paris, 1880).
     William BUSNACH, *Trois pièces, tirées des romans et précédées chacune d'une
préface de Emile Zola : l'Assommoir, Nana, Pot-Bouille* (Paris, 1884).

the volumes *Mélanges, Préfaces et Discours* (" *L'Assommoir* au théâtre ", " *Pot-Bouille* au théâtre ") and *Une campagne* (" *Nana* "). As to the unpublished adaptations, as well as to those which have been published, considerable information of value has been obtained from the *Collection théâtrale Auguste Rondel* in the *Bibliothèque de l'Arsenal*, Paris.

The first work to be discussed will be an early and unimportant collaboration, *les Mystères de Marseille*, after which Busnach's six adaptations will be taken up, followed by consideration of a number of adaptations in which Zola did not actively participate.

« Les Mystères de Marseille »

In 1867, Zola accepted the offer of a Marseille newspaper, *Le Messager de Provence*, to write for serial publication in that journal a novel based upon the records of criminal cases tried before the courts of Marseille and of Aix. The novel, *les Mystères de Marseille*, was pure hack-work, undertaken in a period of financial distress. In his preface to a later edition, Zola himself refers to it as " cette œuvre de pur métier, et de mauvais métier ", pointing out, however, that he profited in his later work from this early experience in writing documentary fiction. How little effort he put into the writing of this novel may be judged from his statement that whereas two pages of *Thérèse Raquin*, which he was writing concurrently, sometimes cost him four hours of effort, one hour sufficed for seven or eight pages of *les Mystères de Marseille* (1).

Zola quickly recognized the theatrical possibilities of his material. While the novel was still being published serially in the *Messager de Provence*, he and his childhood friend, Marius Roux, set to work adapting it for the stage, and succeeded in having it accepted by the *Gymnase* theater in Marseille. A record of the collaboration is preserved in a series of published letters which Zola wrote to Roux between 16 March and 10 October 1867 (2). From these letters, it seems probable that Zola's work was principally of a planning and supervisory nature,

---

(1) Preface dated July 1883, LES ŒUVRES COMPLÈTES, *les Mystères de Marseille* (the novel), p. x. See also ZOLA's letter to Valabrègue, 19 February 1867, *Correspondance (1858-1871)*, p. 296.
(2) LES ŒUVRES COMPLÈTES, *Correspondance (1858-1871)*, letters dated 16 March, 28 May, 3, 4 and 8 June, 16 and 23 July, 14 and 25 August, 4 and 17 September, 4, 6, 7 and 10 October, and telegram of 6 October — all in the year 1867.

and that he left to Roux the task of writing most of the dialogue.
In his letter of 4 June, he describes the basic idea, one of the stock
ideas of melodrama :

Mon idée reste celle-ci. Un prologue dans lequel la naissance des deux
enfants est expliquée ; suivre des routes différentes : la route du vice
et la route de la vertu ; au dénouement tout s'explique, la vertu est
récompensée et le vice puni. Il y a de belles scènes à trouver.
N'importe. Fais ton plan. Ce sera notre base de travail (1).

A few days later, he writes that, having suffered from insomnia
during the night, he has worked on their play :

Je crois avoir trouvé des scènes très saisissantes, toute une intrigue
corsée et poignante. Ne fais rien, ne bâtis rien, avant d'avoir reçu les
notes que je rédige... Tu travailleras sur la donnée que je vais te fournir,
et, mardi soir, nous pourrons arrêter le plan (2).

And the following month he writes :

Voici le dernier tableau.
J'ai arrangé plusieurs choses pour donner quelque vraisemblance à
nos gros mensonges (3).

In August and September, Roux was in Marseille, while Zola
remained in Paris. The latter wrote several anxious letters
urging his friend to obtain a definite production date, to be on
his guard against the manager of the *Gymnase*, whose taste and
scruples Zola distrusted, and to secure as favorable publicity as
possible for the play. Apparently neither of the authors was
present at rehearsals. Zola arrived in Marseille only a day or
two before the opening on 5 October. Roux had meanwhile
returned to Paris. A telegram and three letters from Zola bore
the sad tidings to his friend. The play was too long (having
lasted five hours) and " véritablement ennuyeuse ". There had
surely been " une petite cabale " against it. The actors had been
inadequate (4). Although the second night was an improvement
over the first (" les acteurs n'ont plus eu de manque de
mémoire ") (5), the play was a failure and was withdrawn after
a few performances.

(1) *Ibid.*, p. 309.
(2) *Ibid.*, p. 310. Letter dated 8 June.
(3) *Ibid.*, p. 311. Letter dated 16 July.
(4) *Ibid.*, p. 324. Letter dated 6 October.
(5) *Ibid.*, p. 325. Letter dated 7 October.

This was Zola's first production in the theater, but, except for the loss of prospective income, the failure meant little to him. The enterprise represented merely an interlude of hackwork. Neither his artistic standards nor his faith in his capacities had been compromised. The play, *les Mystères de Marseille*, has not been published.

« L'Assommoir »

L'Assommoir, " drame en cinq actes et dix tableaux, tiré du roman de M. Émile Zola par M. William Busnach et feu Octave Gastineau " (1), opened at the *Ambigu* on 18 January 1879 and had a highly successful run of about 300 performances. The play has been revived a number of times in Paris. According to Alexis and to Zola's preface, an English translation by Charles Reade entitled *Drink* played some 500 performances in London (2). Of all the plays with which Zola was connected as sole or joint author, *l'Assommoir* has been the most popular.

Part I of Zola's preface contains a partial summary or the play, in which he himself points out the principal departures from the novel (3). The play employs a cast of 29 and unfolds in a series of nine different *tableaux* (reduced after the opening from ten, for the sake of greater brevity), in which it may be presumed that Zola's instructions to Busnach were carefully followed :

Il faut des décors exacts, très curieusement plantés, faits exprès, copiés sur nature, et très vastes (4).

The first tableau is in the hotel room occupied by Gervaise and her lover, Lantier, and shows the abandonment of Gervaise

(1) Announcement in the " Courrier des théâtres " of *le Figaro*, 18 January 1879.
(2) ALEXIS, *Emile Zola*, p. 220. ZOLA's preface, in LES ŒUVRES COMPLÈTES, *Mélanges, Préfaces et discours*, p. 224. According to Eileen E. PRYME, " Zola's Plays in England 1870-1900 ", in *French Studies*, vol. 13 (1959), pp. 28-38, this adaptation was Reade's greatest success in the theater and received the commendations of William Archer and George Bernard Shaw for its high moral value.
(3) Part I of ZOLA's preface (*ibid.*, pp. 203-215) first appeared in his " Revue dramatique et littéraire ", in *le Voltaire*, 28 January 1879 — ten days after the opening.
For a detailed comparison of Zola's novels with their stage adaptations, see the work by Werner SCHILDBACH, *Die Dramatisierung des naturalistischen Romans bei Emile Zola* (Halle, 1937).
(4) Letter dated 23 August 1877, in *Correspondance (1872-1902)*, p. 491.

by her lover. Zola admires particularly the simplicity of the action and dialogue, the absence of theatricality, and the human quality of the scene, which he describes accordingly as " du très bon naturalisme " (1). The next *tableau* reveals the laundry and is one of the striking stage settings which contributed in large measure to the success of the play. The scene leads up to the fight between Gervaise and Virginie. There follows a street scene in front of the tavern, *l'Assommoir*, during which Gervaise and Coupeau decide to marry. One of the principal elements of this scene is a long speech by the foundry-manager, Goujet, showing the contrast between the honest worker and the drunkard. Since this was the type of moral preaching for which Zola reproached Dumas it is interesting to see Zola's comment upon it :

> Quant à la tirade de Goujet défendant le vrai peuple, le peuple honnête, et jetant son mépris aux mauvais ouvriers qui désertent le chantier pour le cabaret, elle était nécessaire, dans la pensée des auteurs, pour mettre les spectateurs en garde contre les calomnies répandues sur le roman. On a prétendu que j'attaquais le peuple, que je le salissais à plaisir. MM. Busnach et Gastineau ont jugé qu'il était bon de résumer dans une tirade, et de placer dans la bouche de Goujet, la morale qui se dégage de mon livre. Je constate, je n'apprécie pas (2).

The fourth *tableau* is the garden of a restaurant, in which, co-incidentally, Gervaise and Virginie are each holding their respective wedding dinners. The fifth *tableau* shows Coupeau's fall from the scaffolding before the eyes of Gervaise and their six-year old Nana. Here, in the rôle of Virginie, is the greatest departure from the novel. The Virginie of the play is a starkly melodramatic villain whose passions of vengeance and jealousy cause the downfall of Gervaise and Coupeau. In the novel, Coupeau's fall from the scaffolding was a pure accident, one of those acts of fate that try men's characters, and the deep tragedy of the novel flows from the helplessness of Coupeau to surmount this accident of fate. In the play, however, the accident occurs through the direct intervention of Virginie. From her window in the adjoining house, she watches the preparations of the workers (Mes-Bottes, Bibi-la-Grillade, Bec-Salé) to erect a scaffolding. The scaffolding is found to be defective. The workers leave for their lunch hour, exacting from Virginie the

(1) ZOLA's preface, *ibid.*, p. 207.
(2) *Ibid.*, pp. 207-208.

promise to warn Coupeau, who has not yet arrived, against using the scaffolding. Virginie takes advantage of the opportunity to bring misfortune upon Gervaise, and fails to give the warning to Coupeau.

The sixth *tableau*, which takes place some years later, shows the birthday feast of Gervaise, now the successful owner of a laundry. Her happiness is menaced by the habitual drunkenness of her husband, who, as in the novel, has succumbed to alcohol during his convalescence from the accident. Lantier returns and is welcomed by the drunken husband. Zola points out in his preface the moral lesson to be drawn from this episode :

Je ne croyais pas qu'on pût mettre cette scène au théâtre : la leçon qui s'en dégage est formidable. Toute la déchéance de l'ivrogne est là, hardiment, dans cet homme qui, après avoir voulu tuer l'ancien amant de sa femme quand il a sa raison, l'accueille et plaisante quand il est ivre (1).

The original seventh *tableau*, a scene in Goujet's foundry, was omitted after the first night, and does not appear in the published play. There follows the scene in the bar-room where Coupeau, who has reformed, is maliciously enticed into his former habits by Lantier, acting again under the instructions of Virginie. This was Zola's favorite scene of the play :

C'est le tableau que je préfère. Toutes mes idées sont là, dans cette reproduction exacte de la vie. Les acteurs ne jouent plus, ils vivent leur rôle. La mise en scène est une merveille de vérité ; ces hommes qui entrent, qui sortent, qui consomment assis à des tables ou debout devant le comptoir, nous transportent chez un véritable liquoriste (2).

Zola, as appears from this passage, had a primitive conception of the later " slice of life " technique. His conception of it was limited, however, to individual scenes. It was left to Jean Jullien to make an esthetic formulation of the " slice of life " principle by applying it to a play as a unified whole (3).

The eighth *tableau* (ninth of the first performance) is entitled " La dernière bouteille " and shows the miserable attic to which her husband's drinking has brought Gervaise. But there is still hope for Coupeau's regeneration. He has just been discharged from the alcoholic ward of the hospital, reformed and cured — provided that he abstain from alcohol in the future. He is permitted, however, to drink light wine. Virginie inter-

(1) *Ibid.*, p. 208.
(2) ZOLA's preface, *Mélanges, Préfaces et Discours*, p. 209.
(3) Jean JULLIEN, *Le théâtre vivant, essai théorique et pratique*, pp. 11-13.

venes again. In celebration of Coupeau's return from the hospital, she has thoughtfully sent him a bottle marked " Bordeaux ". Coupeau, in all innocence, takes a sip, and discovers with horror that the bottle is wrongly labeled and that it contains the dread and forbidden beverage. We may let Zola describe the scene :

J'arrive enfin à la fameuse scène de la bouteille, scène qui n'est pas dans le roman et que je puis admirer à mon aise. Je la déclare absolument superbe. Ne cherchons pas comment la bouteille est là : une ficelle l'y apporte, mais elle y est. Coupeau croit avoir une bouteille de bordeaux, et c'est une bouteille d'eau-de-vie qu'il tient entre ses mains. Voilà la situation : s'il boit un petit verre, il est mort. Alors, commence dans cet homme une lutte affreuse. Il tremble comme un enfant : pourquoi l'a-t-on laissé seul avec cette bouteille ? Et il recule, et il se cache, et il claque des dents. Sur la table, la bouteille grandit, grandit ; elle devient démesurée, elle emplit la scène dans son immobilité, tandis que le misérable éperdu tourne autour d'elle. Il boira, il sera pris d'un dernier accès de *delirium tremens*, une crise suprême qui le jettera mort sur la paillasse (1).

In the final *tableau*, a night scene on the Boulevard Rochechouart, the homeless Gervaise dies on a public bench, and justice is rendered to Virginie and her lover, Lantier. Virginie's husband, having discovered their adulterous relations, avenges his honor with their death.

The opening of *l'Assommoir* was one of the most eagerly awaited events of the theatrical season. Even habitual members of first-night audiences were unable to obtain seats for the first night, and — an unusual circumstance for French plays of the epoch — there was a considerable advance sale for later performances (2). In terms of popularity, the play justified expectations. As to the critics, Zola is probably correct in stating that the dominating note of their reviews was astonishment at the play's success (3). The critics, however, were careful to point out the absence of any literary quality in the work. Henry Fouquier writes :

... il est incontestable que cette « première » a été un grand événement parisien. Je me refuse à admettre qu'elle ait été un grand événement littéraire (4).

(1) Zola's preface, pp. 209-210.
(2) According to " Un monsieur de l'orchestre ", in *le Figaro*, 19 January 1879.
(3) Zola's preface, *ibid.*, pp. 210-211.
(4) *Le XIXᵉ siècle*, 21 January 1879, as cited in Les Œuvres complètes, *l'Assommoir* (the novel), " Notes et commentaires, l'Assommoir au théâtre ", p. 491.

Auguste Vitu, calling the play " une œuvre si vantée et cependant si vide ", concludes :

Les arrangeurs du drame, en passant l'éponge sur le style de M. Zola, y ont substitué le leur qui est commun, traînant, sans expression et sans flamme. Les connaisseurs remarquent qu'il y a beaucoup moins d'argot et beaucoup moins de français dans le drame que dans le livre. La littérature n'a rien à voir là-dedans (1).

Sarcey finds it " un drame qui ne soulève aucune question littéraire " (2). Both Vitu and Sarcey, in almost identical terms, observe that the play diminishes in its later stages to the sole question of whether Coupeau will or will not take a drink. Both protest against showing the horror of *delirium tremens* on the stage. As to this scene, Sarcey writes :

Il boit, et ce n'est plus de l'ivresse, c'est de la folie furieuse. Il pousse des cris inarticulés, il saute, il se roule, il se tord, il bave... Non, on me donnerait 1 000 francs pour voir ce spectacle hideux à l'hôpital, je refuserais, et c'est ça qu'on me donne au théâtre pour m'amuser !
Mais c'est horrible ! Mais il n'y a pas ombre d'art dans tout cela ! L'art consisterait, si l'on en arrive à reproduire sur la scène ces ignominies, à choisir un ou deux traits qui donneraient la sensation du reste... Je trouve ce spectacle très répugnant et ne comprends rien à la frénésie d'admiration qu'a marquée le public (3).

Sarcey's judgment, which may be taken as measuring the standards of taste which governed the conventional French theater of the epoch, illustrates the resistance then offered to the exhibition of unpleasant subjects on the stage. The great success of *l'Assommoir* widened the breach in this wall of resistance, but only to a limited extent, inasmuch as the play as a whole followed a conventional pattern. Its novelty was in the detailed realism of its settings — the actresses in the second tableau, for example, washed real laundry with real soap in really hot water — and in the animated picture of working class life presented on the stage. The outcome of the play was somber and tragic, but the tragedy was alleviated by touches of comedy (Mes-Bottes, Bec-Salé, Bibi-la-Grillade), by the picturesque quality of the settings, and by the satisfaction of seeing the prime mover of the tragedy — Virginie — given her just deserts. The

(1) *Le Figaro*, 20 January 1879.
(2) Francisque SARCEY, *Quarante ans de théâtre* (Paris, 1902), t. VI, p. 13 (reprinted from *le Temps*, 20 January 1879).
(3) *Ibid.*, p. 19.

change in Virginie's rôle from that of incidental character in the novel to that of causal agent in the drama is the principal reason for the weakness of the play with respect to the novel. The tragedy of Coupeau and of Gervaise becomes ascribable, in the play, not primarily to their character and environment, but to the malevolence of a human agent. The source of the tragedy is diverted from the conditions of life to the artificial contrivance of the writer, and the impact of the drama is correspondingly lessened.

Zola insisted that he had no part in the adaptation of *l'Assommoir* to the stage. However, his two letters to Busnach (the only letters to Busnach which have been published or are available), as well as Busnach's letters to him, show that he was a real collaborator.

Busnach's first letter in which Zola and *l'Assommoir* are specifically referred to is that of 27 June 1877, in which he states what he and Gastineau undertake to do :

... nous ferons mon collaborateur et moi un scénario détaillé de la pièce. Nous vous l'enverrons. Vous nous direz ce que vous en pensez.
Une fois d'accord nous écrirons la pièce. Mais il sera entendu entre nous que du moment que le scénario aura été adopté par vous, il ne vous sera plus possible de faire la pièce sans notre collaboration...
A quelle époque croyez-vous qu'il faudra arrêter le drame ? Faut-il oui ou non faire Gervaise mère de Nana partie, ou ne pas montrer Nana ? Faut-il faire la pièce en 3 époques... Enfin, enfin... il y a un rude travail à faire (1) !

A few days later, he writes :

Nous avons supprimé un tableau. Nous vous enverrons la semaine prochaine un plan complet de mes 7 tableaux.
La pièce aura 3 époques.
1re époque : 1er acte, 1860.
2e époque : 2e acte, 1869.
3e époque : 3e ,4e et 5e actes, 1877 (2).

The following letter is in reply to one from Zola. Zola's letter has been lost, or at least is unavailable, but it is clear from Busnach's reply that Zola furnished reasons for the complete

---

(1) *Correspondance Emile Zola*, t. IV, feuillets 4-5 (*Nouvelles acquisitions françaises* 24513, in the *Bibliothèque Nationale*, Paris).
(2) *Ibid.*, feuillets 6-7. Letter dated 30 June 1877.

revision of all their work so far accomplished, and that Busnach
yielded to Zola's ideas :

Paris, 17 juillet 1877.

Mon cher Zola. Je viens de recevoir votre lettre et le scénario...
Par malheur vous êtes à Marseille, Gastineau est à Blois et je vais
partir pour Genève samedi prochain. Néanmoins, je suis si convaincu
que les raisons que me donne votre lettre pour les changements à faire
à la pièce en question sont excellentes que je vais aller passer 2 jours à
Blois pour refondre notre travail... J'adopte absolument votre idée de
faire des *scènes populaires*. Je crois qu'il ne faut pas changer trop au
roman ni introduire des personnages inconnus. Cela étonne le spectateur.
Un drame tiré d'un roman a besoin de moins de cohésion qu'une pièce
ordinaire.
Il faut trouver 10 tableaux et quatre grands décors. Je trouve la
forge excellente. Donc, refonte complète du travail (1).

Ten days later, Busnach furnished Zola with a list of 12 tentative *tableaux* for the play (2), and in a letter dated only
" Lundi 30 juillet ", but which was undoubtedly written in 1877,
he submits alternate projects of 1) four acts in twelve scenes,
or 2) five acts in ten scenes, and requests Zola's opinion (3).
On 2 August 1877, he acknowledges receipt of Zola's letter
(lost or unavailable), and answers Zola's suggestions with counter-
suggestions (4). In a letter dated only " Blois 4 août ", written
presumably in 1877, he writes :

Je crois que c'était impossible, sans rendre notre héroïne ignoble
et odieuse aux yeux des spectateurs, de la montrer recouchant avec
Lantier (5).

(This suggestion was followed. The Gervaise of the play,
unlike her prototype of the novel, repulses Lantier when he
tries to resume their relations.)
At this point in the correspondence, we come to the first
of Zola's two published letters to Busnach, written from
L'Estaque 19 August 1877 (6). Zola discusses each of the
twelve scenes of the scenario submitted by Busnach, but only
the most important of his suggestions need be examined here.
Commenting on the first *tableau*, he writes that Lantier must

(1) *Ibid.*, feuillets 10-11.
(2) *Ibid.*, feuillets 12-13.
(3) *Ibid.*, feuillets 663-664.
(4) *Ibid.*, feuillets 14-15.
(5) *Ibid.*, feuillets 672-673.
(6) LES ŒUVRES COMPLÈTES, *Correspondance (1872-1902)*, pp. 480-487.

leave Gervaise for Virginie rather than, as in the novel, for her sister. The reason for the change, he explains later in the letter, is to give Lantier, as Virginie's lover, a motive to join forces with her in seeking the downfall of the Coupeau family. This suggestion of Zola's was fulfilled in the finished play. As to the second scene, Zola advises Busnach to give the principal comic rôle to Mes-Bottes rather than to Bec-Salé, a recommendation which also was observed in the play. His comments on the third scene reveal that it was he, not Busnach, who conceived the idea of expanding the rôle of Virginie to that of villain :

Alors, je fais de Virginie le traître de la pièce. Elle a la fessée du lavoir sur le cœur, elle veut se venger de Gervaise en troublant son ménage, en faisant pousser Coupeau à boire... Et dès lors, c'est Lantier qui sert d'instrument... De cette manière tout s'explique, Lantier, je le répète, est poussé par Virginie... (1).

His, too — and not Busnach's — was the idea of altering the novel so that Coupeau's accident will not be a stroke of fate, but the result of Virginie's intervention :

Seulement, la chute de Coupeau est bête au théâtre, si elle est due au hasard. Il faut absolument qu'il y ait du Lantier là-dessous, de la Virginie (2).

He suggests that Virginie's house be adjacent to the scene of the construction, and that she herself lean from the window to untie a rope of the scaffold. This suggestion was amended in the play, where her intervention consists in her intentional failure to warn Coupeau of the danger, but the essential element of her intervention, her motivation, and the structure of the scene were fully established by Zola in his letter to Busnach. " Tout ceci ", he writes, " est pour dramatiser un peu la pièce qui manque de tout intérêt dramatique ". At the conclusion of his letter, he sums up the matter :

Mon opinion définitive maintenant, c'est que le drame est possible, si on le dramatise un peu dans le sens que j'indique... Dites-moi si les modifications que je demande vous plaisent à vous et à votre collaborateur. Dites-moi cela le plus vite possible, et alors, brièvement, j'écrirai un résumé du scénario tel que je le comprends. Vous pourrez ensuite vous mettre tout de suite à écrire la pièce (3).

(1) *Ibid.*, p. 482.
(2) *Ibid.*, p. 483.
(3) *Ibid.*, p. 487.

Busnach's reply shows that he relied strongly upon Zola's recommendations :

21 août 1877. Mon cher Zola, Je viens de recevoir votre lettre. Je vous dirai d'abord qu'elle m'a rendu un peu de courage. En vous envoyant le nouveau scénario j'étais fort embêté. Je voyais dans tout ce fatras des tableaux et pas de pièce. Vous commencez à éclairer les lanternes. Vos observations me plaisent presque toutes. La suppression du tableau chez les Goujet me va. Mais ce qui me plaît c'est que la pièce consiste en une conspiration de Virginie *maîtresse de Lantier* contre Gervaise.
... Maintenant je prends votre lettre. Je suis vos observations... Je ne demande pas mieux — au contraire ! — que de marcher sur un plan fait par vous sur le nôtre (1).

In this letter, a long one, Busnach makes some counter-suggestions of his own, but agrees to be guided by Zola. Zola's reply (the second and last of his *published* letters to Busnach) shows him still arguing in favor of changing the rôle of Virginie to that of a melodramatic villain :

Je sais qu'il est raide de faire de Virginie une assassine... nous sommes au boulevard, il est entendu que nous faisons de Virginie un traître de mélodrame (2).

Before the opening, which took place some fifteen months after this correspondence, Busnach sent to Zola the suggested draft of a press announcement to be signed by Zola, from which it appears that Zola's refusal to be named as collaborator was a matter of policy. Busnach gives the matter a flavor of conspiracy by requesting that his letter be kept secret. The letter is dated only " Mercredi 13 9bre " (i. e., 13 November), and was undoubtedly written in 1878 :

... Si vous êtes d'accord avec moi que l'on doit dire au public et aux journalistes que la pièce a été faite par Gastineau et moi sous votre direction, envoyez au *Figaro* ou M. Préval.
« Vous annoncez, hier, en parlant de *l'Assommoir* que la pièce de MM. Zola et Busnach est reculée d'un jour. Je n'ai point collaboré au drame en question. J'ai simplement autorisé MM. Busnach et Gastineau à tirer une pièce de mon roman, à la condition qu'elle me serait soumise et que je l'approuverais, ce qui a été fait..., etc. E. Zola. »
Ce que je vous dis doit rester entre nous deux (3).

(1) *Correspondance Emile Zola*, t. IV, feuillets 16-17.
(2) LES ŒUVRES COMPLÈTES, *Correspondance (1872-1902)*, p. 490.
(3) *Correspondance Emile Zola*, t. V (*Nouv. acq. fr.* 24514), feuillet 101.

And from a letter dated only " Samedi 21 " — which may be presumed to have been written on 21 December 1878 — it appears that the withholding of Zola's name was at least partly a matter of expediency, arising from the unpopularity which had attached to him because of his recently published article on contemporary novelists (1). The letter reads :

Samedi 21. Mon cher Zola, Je vous ai déjà répondu hier... La pièce passera le 10 ou le 11 janvier.

Dans vingt jours.

Les vraies générales ne commenceront que le lundi 6.

Mais il serait bien, je crois, que vous en vissiez une ou deux auparavant.

Tout va bien.

Mais les luttes que vous soutenez avec les romanciers dans *le Figaro* rendent la première plus dangereuse encore.

Il faudra bientôt trouver le moyen de vous désintéresser un peu de la pièce.

Dans l'intérêt de la première. Après, nous dirons toute la vérité... plus même que la vérité, si ça vous fait plaisir. Il nous faut un succès (2) !

The correspondence which has been cited indicates that the writing of the dialogue was left to Busnach and Gastineau, and that Zola's participation in the play was principally that of collaborating on the scenario. It would be correct to say that Busnach and Gastineau wrote the play under Zola's direction, provided it be understood that Zola's direction was the major influence which determined the nature and structure of the play. Zola was under no obligation to name himself as collaborator. But his denial that he had exercised any influence at all upon the production is misleading and raises the false implication that his colleagues were responsible for making concessions to popular theatrical conventions, whereas, on the contrary, it was Zola himself who insisted that these concessions be made.

Zola rightly attributed the success of the play to its naturalist scenes of every-day life. " Certes, ce n'est pas une victoire décisive pour le naturalisme ", he concludes, " mais c'est un grand pas vers la vérité des personnages et du milieu " (3).

---

(1) In *le Figaro, supplément littéraire du dimanche,* 22 December 1878, reprinted in LES ŒUVRES COMPLÈTES, *les Romanciers naturalistes,* " les Romanciers contemporains ", sections I-VII (Section VIII of this article is reprinted from *le Voltaire* of 31 December 1878). It may be presumed that the Sunday supplement of the *Figaro* was on sale by Saturday, the day Busnach wrote this letter.

(2) *Correspondance Emile Zola,* t. VI, feuillet 44.

(3) ZOLA's preface, *Mélanges, Préfaces et Discours,* p. 213.

The successful adaptation of *l'Assommoir* to the stage brought naturalism before the public mind more effectively than any other single event. The play has been frequently revived in Paris. The *Collection Rondel* contains theater programs of a number of these revivals, of which the most important were at the *Porte-Saint-Martin* in Novembre 1900, at the *Odéon* in September 1915, at the *Ba-ta-clan* in May 1921 and at the *Odéon* in September 1927 (1).

« Nana »

Zola's novel, *Nana*, began to appear serially in *le Voltaire* on 16 October 1879 and was published in volume the following year. The stage adaptation, with Busnach named as author, opened at the *Ambigu* on 29 January 1881 and ran for more than 100 performances. Busnach's letters to Zola establish that Zola collaborated not only on the scenario of the play, but on the dialogue as well, and that the collaboration was, therefore, still closer than in the case of *l'Assommoir*. Pertinent excerpts from Busnach's letters follow :

On 26 March 1880, he wrote to Zola :

Si vous voulez faire le plan des scènes du 8ᵉ tableau, il faut que vous veniez me voir (2).

In a letter dated only " 27 juin ", written undoubtedly in 1880, he says :

Je vous envoie les 3 premiers tableaux de *Nana*... Relisez ces trois tableaux, cherchez comment vous ferez les modifications et le mois prochain en un jour ou deux nous ferons le travail (3).

On 4 July 1880, he writes :

Je vous propose ceci : aller à Médan le lundi 12 avec 2 tableaux. Faire le scénario avec vous des 7ᵉ, 8ᵉ, et 9ᵉ et repartir le 13 à 5 heures du soir.
Puis vous porter les 6ᵉ, 7ᵉ, 8ᵉ et 9ᵉ à la fin du mois. Dès que vous aurez mis sur pied les 5 premiers, vous remettrez sur pied les 4 derniers du 1ᵉʳ au 15 août. Du 20 au 25 ou 26 août j'irai à Médan revoir le tout avec vous et nous l'enverrons à Chabrillat le 1ᵉʳ 7bre (4).

(1) *Collection théâtrale Auguste Rondel*, RF 49094, Bibliothèque de l'Arsenal.
(2) *Correspondance Emile Zola*, t. IV, feuillet 57.
(3) *Ibid.*, feuillets 600-601.
(4) *Ibid.*, feuillet 63.

It appears from this letter that Zola was to have the task of finishing the script immediately prior to its despatch to the manager of the *Gymnase*, Chabrillat. Then in a letter dated only " 16 juillet ", written presumably in 1880, Busnach writes :

> Mon cher Zola, Je viens de rebâcler le 4 en entier. J'en suis très content. Je n'ai pas fait la scène de Georges et de Nana. Vous la ferez mieux que moi (1).

And on 18 July 1880 :

> Je vous envoie par la poste le 4e tableau. Lisez-le. Et si vous en avez le temps, faites la scène de Georges et de Nana.
> Nous en causerons jeudi. Je vous porterai les 5 et 6e (2).

It is clear from these two letters that Busnach relied wholly upon Zola for the scene between Georges and Nana.

Other letters confirm the existence of a very close collaboration in which both Zola and Busnach wrote dialogue on specific scenes and revised each other's work. For example, on 17 August 1880, Busnach writes :

> Je veux vous voir dimanche. Si vous avez fini le 5e vous me le lirez. Ce me fera grand plaisir. Et le 31 j'irai entendre les 6 et 7. Vous savez que j'ai juré à Chabrillat qu'il aurait 7 tableaux achevés le 1er 7bre (3).

On 21 August 1880 :

> Je vous envoie par la poste aujourd'hui les 8e et 9e tableaux. Je pense recevoir demain pour emporter à Dieppe les 5 et 6 (4).

And on the following day :

> J'ai reçu votre lettre. Je compte recevoir les 5e et 6e aujourd'hui...
> ... Je viendrai le 4 8bre à Médan, puisque c'est la date que vous me fixez. Vous me donnerez les 3 derniers tableaux et nous causerons du tout. J'aurai peut-être à rester 1 jour chez vous à causer de l'ensemble. J'apporterai les 6 premiers avec moi pour s'il y avait certaines choses à modifier (5).

Nana was originally produced in nine *tableaux*. The number of stage sets was, after a time, reduced to five (6), and a few of

(1) *Ibid.*, feuillets 637-638.
(2) *Ibid.*, feuillet 65.
(3) *Ibid.*, feuillets 69-70.
(4) *Ibid.*, feuillets 71-72.
(5) *Ibid.*, feuillets 73-74.
(6) Concerning the reduction of the number of *tableaux* from nine to

the characters eliminated ; it is in this reduced form that the play
was published (1). The critics' reviews of the opening night, in
particular the account by " un Monsieur de l'orchestre " in the
Figaro (2), indicate that the original production was considerably
more spectacular than the later published version. The first
scene shows Nana in her modest lodgings the day after her
triumph on the stage as a stellar show-girl, and introduces the
new admirers whom success has brought her. The second
tableau, eliminated in the published version, continues the exposition in the drawing room of the Countess Muffat. Neither the
Countess nor her lover Fauchery appear in the later version of
the play. The third *tableau* in the original production was a
backstage scene at the theater where Nana was playing. This,
too, was dropped from the later version. There follows a picturesque scene in the country, which became Act II of the published
play. The curiosity of the audience was particularly aroused
by the mechanics of the setting, which included a brook with
real, running water, edible apples dropping from a card-board
tree, and the song of a nightingale. These were taken as tokens
of naturalism, but their mechanical nature was so apparent that
they tended to destroy, rather than to enhance, the illusion of
reality. The trills of the nightingale were particularly unfor-
tunate, as they inspired the audience with feelings of mirth
during the one tender scene of the play, between Nana and the
adolescent Georges (3) — undoubtedly the scene to which
Busnach refers in his letters of 16 and 18 July. It is typical
of the idyllic love scenes which occur in a number of Zola's
novels (for example, in *la Fortune des Rougon, la Faute de l'abbé
Mouret, Une page d'amour, la Joie de vivre, le Rêve, le Docteur
Pascal*), and it is unlikely that Busnach would have presumed
to change a word of it. Nana, touched by the infatuation of a
seventeen year old boy, dreams for a moment of escaping from
her sordid life in Paris. She remembers the days of her lost
innocence, and reflects wistfully upon her childhood, to which
she longs to return. Into this scene of essentially lyric feeling,
Zola sought to introduce elements of real life dependent upon
his stage set and properties. Georges climbs an apple tree and
picks an apple for Nana, which she ostentatiously eats. Then

five, see Busnach's letters to Zola dated 10 and 26 October 1881, in *Correspondance Emile Zola*, t. IV, feuillets 124-125 and 130-131.
(1) In William Busnach, *Trois pièces* (Paris, 1884).
(2) " La Soirée théâtrale ", *le Figaro*, 30 January 1881.
(3) *Nana*, Act II, scene V, in William Busnach, *Trois pièces*, pp. 251-253.

he shakes the tree, and they gather a harvest of the fruit.   It will be recalled that Zola had admired, in his dramatic criticism, the live cherry tree in Erckmann-Chatrian's *l'Ami Fritz*.   He felt that the reality of a play could be augmented by reality of scenery, but failed to appreciate that stage devices would divert the attention of the audience from the emotional overtones of the action.   The use of such devices for comic purposes is less objectionable.   The real water of the brook furnishes a farcical conclusion to this Act II, when the banker, Steiner, falls into it and is physically drenched.   " Ce bain froid ", writes *un Monsieur de l'orchestre*, " a causé dans la salle une joie indescriptible " (1).   The comic rôle of Steiner was played by the actor, Dailly, whose interpretation of Mes-Bottes had contributed to the success of *l'Assommoir*.

Act III of the published play shows Nana in her sumptuous mansion, at the apex of her career.   There follows, in the original production, a scene at the race-track, omitted in the later version.   Next comes the scene in Nana's boudoir (Act IV of the published play) in which are shown the suicide of Georges and the ruin of the comte Muffat.   The eighth *tableau* of the original production, omitted in the later version, takes us to Muffat's home.   He seeks to be reconciled with his wife, but she confesses to having taken a lover.   They agree upon a suicide pact and set fire to the house, which burns in view of the audience, while they perish in the flames.   The final scene (Act V), shows Nana sick and disfigured with smallpox, and ends with her death in a lonely hotel room.

In dramatizing the novel, the authors were careful to leave the shocking passages alone, and the play emerges as an inoffensive melodrama, depending largely for its appeal upon its spectacular stage settings.   Thus Auguste Vitu writes in *le Figaro* :

Reste un médiocre mélodrame... Mais la mise en scène, qui est très belle, très riche et très artistiquement comprise, ainsi que l'inestimable appui d'une interprétation excellente, assureront peut-être à *Nana* un succès de curiosité (2).

And Sarcey in *le Temps* :

Nana... ne soulève pas, comme on aurait pu le croire, de hautes questions d'esthétique. C'est un mélodrame vulgaire, découpé avec

(1) *Le Figaro*, 30 January 1881.
(2) *Ibid.*

adresse dans le roman par un habile metteur en scène qui possède et manie avec une dextérité rare toutes les ficelles du métier. Ce n'est pas encore cette fois que M. Émile Zola a livré sa grande bataille ; la fameuse question du naturalisme n'a rien à voir dans cette pièce, qui est de fabrication courante. Il ne s'agit ici que d'argent à gagner et non de principe littéraire à défendre...

Ces six premiers tableaux ne valent que par la mise en scène, qui est très soignée et très curieuse. Oh ! c'est là que le naturalisme triomphe ! Les sentiments sont faux, et faux les événements et faux le langage, mais les accessoires sont vrais...

Je crois à un grand succès d'argent. C'est tout ce que voulaient sans doute les auteurs... Mais, je le répète, l'art n'a rien à voir en cette affaire. Il n'y a de littéraire en tout cela que le nom d'Émile Zola. Peut-être s'amoindrit-il à ces tentatives (1).

Zola, in his preface to the play did not deny that he had worked on it, but he insisted upon his right to withhold his name if he chose. Having withheld his name, he felt that the play could not properly be considered as representing his ideas of dramatic art (2).

Nana has been revived a number of times. The *Collection Rondel* has newspaper clippings and theater programs of revivals which took place at various theaters in 1896, 1904, 1912, 1920, 1926 and 1927 (3).

« Pot-Bouille »

The novel was published in volume in 1882, and the stage adaptation, signed by Busnach, opened at the *Ambigu* on 13 December 1883. A letter from Busnach dated 19 April 1882 indicates that the adaptation was contemplated soon after publication of the novel :

Mon cher Zola, Vous avez raison ! Je viens de lire *Pot-Bouille* en volume.

Quelle différence avec le roman en feuilleton ! Il y a un drame terrible. 4 actes sur l'adultère. *Les Josserand*, si le titre *Pot-Bouille* était trop cru

(1) SARCEY, " Chronique théâtrale ", *le Temps*, 31 January 1881. For some other comments on the play, see LES ŒUVRES COMPLÈTES, *Nana* (the novel), " Notes et commentaires ", pp. 443-444.

(2) ZOLA's preface to *Nana* is published in *Trois pièces*, by William BUSNACH and in LES ŒUVRES COMPLÈTES, *Une campagne*, " Nana ". It was first published in ZOLA's column in *le Figaro*, 7 February 1881, about ten days after the play opened.

(3) *Collection théâtrale Auguste Rondel*, RF 49107, Bibliothèque de l'Arsenal.

pour le théâtre. Quand vous voudrez... Dans un, deux ou trois ans, je suis à vous (1).

However, work on the play was not begun until a year later. In April 1883, Busnach wrote to Zola :

Depuis 48 heures je vis avec *Pot-Bouille*... Je vous envoie ci-contre la liste des personnages qui me semblent nécessaires à l'action... action que je ne vois pas encore nettement. Envoyez-moi donc *tout de suite* la division à faire. Mais pour impossible, non (2).

From the following letter, dated 2 October 1883, it appears that Busnach wrote the first draft of the dialogue, leaving final revisions to Zola :

Mon cher Zola, Je pense vous envoyer le 2e et le 3e de *Pot-Bouille* cette semaine.

Si vous le voulez, j'irai, lundi 8, causer avec vous des trois premiers actes dès que vous les aurez lus avant que vous ne fassiez votre travail.

Cela sera peut-être utile.

Mon objectif — aidez-m'y — serait de livrer la pièce terminée le 2 9bre.

C'est possible, si vous le voulez ou si vous le pouvez (3).

A published letter dated 10 October 1883 from Zola to his friend Henry Céard confirms the collaboration which Zola was giving to this play. Zola asks Céard to postpone a prospective visit to Médan, explaining that all his time is taken up with work on a novel *(la Joie de vivre)* and the adaptation of *Pot-Bouille* :

Imaginez-vous que je veille chaque soir jusqu'à 2 heures du matin pour mettre sur pied les trois premiers actes de *Pot-Bouille*, que j'ai formellement promis de donner à l'Ambigu dans dix jours. J'ai un mal de chien, je vous expliquerai cela. Et, comme je ne veux pas lâcher mon roman le matin, de façon à m'en débarrasser et à rentrer à Paris, je travaille à la pièce le soir, ce qui me prend mes journées entières. Ce n'est d'ailleurs que le coup de collier d'un moment (4).

A letter from Busnach to Zola a week later shows that the former assumed the responsibility of making minor changes in the script, pending Zola's approval :

J'ai fait les coupures qui ne peuvent vous gêner en rien. J'ai fait copier.

(1) *Correspondance Emile Zola*, t. IV, feuillets 170-171.
(2) *Ibid.*, feuillets 184-185.
(3) *Ibid.*, feuillets 197-198.
(4) Les Œuvres complètes, *Correspondance (1872-1902)*, p. 599.

Je vais lire à Simon ce matin.
Je vous envoie les 2 actes ce matin.
Lisez-les.
J'apporterai samedi avec moi le manuscrit copié. Si dans ce que je vous envoie il y a des changements qui vous gênent nous remettrons. Mais je ne crois pas. Vous verrez (1).

But, as the following extract from a later letter shows, Busnach did not have authority to change even one line which Zola might consider important :

Il faut dans le 4ᵉ acte couper la phrase de Berthe... *ça ne vaut que 100 f.* C'est vilain décidément. Mais je ne le ferai pas sans votre autorisation (4).

Letters from Zola to Alexis and Hennique show that he attended rehearsals of the play (3). And a letter to Paul Bourget informs us that Zola had been " terriblement bousculé par la fin de mon roman et par la pièce de l'Ambigu " (4). According to the evidence of Busnach's letter to Zola, written after the disappointing opening, Zola's collaboration on *Pot-Bouille* was greater than that on either *l'Assommoir* or *Nana* :

Pot-Bouille est certainement le mieux fait de nos trois ouvrages. C'est celui auquel vous avez le plus travaillé ! C'est le plus hardi. Le plus littéraire. Le plus neuf. *Nana* avait fait 400 000 F de recettes. *L'Assommoir* 600 000 F... *Pot-Bouille* ne fera qu'à peine 100 000 F... Cur (5) ?

The reason for the comparative failure of *Pot-Bouille* is not difficult to find, although Zola himself failed to appreciate it at the time. Zola attributed the failure to critics, such as Sarcey, who found some portions of the play immoral (6), and

---

(1) *Correspondance Emile Zola*, t. IV, feuillets 202-203, letter dated 17 October 1883.
(2) *Ibid.*, feuillets 207-208, letter dated 9 November 1883.
(3) Letters dated 7 and 25 November 1883, in Les Œuvres complètes, *Correspondance (1872-1902)*, p. 600 and 603.
(4) *Ibid.*, p. 603. Letter dated 25 November 1883.
(5) *Correspondance Emile Zola*, t. IV, feuillets 411-412. This letter is dated only " Vendredi 4 janvier ", but must be presumed to have been written in 1884.
(6) See Zola's preface to *Pot-Bouille*, published in the volume *Trois pièces*, by William Busnach, and in Les Œuvres complètes, *Mélanges, Préfaces* et *Discours*, " Pot-Bouille au théâtre ", pp. 228-236. The preface first appeared, except section vi thereof, in *le Figaro*, 29 December 1883 (some two weeks after the play opened), under the title " De la moralité au théâtre à propos de Pot-Bouille ".

to the disinclination of bourgeois playgoers, who constituted
the financial mainstay of the theater, to see themselves satirized
on the stage (1). Neither of these reasons appears to be valid.
On the score of immorality, Sarcey criticized only the behavior
of two minor characters (Bachelard, Trublot) and occasional
vulgarities in the dialogue (" infection ", " garce "), and concluded
his review of the play in far more favorable terms than Zola's
preface would lead one to believe :

> En somme, *Pot-Bouille*, si l'auteur consent à en retirer quelques
> ordures inutiles, sera une pièce intéressante à voir. Les deux premiers
> actes sont gais, bien que le comique ait toujours chez Zola un arrière-
> goût d'amertume ; le troisième est plein de mouvement, et il s'y trouve
> deux scènes excellentes, faites de main de maître. Passons sur le qua-
> trième, que je n'aime pas, mais enfin qui n'est pas ennuyeux à entendre.
> Le cinquième est d'un pathétique rare. En voilà plus qu'il ne faut pour
> attirer le public à un drame. Ah ! si Zola voulait se résoudre à ne point
> faire faire de pas à l'art (2) !...

The explanation of the failure of *Pot-Bouille* to measure up
to the popularity of *l'Assommoir* and of *Nana* is probably to be
found in the absence of those spectacular qualities which brought
success to the first two adaptations. The five acts take place,
respectively, in a dining room, a parlor, a store, a bedroom, and
again the parlor of the second act. The settings, with the
possible exception of the store, are conventional, lacking the
novelty of many scenes of *l'Assommoir* and of *Nana*, and the
success of this adaptation, offering less visual appeal than its
predecessors, was wholly dependent upon the characters, story
and dialogue. Zola and Busnach have followed the novel
closely in depicting the tragi-comic efforts of the Josserands to
find husbands for their dowerless daughters, and the principal
characters are well projected on the stage. As Sarcey points
out, in the excerpt from his review quoted above, the play has
moments of gayety, mixed with an aftertaste of bitterness ; if
the play as a whole had risen to the level of its best moments,
the adaptation would have attained the highest level of comedy.
Unfortunately, Zola's satire appears labored on the stage.
Irrelevant characters (such as the obnoxious Trublot) and bits

(1) See Zola's letter to Antoine Guillemet, 30 December 1883, in Les
Œuvres complètes, *Correspondance (1872-1902)*, pp. 605-606.
(2) Sarcey, *Quarante ans de théâtre*, t. VII, pp. 21-38, reprinted from
le Temps, 17 December 1883. In *ibid.*, pp. 38-42, there is a second article
on *Pot-Bouille*, written several weeks later in reply to Zola's preface.

of dialogue (such as the servants' comments upon the faults of
their masters) are introduced for the sole purpose, which the
audience too clearly perceives, of disparaging bourgeois morality.
Moreover, the authors have frequently placed their own moral
comment in the mouths of the characters. Among examples
of this forced satire, the following are typical :

Act II, scene IX.

TRUBLOT

Mon cher, il ne faut pas regarder derrière les portes. La moralité
d'une maison est une question d'escalier.

Act IV, scene VI.

BERTHE *(reproaching her lover for neglecting her)*

Ce n'est pas la peine de prendre un amant, si l'on doit retrouver avec
lui les ennuis de son ménage. Ma parole ! il y aurait avantage à rester
honnête femme.

OCTAVE

Oh ! oui, c'est la première chose sensée que tu dises.

Pot-Bouille has been revived infrequently. The *Collection
Rondel* contains information of a revival at the *Menus plaisirs* in
Paris in 1890 and at the *Théâtre des Variétés* in Marseille in 1894 (1).

« Le Ventre de Paris »

After *Pot-Bouille*, the collaborators turned their attention
to the dramatization of *Germinal*, but censorship difficulties
caused postponement of the production until 1888. The fourth
Busnach-Zola adaptation to reach a stage was *le Ventre de Paris*
(based upon the third novel of the *Rougon-Macquart*, published
in volume in 1873), which opened at the *Théâtre de Paris* on
18 February 1887. Except for one *tableau* published in *le Figaro,
Supplément littéraire*, to which reference will be made below,
the play has not been published.

There is some question as to whether Zola signed the play
as co-author. No program of the production at the *Théâtre de
Paris* is available. Notices of the opening in *le Figaro* and *le*

(1) *Collection théâtrale Auguste Rondel*, RF 49113, Bibliothèque de l'Arsenal.

Temps name Busnach as sole author of the adaptation (1). On the other hand, Gaston Calmette, a reporter who interviewed Zola immediately prior to the opening states categorically that the play is signed by Zola and Busnach (2), and the play is listed with joint authorship by the editor of Zola's LES ŒUVRES COMPLÈTES (3). In any case, Zola's collaboration is proved not only by Busnach's correspondence and Calmette's interview, but also by the fact that the *tableau* of the play published in the literary supplement of the *Figaro* is signed " Émile Zola " (4).

Busnach's correspondence to Zola indicates that the play was thrown together hastily. His first specific mention of it occurs in a letter dated 4 October 1886, less than five months before the opening, in which he writes :

Cher Ami, Répondez vite pour *le Ventre*. La pièce sera reçue sur un simple plan que nous pouvons faire à Médan en une demi-journée... Il y a là une affaire et de l'argent (5).

It appears from his next letter, written two weeks later, that the assistance of a third collaborator — Zola's friend, Henry Céard — had originally been contemplated. The letter is interesting as showing the respective shares of the receipts which the collaborators were to be given : 4 % to Zola and 3 % each to Busnach and Céard. Busnach writes to ask that his share be increased to 4 % at the expense of Céard (6). There is nothing, either in theatrical notices or in correspondence between Zola and Céard, to indicate that Céard did in fact collaborate, and it is probable that he withdrew from the production. On 20 December 1886, Busnach writes that he has just read the play to the actors, and makes an urgent appeal for Zola's authority or assistance in making necessary changes in the script (7).

Busnach's correspondence in regard to this play is meager, but the fact of Zola's collaboration is amply confirmed by an

---

(1) " Courrier des théâtres ", *le Figaro*, 18 February 1887. " Spectacles et concerts ", *le Temps*, 19 February 1887 (*le Temps* appears on the newsstands on the day preceding the stated date).

(2) Interview of ZOLA signed " Gaston Calmette ", in *le Figaro, Supplément littéraire*, 19 February 1887.

(3) LES ŒUVRES COMPLÈTES, *le Ventre de Paris* (the novel)" Index bibliographique ", p. 368. The date of the opening is erroneously given here as 25 February 1887. The correct date is 18 February.

(4) *Le Figaro, Supplément littéraire*, 19 February 1887.

(5) *Correspondance Émile Zola*, t. IV, feuillets 267-268.

(6) *Ibid.*, feuillets 269-270.

(7) *Ibid.*, feuillets 271-273.

interview which he gave to Gaston Calmette and which was published in the literary supplement of the *Figaro* on 19 February 1887. The interview is important also in that it shows the subsistence of his previously-expressed ideas for a new theater, and his reasons for offering so trivial a play as *le Ventre de Paris*. According to the report of this interview, Zola stated :

Certes, j'ai de nombreuses raisons, d'excellentes raisons pour adjoindre un collaborateur à mes travaux de théâtre, et celui que je préfère, vous le connaissez, c'est mon ami Busnach, un homme de talent, expert en matière de théâtre, et dont l'éloge n'est plus à faire.

Oui, je voudrais être l'homme nouveau qui balayât les planches encanaillées, enjambant les ficelles des habiles, crevant les cadres imposés, élargissant la scène jusqu'à la mettre de plain-pied avec la salle, donnant un frisson de vie aux arbres peints des coulisses, amenant enfin, par la toile de fond, le grand air libre de la vie réelle ; Une révolution s'impose, et je voudrais être l'homme de la révolution. C'est mon rêve ! Malheureusement, ce rêve ne se réalisera pas de sitôt ! Car je suis engagé dans une série de romans qui me prennent tout mon temps et j'ai encore cinq ouvrages que je veux absolument terminer avant que l'âge et les fatigues m'aient achevé.

Le théâtre ne doit venir qu'après cette œuvre entamée depuis longtemps, j'attendrai.

Et puis, je l'avoue sans crainte, quand je me suis décidé à faire du théâtre, on n'en a pas voulu.

Zola then speaks of the refusal of theater managers to stage his own play, *Renée*, which he has been unsuccessfully trying to place in production during the past six years. He also complains of the failure of producers to revive his *Thérèse Raquin*, although this drama which failed in Paris in 1873 has been played throughout Europe. And he continues :

Donc, vous le voyez, impossibilité absolue de me faire jouer en France et, par conséquent, nécessité absolue d'une collaboration.

J'ajouterai cependant que j'ai encore en portefeuille une pièce signée de moi tout simplement [he is referring to *Renée*], et que je reste plein de projets.

Then he refers to his collaboration with Busnach and to his intentions in offering *le Ventre de Paris* :

En attendant, cette collaboration avec un homme de talent, un « carcassier » me permet certaines concessions momentanées dans le mélodrame. Busnach et moi, nous ne faisons pas en ce moment cette grande révolution populaire que je rêve, et pour laquelle il serait nécessaire d'appliquer toutes mes idées, rien que mes idées, à moi : non certes, nous faisons des pièces *mixtes*, dans lesquelles il y a des choses que je réprouve, des conventions que je condamne, mais dans lesquelles il y a aussi des tableaux que j'aime et que je signerais volontiers si j'étais seul. En prenant un collaborateur, je fais donc une étude du théâtre, une éducation de la foule ; en résumé, c'est une expérience, c'est un acheminement, c'est un progrès, enfin c'est l'opportunisme !

. . . .
Quant au *Ventre de Paris* représenté sur un théâtre, c'est la réalisation d'une vieille idée de moi. Le titre était splendide. Le milieu excellent : *les Halles* n'avaient jamais été jetées sur la scène dans toute leur vérité, une fois, cependant, avec *la Poissarde*, un drame joué par Mme Marie Laurent, il y a vingt-cinq ans. J'avoue que l'action manquait ; Busnach refusait cette collaboration que je lui demandais [compare this statement, however, with Busnach's letter of 4 October 1886] ; ce qui nous a décidé, c'est encore Mme Marie Laurent, dont je vous parlais tout à l'heure.

La grande artiste voulait un rôle à la Frederick Lemaître, rôle à la fois comique et dramatique, nous avons essayé de le faire et nous croyons l'avoir trouvé dans cette pièce « bon enfant ».

Oui, je tiens beaucoup à cette qualification de « bon enfant » pour cette œuvre sans prétention littéraire et sans parti pris ; ce n'est pas une bataille, c'est une halte, nous avons laissé au vestiaire toutes nos grandes réformes qui effraient, nos doctrines d'école ; vous ne trouverez là ni le delirium, qui effrayait dans *l'Assommoir*, ni la petite vérole qui rendait horrible la mort de Nana, ni l'attaque foudroyante de Josserand, dans *Pot-Bouille*. Le *Ventre de Paris* est tout différent ; et le public sera renvoyé content, je l'espère du moins ; il pourra applaudir, au dernier tableau, le mariage du héros et de l'héroïne. La vertu est récompensée, le crime est puni. Nous avons voulu amuser le peuple, le faire beaucoup rire et beaucoup pleurer (1).

The play is in five acts and seven *tableaux*, designated as follows : 1. La Belle Normande. — 2. Mourant de faim. — 3. Le Réveil des Halles. — 4. La Charcuterie Quenu-Gradelle. — 5. Au Café Charles. — 6. L'Enfant. — 7. Le Pavillon de la Marée (2). Whereas in their previous adaptation, *Pot-Bouille*, the collaborators had sought to win public approval without recourse to spectacular settings, it appears from the critic's reviews that in *le Ventre de Paris* they went to the other extreme and presented a series of spectacles with little drama. The theatrical news reporter of *le Temps* (not Sarcey) describes the play as " moins un drame qu'une succession de tableaux pittoresques, de décors à sensation ", and mentions particularly a

(1) *Le Figaro, Supplément littéraire*, 19 February 1887.
(2) According to " Courrier des théâtres ", in *le Figaro*, 18 February 1887.

night scene at the *porte Maillot*, a view of the *Halles* by dawn, showing the arrival of the market-gardeners with their vegetables, and the interior of a butcher shop, where the art of stuffing a *galantine* is exhibited to the audience (1). But the scenery, picturesque as it was, had little relation to the action of the play, which, as Sarcey observed, " pourrait se passer tout autre part qu'aux Halles " (2). The irrelevance of the scenery to the action was Sarcey's principal objection to the play, which he found far inferior to *l'Assommoir*, where the spectacular settings were logical and purposeful. Zola's theory of stage scenery required that it be more than picturesque — that it be comparable to the novelist's description, which he defined as " un état du milieu qui détermine et complète l'homme " (3). Although the settings of *le Ventre de Paris* afforded an opportunity of showing scenes of ordinary life — and to this extent they were in accord with Zola's naturalist theory of scenery (4) — Sarcey's accusation of irrelevancy drew a quick response from Zola. " Jamais ", he protests in the *Figaro* a few days later, " milieu n'a fait corps avec l'action comme dans *le Ventre de Paris* (5). " Here Zola's defense of his stage settings introduces a significant departure from his previously-expressed theories. He declares the settings to be relevant not in a literal sense, as might be expected from a proponent of naturalism — but in a symbolic one. Such appears to be a reasonable interpretation of the following passage of his reply to Sarcey :

Florent, ce proscrit, ce maigre, cet affamé, qui incarne la foi au serment, qui est la protestation de l'idéal, le rêve de la justice et de la fraternité, tombe au milieu de la bombance du second Empire, dans la satisfaction et le triomphe des appétits du ventre ; et où voulez-vous qu'il débarque pour que l'antithèse soit forte, aisée à dramatiser ? Il débarque dans les Halles, parmi ce peuple de boutiquiers satisfaits, il agonise de faim dans la formidable indigestion de Paris...

C'est comme le tableau dans la charcuterie Quenu-Gradelle, le plus original, celui que je préfère, n'est-il pas une évidente tentative de théâtre nouveau, avec son allure symphonique, l'opposition de ce maigre jetant sa plainte au milieu du débordement des gras ? Supprimez la

---

(1) " Spectacles et concerts ", *le Temps*, 20 February 1887.
(2) SARCEY, *Quarante ans de théâtre*, t. VII, p. 47, reprinted from *le Temps*, 28 February 1887.
(3) See *supra*, Chapter III.
(4) See *supra*, Chapter III.
(5) *Le Figaro*, 2 March 1887, reprinted in LES ŒUVRES COMPLÈTES, *le Ventre de Paris* (the novel), " le Ventre de Paris au théâtre ", p. 363.

charcuterie, vous supprimez le fond de prospérité ventrue sur lequel
doit se détacher la noire figure de Florent (1).

Louis Ganderax, reviewing this play in the *Revue des deux
mondes*, commented on the symbolism of the novel from which
the play was adapted, and quoted the first quatrain of Baudelaire's *Correspondances* as a source of Zola's method in this
respect (2). Certainly in many of the *Rougon-Macquart* novels,
Zola magnified descriptive passages for the purpose of giving
them allegoric connotations — for example, the tree of life in
la Faute de l'abbé Mouret, the bar-room of *l'Assommoir*, the description of Nana as " la mouche d'or ", the artist's view of Paris
in *l'Œuvre*, the locomotive of *la Bête humaine*, the burning of the
manuscripts in *le Docteur Pascal*, among others. Hitherto, in
his dramatic criticism, he had limited the scope of stage settings
to the surface reality of action and characters. In this answer
to Sarcey, he is extending the function of scenery to a symbolic
expression of the play's deeper meaning. He was to pursue this
path in the following decade and to turn frankly from naturalist
to lyric dramas requiring symbolic or connotative settings.

The only part of *le Ventre de Paris* to be published was the
sixth tableau, entitled " L'Enfant ", which appeared in the
literary supplement of the *Figaro* concurrently with the opening
of the play, and which was signed by Zola himself (3). This
scene was generally praised as the most powerful one of the play,
and as it was a further subject of dissension between Sarcey and
Zola, it is profitable to examine it. Although it appeared over
Zola's name, it is unlikely that Zola could, or would, have
contrived so perfect an example of ancient melodrama without
the guiding hand of Busnach. Indeed, both Sarcey and Zola
himself appear to consider the scene as pure Busnach, and it is
quite possible that Zola permitted publication over his signature
for publicity reasons, or even that the newspaper published
the fragment over his name without specific authorization.
What particularly nettled Zola was Sarcey's designation of the
scene as " le coup de l'enfant ", coupled with his evident satisfaction that failure of the play had been averted only by a scene
of classic melodrama, the outcome of which was known to every
experienced theatergoer (4).

(1) LES ŒUVRES COMPLÈTES, *le Ventre de Paris*, " le Ventre de Paris au
théâtre ", pp. 363-364.
(2) *Revue des deux mondes*, 15 March 1887, p. 456.
(3) *Le Figaro, Supplément littéraire*, 19 February 1887.
(4) SARCEY, *Quarante ans de théâtre*, t. VII, pp. 50-51.

The situation developed in the first five *tableaux* of the play
is this : Louise Méhudin has, unknown to her mother, borne a
child to Florent, a radical who was subsequently imprisoned
following the Coup d'Etat of 1852. The child has been secretly
brought up by Père François, a market-gardener and family
friend. Florent escapes from the Cayenne prison and returns
seven years later. Mme Méhudin, ignorant of the true situation
and resenting his attentions to her daughter, has reported him
to the police. In the sixth *tableau*, Louise learns of her mother's
action and reproaches her. The mother is about to strike Louise,
when the little boy, who has been listening from the adjoining
room, rushes onstage to protect his mother. The rest of the
tableau, with its perfect example of the " coup de l'enfant ",
follows :

JEAN

Méchante ! ne faites pas de mal à maman !

MADAME MÉHUDIN, *hors d'elle*

Cet enfant trouvé !... Ah ! il est le tien ! Ah ! voilà donc ce que je
sentais, ce que tu cachais ! une honte inavouable, un enfant de cet
homme ! Et, pendant sept années, tu t'es moquée de moi, tu m'as
trompée, le matin, le soir, à table, partout, à toute heure !... Tiens ! tu
n'es plus ma fille, tu es une gueuse, je te chasse ! Emporte-le ton fils de
forçat !

LOUISE, *serrant son fils entre ses bras*

Mon pauvre petit... Punissez-moi, mais lui n'a rien fait.

FRANÇOIS, *qui est entré par la porte du fond*

Qu'y a-t-il donc ?

MADAME MÉHUDIN, *l'apercevant*

C'est vous, ça me fait plaisir, entrez !... Il y a que ma fille prend des
amants ; et moi, parbleu, faute d'être prévenue, je viens d'en dénoncer
un à la police. Oui, j'ai dénoncé le père de son enfant ! Voilà... Car elle
a un enfant, ma fille, vous connaissez cette histoire ?... Le père François ?
Oh ! un bien brave homme, la crème des honnêtes gens ! Le père François, allons donc ! Du temps de sa femme, il cachait les filles mères, et
depuis qu'il est seul, il garde les bâtards en sevrage !

FRANÇOIS

Madame Méhudin, vous n'avez pas la tête à vous. Tout à l'heure
vous regretterez ce que vous dites... Si nous avons reçu Louise, c'est
qu'elle faisait pitié et qu'elle parlait de mourir... Et puis, regardez-le
donc, cet enfant, est-ce que vous auriez eu le cœur de le jeter à la rue ?

MADAME MÉHUDIN

Je ne veux pas le voir. C'est fini, le mensonge a tout tué... Entendez-vous, père François, vous m'avez trompée comme Louise, il n'y a plus de vieille amitié, il n'y a plus rien !... Reprenez l'enfant, prenez la mère avec, si ça vous amuse ! Allez-vous-en !

LOUISE

Je t'en prie... Nous ne pouvons nous quitter ainsi.

MADAME MÉHUDIN

Mais allez-vous-en donc tous les trois, puisque je vous chasse ! *(François, Louise, et Jean remontent lentement et s'arrêtent au fond, près de la porte.)*

FRANÇOIS, *bas à Jean*

Va, mon petit, va lui parler. *(Il le pousse vers elle.)*

JEAN, *s'avançant*

Dis, grand-mère, c'est pour toujours que tu nous renvoies ?

MADAME MÉHUDIN

Pourquoi ça ?... Que dit-il donc, ce gamin ?

JEAN, *s'avançant*

Parce que, si c'est pour toujours, veux-tu alors que je t'embrasse, dis, grand-mère ?

MADAME MÉHUDIN, *émue, se mettant à trembler*

Emmenez-le, emmenez-le... Vous voyez bien que je ne veux pas, que ça me fait du mal.

JEAN, *près d'elle*

Non, grand-mère, je ne te ferai pas du mal, va !... Pourquoi es-tu méchante ? Moi, je ne suis pas méchant, et si tu voulais un tout petit peu, je t'aimerais bien, grand-mère !

MADAME MÉHUDIN

Ah ! mon Dieu ! qu'est-ce que j'ai ? Voilà que ce chéri me retourne, avec ses petites mains !... Je suis donc méchante, moi qui n'écraserais pas une mouche ! je fais peur à ce chérubin, c'est en tremblant qu'il s'approche ! et si mignon !... *(Elle embrasse Jean avec passion.)* Mais alors, je suis une coquine, moi ! aller dénoncer ce pauvre diable ! Faut que ma tête déménage, des fois ! Est-ce affreux de se mettre dans de pareilles colères ! Ah ! mauvaise, mauvaise, mauvaise femme !

LOUISE, *à genoux près d'elle*

Non, mère, tu es bonne !

MADAME MÉHUDIN

Allons, puisque vous vous aimez, toi, ton Florent et le gamin, je vais être forcée de vous aimer aussi. *(Elle les embrasse.)*

FRANÇOIS

Bravo ! la belle Normande ! Je savais que ça finirait comme ça !

MADAME MÉHUDIN

Toi, grande bête, je t'aimais bien, mais je t'aime encore davantage !
(Elle lui saute au cou.) Ce n'est pas tout ça, puisque j'ai livré Florent,
il faut que je le sauve ! Du diable si je sais comment, mais je le sauverai !
(Elle sort en courant.)

Émile ZOLA.

In his reply to Sarcey, Zola defends this scene against the
charge of melodrama (it should be noted that neither Zola nor
Sarcey attribute authorship of the scene to Zola — a circumstance which confirms the view that Zola's name was appended
either in error or for purposes of publicity) (1) :

... le sixième tableau est du bel et bon drame, et nullement du
mélodrame. J'en puis parler d'autant plus à l'aise que ce tableau ne se
trouve pas dans le roman. Vous écrivez que « M. Émile Zola répudiera
sans doute cette scène, car c'est une scène qui sent à plein nez son vieux
mélodrame, une scène en quelque sorte classique ». Loin de la répudier,
je la trouve très belle, très grande, très humaine...

Quoi ! parce qu'il y aura là une mère qui pleure, un enfant qui
implore, une grand-mère qui pardonne, ce sera du mélodrame ? Où
avez-vous encore pris ça ? Ce qui fait du mélodrame une basse littérature,
c'est l'imbécillité de la forme et des moyens. Le sixième tableau du
Ventre de Paris n'est pas du mélodrame, parce que jamais moyens plus
simples, forme plus simple ne sont arrivés à une pareille intensité
d'émotion. Cela est très grand, et je le dis (2).

And he challenges Sarcey to justify the accusation that the
scene is " classic " melodrama by naming a play in which it has
occurred — a challenge which Sarcey took up in his next weekly
article by naming, not a play, but a novel which appeared
in 1870, *les Pauvres*, by Alexis Bouvier (3).

Zola's views in regard to *le Ventre de Paris* are clarified in a
letter written a week after the opening to the editor of the
Gaulois, from which it appears that he had no illusions as to the

(1) In a further article by SARCEY, " Réponse à M. Emile Zola ", in
le Temps, 7 March 1887 (reprinted in vol. 7 of *Quarante ans de théâtre*, pp. 53-68),
Sarcey's observation : " M. Emile Zola, qui a laissé imprimer cette longue scène
sous son nom dans le supplément du *Figaro*, reconnaît modestement qu'elle
est très belle et très grande ", indicates some uncertainty in his mind as to
whether or not the scene actually was of Zola's authorship.

(2) LES ŒUVRES COMPLÈTES, *le Ventre de Paris*, " le Ventre de Paris
au théâtre ", pp. 364-365.

(3) SARCEY, *ibid.*, p. 61.

literary merits of the play, but felt that it was a justifiable venture in popular drama. He again defends himself against the charges of misusing scenery and of resorting to melodramatic effects :

> Eh bien, mon sentiment est que j'ai dû me fort mal expliquer ou qu'on m'a fort mal lu, lors de mes longues polémiques d'autrefois, puisqu'on paraît croire que mon désir, au théâtre, est la vie banale et sans lien, le dédain de l'action, l'envahissement du décor.
>
> Je ne suis de l'école de rien, ni dans le roman, ni dans le drame ; je suis au contraire pour la passion, pour ce qui agit et ce qui émeut ; et, à mon sens, le décor n'est que le milieu qui complète et explique le personnage.
>
> Je dois ajouter que j'ai, au sujet du drame populaire, des idées plus accommodantes, ce que j'appellerai des idées opportunistes, qu'il serait beaucoup trop long d'exposer ici. Qu'on me permette seulement de sourire, lorsqu'on rappelle le bon vieux mélo, à propos du sixième tableau du *Ventre de Paris*.
>
> Moi aussi, j'ai traité de mélodrame les épopées lyriques de Victor Hugo. J'avais raison et j'avais tort. Ce ne sont pas les éternels sentiments du cœur, les éternelles joies et les éternelles douleurs humaines qu'il faut blâmer dans le mélodrame ; ce sont les imbécillités de la forme et des moyens (1).

A number of critics had expressed their surprise at Zola's failure to enter the theater with a play of his own. In this same letter, Zola explained that he did indeed have a play from his pen alone — *Renée* — which had been awaiting a sympathetic producer for six years, and he challenged his critics, notably Henri de Lapommeraye, to find a theater for it. Lapommeraye accepted the challenge and succeeded in placing *Renée* at the *Vaudeville*, where it opened less than two months after *le Ventre de Paris*, with the results examined *supra* in Chapter II (2). With all its faults, *Renée* illustrates the superiority in characterization of Zola's own work over that in which he collaborated with Busnach, and explains Zola's reluctance to be named as co-author with him. Zola's own dramas aspire to a higher level of character analysis and poetic feeling than those upon which he collaborated, but the latter were more popular. *Le Ventre de Paris*, the weakest as yet of Busnach's adaptations, had difficulty

---

(1) Letter to L.-P. LAFORÊT, rédacteur au *Gaulois*, 25 February 1887, in LES ŒUVRES COMPLÈTES, *Correspondance (1872-1902)*, pp. 671-672.
(2) For ZOLA's own account of LAPOMMERAYE's efforts in behalf of *Renée*, see LES ŒUVRES COMPLÈTES, *Théâtre II*, preface to *Renée*, p. v.

making its way (1), but managed to play through the season and remained until the first of June, whereas *Renée* closed after 38 performances.

« Germinal » and the censorship

The novel was published in volume early in 1885, the script of the stage adaptation completed in August of that year (2), and the play was in rehearsal in October (3) for an opening at the *Châtelet.* Then the censorship intervened and caused postponement of the production. The play did not open until 21 April 1888, with Busnach named as the sole author. It has not been published.

The fact of Zola's collaboration is established by Busnach's letters and by Zola's own correspondence with other friends. Before publication of the complete novel, Busnach had misgivings as to the stage possibilities of *Germinal*, based on a reading of the early installments :

Mon cher Zola, J'ai lu hier jusqu'au 20ᵉ feuilleton de *Germinal.* Des détails superbes, un roman étrange... mais jusqu'à présent pas l'ombre de l'ombre d'une pièce. J'espère que cela va venir. *(Letter dated 15 December 1884)* (4).

But the collaboration was under way by the following July, when Busnach wrote to Zola :

J'irai vous voir très probablement le lundi 20 juillet. J'espère trouver 2 tableaux de *Germinal* achevés (5).

and some ten days later :

Trouverai-je les 2 premiers tableaux de *Germinal* finis ? Qu'il me tarde de savoir que vous êtes à la besogne (6) !

---

(1) Busnach's letter of 3 March 1887 describes the receipts of the preceding night, 1 300 F, as execrable (*Correspondance Emile Zola*, t. IV, feuillets 274-275). See also feuillets 282-283.
(2) See Zola's letter to Céard of 23 August 1885, in Les Œuvres complètes, *Correspondance (1872-1902)*, p. 643.
(3) See Busnach's letters of 5 and 11 October concerning casting problems, *Correspondance Emile Zola*, t. IV, feuillets 232-235.
(4) *Ibid.*, feuillets 221-222.
(5) *Ibid.*, feuillets 225-226. Letter dated 3 July 1885.
(6) *Ibid.*, feuillets 227-228.

Further confirmation of Zola's collaboration may be found in letters to his friends, Céard and Coste.   He wrote to the former on 23 August 1885 :

J'avais laissé à Paris les sept premiers tableaux de *Germinal* et j'ai voulu abattre les cinq derniers. Ils sont finis d'hier. C'est un gros ennui de moins. Je serais très content, si j'avais la moindre illusion sur les gifles que mon travail va recevoir au Châtelet. Ainsi j'ai donné à la foule un rôle important qui sautera évidemment aux répétitions, car il faudrait que je perdisse moi-même deux mois pour tâcher de mettre sur pied cette tentative. On m'a déjà fait remarquer avec effroi que des figurants à vingt sous la soirée « ne pouvaient pas jouer ». C'est dommage, il y aurait là quelque chose de très saisissant à tenter (1).

And, evidently referring to the forthcoming rehearsals, he wrote to Coste a few days later :

Puis, *Germinal* au Châtelet va me tracasser, malgré mon désir de m'en occuper le moins possible (2).

Rumors of censorship precede the official ban.   On 15 October, the theatrical news section of *le Temps* carried a denial by Busnach that the play had been prohibited, but the rumors turned out to be well-founded.   The council of ministers, meeting on 27 October, upheld the recommendation of the censorship authorities (designated euphemistically, under the Republican government, as the " commission d'examen ") and formally banned the play for, as reported in *le Temps*, " la tendance socialiste de l'œuvre, et particulièrement le septième tableau, la grève des mineurs, où les gendarmes sont amenés à tirer sur les ouvriers en révolte " (3).

During the course of his career, Zola had had a number of encounters with the censorship, but none which had seriously interfered with his work.   Under the Empire, his first novel, *la Confession de Claude*, had attracted the attention of the public prosecutor in 1865, but was allowed to pass unchallenged (4). In his " *Causerie* " in *la Tribune*, 9 August 1868, he protested against the failure of the " commission du colportage " to authorize the sale of his *Thérèse Raquin* in book-stalls over which the commission had jurisdiction.   A few months later, the

---

(1) LES ŒUVRES COMPLÈTES, *Correspondance (1872-1902)*, p. 643.
(2) *Ibid.*, p. 646.   Letter dated 1 September 1885.
(3) *Le Temps*, " Spectacles et concerts ", 28 October 1885.
(4) See the report of the *procureur général*, in LES ŒUVRES COMPLÈTES, *la Confession de Claude*, " Notes et commentaires ", pp. 144-145.

threat of censorship proceedings caused publication of his
Madeleine Férat, which was then appearing serially in *l'Événement*
under the title *la Honte*, to be suspended, without, however,
impeding the later publication of the novel in volume. Zola
devoted a " Causerie " in *la Tribune* to a caustic comment upon
this abuse, as he considered it, of the censorship power (1).
Three years later, after the Empire had given way to the Republic, Zola expressed his astonishment that the new government
should seek to suppress *la Curée*, a satire of the old regime (2).
Later, in his preface to the stage adaptation of *Nana*, he ridiculed
the picayune changes demanded by the censorship, in particular
the elimination of the word " nuit " wherever it appeared in the
dialogue (3).

Zola's most comprehensive study of the relations between
government and literature is to be found in his article " La
République et la littérature " (4). Why, he enquires, should one
seek liberty in government, and dispute the right of literature to
enlarge the horizon ? Each time that political leaders in France
have attempted to bring new freedom to the nation, they have
begun by distrusting the writers and seeking tc enclose them
in ancient formulas. The Revolution of 1789 brought no
contemporaneous revolution in literature, and when the romantics of 1830 finally succeeded in breaking free of the classic mold,
it was against the opposition of political liberals. Similarly,
contemporary liberals are opposed to the new movement,
naturalism. Zola accuses political leaders of nourishing " la
haine de la littérature ", and explains this phenomenon by a
principle common to all governments :

Ces causes agissent sous tous les gouvernements. Dès que les républicains sont arrivés au pouvoir, ils n'ont pas échappé à cette loi commune
qui veut que tout homme devenu le maître, se mette à trembler devant
la pensée écrite. Quand on est dans l'opposition, on décrète avec enthousiasme la liberté de la presse, la mort de toute censure ; mais, si, le lendemain, une révolution assoit notre homme dans un fauteuil de ministre,
il commencera par doubler le nombre des censeurs et par vouloir régenter
jusqu'aux faits divers des journaux. Certes, je le sais, il n'est pas de

(1) *La Tribune*, 29 November 1868, reprinted in LES ŒUVRES COMPLÈTES,
Madeleine Férat, " Notes et commentaires ", pp. 298-302.
(2) See, in LES ŒUVRES COMPLÈTES, Zola's letter to Ulbach, 6 November 1871 (*Correspondance (1858-1871)*, pp. 382-386) and the volume *la Curée*,
" Notes et commentaires ", pp. 314-317.
(3) LES ŒUVRES COMPLÈTES, *Une campagne*, " Nana ", p. 120.
(4) In the volume *le Roman expérimental*. ZOLA studies the question
of censorship in section II of the article " la République et la littérature ".

ministre éphémère qui ne semble brûler du beau zèle de rouvrir sous son nom le siècle de Louis XIV ; c'est là un air de musique qu'il joue pour la fête de son avènement, les arts et les lettres au fond ne comptent pas, la politique le possède tout entier. Puis, s'il est tourmenté du besoin de faire parler de son règne, s'il s'occupe réellement des écrivains et des artistes, c'est une véritable calamité, il patauge dans des questions qu'il ne connaît pas, il stupéfie ses administrés par des actes extraordinaires, il distribue des récompenses et des rentes à de telles médiocrités, que la foule elle-même finit par hausser les épaules. Voilà où aboutit tout homme qui entre au pouvoir, quelles que soient d'ailleurs ses bonnes intentions du début : il encourage fatalement les médiocres, tandis qu'il laisse les forts à l'écart, lorsqu'il ne les persécute pas. Il y a peut-être là une raison d'État. Les gouvernements suspectent la littérature parce qu'elle est une force qui leur échappe (1).

" La liberté ", Zola affirms, " voilà tout ce qu'un gouvernement peut nous donner " (2).

The ban of *Germinal* brought an immediate response from Zola. For the medium of his reply, he chose the *Figaro*, whose editor, Francis Magnard, had supported the prohibition of the play on the grounds that :

Les coups de fusil de *Germinal* eussent été comme un commentaire vivant des discours enflammés, des déclamations des clubs, des provocations haineuses de la presse anarchiste. Il fallait les supprimer... (3).

Despite his opposition, Magnard consented graciously to print Zola's protest, which appeared in the *Figaro* on 29 October (4). Zola begins by pointing out that the work was banned not for immorality but for political reasons. " On nous a condamnés uniquement parce que la pièce est républicaine et socialiste (5). " The prohibition was made despite the willingness of the authors to comply with any suggested changes which the authorities might desire. The controversial seventh *tableau*

---

(1) *Ibid.*, p. 316.
(2) *Ibid.*, section III, p. 322. Hemmings lists three other articles where Zola develops the idea that the writer is superior to the politician, and suggests that Zola's scorn of this class of people may have been due, at least in part, to his own frustrations in the field of politics (F. W. J. HEMMINGS, *Emile Zola*, pp. 68-69).
(3) Front-page article signed " F. M. ", *le Figaro*, 27 October 1885.
(4) A preliminary letter from Zola to Magnard appeared in the *Figaro* 28 October 1885, and Zola's protest on the day following. The protest to the censorship of *Germinal* is reprinted in LES ŒUVRES COMPLÈTES, *Mélanges, Préfaces et Discours*, " Germinal " (1st article), pp. 133-139.
(5) *Ibid.*, p. 133.

had already been modified.   As Zola describes the amended
version of this scene :

Je tiens à dire, avant tout, que nos fameux gendarmes dont on a
mené tant de bruit traversaient simplement la scène, au milieu des
grévistes, et qu'ils ne tiraient que de la coulisse, où leurs fusils partaient
tout seuls, dans la bagarre. Nous avions mis toutes les atténuations
possibles, ôtant l'armée pour la remplacer par une troupe de police,
expliquant que ni les mineurs ni les gendarmes ne se détestaient, qu'ils
étaient de part et d'autre les victimes d'une fatalité. La pièce est une
œuvre de pitié, et non de révolution (1).

The case had been reviewed by successively higher levels of
the government.   Passing out of the hands of the *commission
d'examen* (the censorship board), the matter had gone to Edmond
Turquet, under-secretary of the Beaux-Arts, and finally to Goblet,
Minister of Public Instruction, who, according to Zola, had in all
probability misrepresented the nature of the play to the council
of ministers and caused the ban to be applied.   The article
closes with a petulant attack on Goblet's competence.

The prohibition of *Germinal* aroused considerable public
interest, particularly since an important miner's strike had
occurred at Anzin in the preceding year, on the scene of which
Zola had gathered some of the material for his novel (2).   Zola's
protest in the *Figaro* was reprinted by *le Cri du peuple* on
31 October 1885, and the latter journal published, on 1 November
an interview with Zola together with short passages from the
play to which the censorship had objected, and, on 6 November,
an article " Pas de trêve " by Duc-Quercy comparing the miner's
strike in *Germinal* with the recent violence at Anzin (3).

A few days later, Zola published in the *Figaro* a second article
on the censorship, in which he urged the substitution of " repressive " censorship for the present " preventive " system.   Under
the repressive system, advocated by Zola, plays would receive
the same treatment as novels and newspapers.   No prior examination or permit would be required, but if a work exhibited on
the stage involved a breach of the law, the responsible persons
would be brought to trial.   Zola finds the campaign for liberty
of the theater analogous to the successful campaigns for liberty
of the press and of assembly.   These liberties had been esta-

(1) *Ibid.*, p. 135.
(2) See LES ŒUVRES COMPLÈTES, *Germinal* (the novel), " Notes et
commentaires ", p. 547.
(3) *Le Cri du peuple*, 31 October, 1 and 6 November 1885.

blished without the aftermath of violence which their opponents had predicted. Similarly, Zola argues, liberty of the stage would not endanger the fabric of government, and, if the liberty were abused to the extent of breaking the law, the offenders would be prosecuted in the courts. He cites with approval the stand which Hugo, Dumas *père* and Gautier took against the censorship during a public hearing in 1840, and contrasts their championing of liberty with the servile attitude of his contemporaries, Dennery, Meilhac, Halévy, Sardou, Augier and Dumas *fils*, who, with the exception of Dumas, have expressed themselves in favor of the censorship, the position of Dumas being doubtful. " Le livre a été affranchi, le journal a été affranchi. Est-ce que le théâtre est condamné à l'éternel servage ? " he enquires, and predicts at the conclusion of his article that a republican government will scarcely dare to maintain the shame of stage censorship (1).

Dumas *fils*, whom Zola had mentioned in his article, clarified his position as to the censorship in the *Figaro* two days later (2). As between " preventive " and " repressive " censorhip, he would choose the former, preferring to deal with the government's agencies of culture than with the police. He believes complete liberty of the stage to be an impossible dream, and imagines the hypothetical case of his writing a play dealing with the return of Alsace-Lorraine and showing Bismarck and the German emperor on the stage. The German ambassador would demand the suppression of the play, or the return of his passport, and Dumas concludes :

> Et ma pièce sera supprimée et ce sera bien fait, parce qu'il y a bien d'autres personnages à mettre en scène que S. M. l'empereur d'Allemagne et S. A. le prince de Bismarck, et qu'il n'y a aucune raison pour que deux cent mille hommes soient égorgés parce qu'il m'aura plu de faire une pièce sur un sujet inopportun.

Even if Zola himself were Minister of Public Instruction :

> ... il sera forcé de reconnaître que cet idéal, « un gouvernement sans une censure théâtrale », est impossible et que, quand la censure n'est pas faite par les lois, comme chez nous, elle est faite, comme en Angleterre, par les mœurs, représentées par un chambellan qui décrète tout ce qu'il veut, et que quand elle n'est faite ni par les lois ni par les mœurs, elle est faite par les convenances et par le droit des gens, c'est-à-dire

---

(1) *Le Figaro*, 7 November 1885. Not reprinted in Les Œuvres complètes.
(2) *Ibid.*, 9 November 1885.

qu'à un certain moment elle peut être dans la main de l'étranger, qui est rude.

And Dumas suggests that if Zola had shown more patience and intelligence, he might have obtained authorization for his play without having to sacrifice anything essential. " Il en est de la censure comme des belles-mères ; on s'y fait. Seulement, il y faut beaucoup de patience et un peu d'esprit. " Zola's reply to Dumas was carried in the *Figaro* on the following day :

... laissez-moi simplement ajouter que la pièce n'est pas de moi, qu'elle a été tirée par M. Busnach de mon roman, et que c'est pour cela que je n'avais pas à apporter devant la censure les raideurs qu'on me suppose. Encore une fois, nous consentions à toutes les atténuations demandées. C'est l'esprit même de la pièce qu'on a frappé, le cri de pitié pour les misérables. Et quant à cet art qui dit tout sans rien sacrifier, je le connais : c'est l'art bâtard et juste milieu, c'est la formule moyenne et décente des Casimir Delavigne et des Paul Delaroche (1).

Some five years later, Dumas *fils* and Zola were invited to testify before a parliamentary commission investigating the matter of theatrical censorship. An account of their testimony follows :

MM. Dumas et Zola ont répondu verbalement à l'appel de la commission.

Alexandre Dumas ne croit pas que la censure préventive puisse être écartée. On a fait des tentatives pour la supprimer. Tous les gouvernements ont fini par la rétablir. Les auteurs dramatiques ne s'en plaignaient pas.

Seulement, l'autorisation étant donnée, il demande que la garantie subsiste. La censure a laissé derrière elle des souvenirs vexatoires et ridicules ; mais les relations se sont bien améliorées et les auteurs ne se plaignent plus généralement des censeurs. Ils se plaignent uniquement que leur décision soit définitive.

Émile Zola rappelle qu'il a demandé à Gambetta « la liberté des lettres » et dit s'en référer absolument aux déclarations récentes de M. Vacquerie, la demandant aussi, entière, absolue.

« Je ne puis donc, ajoute-t-il, que me prononcer très catégoriquement pour l'abolition de la censure. Je ne cacherai pas, d'ailleurs, la stupéfaction que me cause, après vingt années de république, le maintien d'une telle chinoiserie. Je suis un républicain de l'avant-veill e. Sous l'Empire, j'ai écrit dans tous les journaux de l'opposition ; j'étais le collaborateur de tous les personnages politiques aujourd'hui au pouvoir.

(1) *Ibid.*, 10 November 1885.

Or, un des articles qui se trouvait en tête de notre programme était précisément l'abolition de la censure. Cependant on ne l'a pas supprimée et les programmes élaborés par ceux qui pourraient aujourd'hui les exécuter sont restés lettre morte (1). »

Sarcey, as well as Dumas, raised his voice in favor of the institution of the censorship, but deplored the manner of its use against *Germinal*. He criticized the failure of the *commission d'examen* to decide the matter of their own initiative, as was their duty under the law, and accused them of following the practices of the Empire in referring the question up to the under-secretary, Turquet, who in turn referred it up to the minister, Goblet. " Il en devrait être autrement en république ", he observes, " où chaque fonctionnaire devrait exercer, sous sa responsabilité propre, les attributions dont il a été jugé digne " (2).

For a month or so after the interdiction, the authors maintained hopes that the ban might be lifted. Writing to Zola on 26 November, Busnach mentions that he has met the first president of the Court of Appeals, who has expressed an interest in *Germinal*, and asks Zola to send him the seventh *tableau* " avec gendarmes " so that he may show it to the influential jurist. And on 2 December, he writes that the judge has high compliments for the play, and requests the *tableau* " sans gendarmes " (3). Nothing came of these negotiations, however, and the matter was left in abeyance for nearly two years (4). On 1 November 1887, Busnach wrote to Zola requesting a manuscript of the play, and suggesting :

Si vous voulez prendre une journée et venir déjeuner avec moi, nous travaillerons toute la journée de dimanche. Nous ferons les remodifica-

---

(1) *Ibid.*, 12 March 1891.
(2) SARCEY, " Chronique, à propos de la censure ", in *la Revue des journaux et des livres*, 2e Année, n° 55, 8-14 novembre 1885, pp. 42-44. Reprinted from *la France*.
(3) *Correspondance Emile Zola*, t. IV, feuillets 247-248 and 253-254.
(4) John C. LAPP has recently brought to light and published (in *French Studies*, vol. 15, 1961, pp. 47-48) a previously unpublished letter of Zola believed, from a notation in pencil, to be addressed to a Mr. Johnson, London correspondent of the *Figaro*, in reply to an inquiry from Johnson concerning the availability of *Germinal* for the London stage. The letter is dated 25 February 1886, some four months after the censorship ban in Paris, and is particularly interesting as a further revelation of Zola's feelings concerning the social value of his play and of his belief that it was suppressed in France for political reasons. Zola is receptive to the idea of a London production, but as a preliminary question, he asks whether the theater in London is free from a political and social point of view. No production of *Germinal* took place in London and Lapp concludes : " One may assume he (Zola's correspondent) soon discovered that the London theatre in 1886 was far from " libre au point de vue politique ou socialiste "... "

tions que Deforges me demandera. Nous causerons de la partie comique et des moyens de satisfaire Floury [*director of the Châtelet*].

Vous emporterez le manuscrit à Médan et ferez les coupures que vous verrez encore.

Ensuite je m'occuperai à mon retour de Bruxelles — d'où je repartirai lundi 7 — de la partie comique convenue et je vous la soumettrai (1).

Zola not only collaborated further on the script, but took an active part in the rehearsals.   On 1 April 1888, he wrote to Coste :

Ici, je suis dans une bousculade terrible, *Germinal* passera dans trois semaines et les répétitions sont très laborieuses (2).

However, on the day of the opening, he wrote to de Goncourt :

Mon cher Ami, le Châtelet joue ce soir *Germinal* contre mon absolue volonté. Je n'irai pas au théâtre, j'ai refusé mon service de première, et je regrette de ne pouvoir vous envoyer le fauteuil que je vous destinais (3).

Many commentators have misinterpreted this letter of Zola and attributed his absence from the opening night of *Germinal* to his dissatisfaction with the censorship (4).

It is doubtful, however, that the censorship at this time demanded any essential changes in the play, and it seems clear that Zola acquiesced in such modifications as the censorship did require.   The true reason for Zola's absence is given in the account of the opening by " un monsieur de l'orchestre " in the *Figaro* (5), from which it appears that by the time of the " répétition générale " (the formal dress rehearsal which is customarily open to invited members of the public), several important stage effects, such as the sabotage explosion of the mine shaft, the inundation of the pits by underground waters, and the escape of the trapped miners, remained unrehearsed.   Zola, believing the play not yet ready for the public, secured the promise of the management to exclude it from the dress rehearsal and, if necessary, to postpone the opening.   The management failed to keep its promise and admitted an audience to the dress rehearsal. Zola absented himself from the opening on the following night, not at all in protest against the censorship, but because he felt that the opening was premature.

(1) *Ibid.*, feuillets 287-288.
(2) Les Œuvres complètes, *Correspondance (1872-1902)*, p. 696.
(3) *Ibid.*, p. 696.
(4) For example, see *ibid.*, p. 696, footnote.
(5) *Le Figaro*, 22 April 1888, " la Soirée théâtrale ", by " Un monsieur de l'orchestre ".

Although the play has not been published, it appears from the accounts of the critics and from an article by Zola himself that it follows closely the main action of the book (1). Divided into twelve *tableaux*, it exhibited spectacular stage effects, particularly in scenes showing the interior of the mine. In deference to the censorship, the police do not appear visually in the controversial seventh tableau — " le seul épisode au sujet duquel la censure se soit montrée inflexible " (2) — but their shots are heard in the wings, and their victims, Maheu and la Mouquette, fall in view of the audience. The play ends with the moving line : " Pitié pour les déshérités. "

The critics found the stage adaptation of *Germinal* far inferior to the novel, and the production closed after 17 performances (3). Sarcey, who admired the novel, complains that he has seldom been so bored and describes the play as " crevante ", " assommante ", and lacking in artistry (4). Auguste Vitu speaks of " l'ennui mortel " into which the suffering audience was plunged for five hours, and, further, condemns the authors' intentions in writing the play :

En somme, *Germinal* est le plus mince des mélodrames qu'on ait construit pour peindre les souffrances de la classe ouvrière : il n'est remarquable que par ses mauvaises intentions. Pas une scène qui ne fasse appel aux passions aveugles de ceux qui souffrent contre ceux qui possèdent, et qui n'envenime le mal qu'il s'agirait de guérir (5).

And Henry Fouquier, who was stirred by the play to write a front-page article in the *Figaro* in behalf of victims of social inequities, found, nevertheless, that the theater was necessarily incapable of doing justice to a novel such as *Germinal* :

Admirateur passionné du roman de M. Zola, j'étais navré de voir ce qu'une funeste manie d'adaptation en avait fait. La leçon, au moins,

---

(1) At least two modern scholars — Guy Robert and Martin Kanes — have been more fortunate than I in locating the censor's manuscript of the play in the Archives Nationales, série F¹⁸, nᵒ 981 (ROBERT, *Emile Zola*, pp. 49, 187 ; KANES, " Zola and Busnach : The Temptation of the Stage ", *PMLA*, LXVII, No. 1, March 1962, p. 109). Kanes points out in his article (p. 111) some interesting differences in the novel and stage versions of *Germinal*.
(2) " La Soirée théâtrale ", *Le Figaro*, 22 April 1888.
(3) " Les castrations imposées par la censure avaient atteint leur but : la pièce eut dix-sept représentations. " — LES ŒUVRES COMPLÈTES, *Germinal* (the novel), " Germinal au théâtre ", p. 552. In our view, however, the censorship did not impose any essential restrictions on the play, and cannot justly be held accountable for its failure.
(4) SARCEY, " Chronique théâtrale ", *le Temps*, 23 April 1888.
(5) Auguste VITU, " Premières représentations ", *le Figaro*, 22 April 1888.

sera-t-elle comprise ? Comprendra-t-on que le livre et le théâtre sont
choses différentes, que ce qui est légitime là devient criminel ici ? Le
livre prépare, encadre, explique tout ; le théâtre, dans sa brutalité
nécessaire, ne peut que résumer, sans atténuation ni réserve, les choses
grossies à son optique (1).

Among the hostile criticisms, that of Albert Wolff moved
Zola to a reply. Zola's part in the production of *Germinal*, says
Wolff, is too great to permit him any longer to hide behind
Busnach :

Cette fois, le maître ne s'en cachait pas ; il suivait les répétitions,
il se chamaillait avec les artistes, il inspirait les décorateurs ; finalement,
il rentra sous sa tente, blessé au vif parce qu'un détail n'était pas au
point. [*An allusion to Zola's abstention from the opening night.*] C'est
donc bien Zola qui est l'auteur de cette lourde machine, et nous ne lu
permettrons pas cette fois de se soustraire à la responsabilité en poussant
en avant le vaudevilliste Busnach, un aimable gros homme qui, philo-
sophiquement, reçoit les gifles quand cela ne marche pas et qui s'éclipse
derrière la gloire de Zola quand cela réussit (2).

Wolff points out that *Germinal* makes no original contribution to humanitarian questions, and that Zola " se montre ici
enfonceur de portes ouvertes ". As to the artistic qualities of
the play, they reside only in the scenery :

M. Zola n'a donc rien inventé au théâtre : son talent considérable
se fait sur les planches le valet des peintres de décors... sa littérature,
si brillante dans le roman, descend sur la scène au rôle d'une bonne à
tout faire chez le peintre.

Wolff then points out the incongruity between Zola's severity
to his fellow-dramatists and the poverty of his own theatrical
offerings :

Zola a été sans pitié pour tous les écrivains dramatiques de ce siècle.
Comme tous ceux qui crient plus fort que les autres, il a eu gain de cause
dans un petit clan de fanatiques. Jamais son naturalisme au théâtre
n'a eu la haute portée philosophique du deuxième acte du *Mariage
d'Olympe* d'Émile Augier ; pas un tableau de son théâtre déjà volumineux
ne va à la cheville de *la Visite de noces*, la pièce la plus naturaliste
d'Alexandre Dumas fils. Sardou, dans *Rabagas*, a été autrement naturaliste que Zola ; le sous-préfet dans *Décoré*, de Meilhac, est une figure
naturaliste autrement trouvée que Mes-Bottes, un cousin de *Bruno le
Fileur* qui a égayé nos aînés. Aucun des auteurs dramatiques de ce siècle

(1) Henry Fouquier, " la Pitié ", in *le Figaro*, 23 April 1888.
(2) Albert Wolff, " Courrier de Paris ", *le Figaro*, 24 April 1888.

n'a trouvé grâce devant M. Zola ; il a déchiré à belles dents tous ceux qui nous ont amusés ou émus ; il a consacré un volume, plein de talent je l'avoue, à mettre en morceaux toute la littérature dramatique depuis un demi-siècle. Et tout cela aboutit à un pitoyable mélodrame.

And Wolff challenges Zola to justify his theories with a play of his own, which, should other theaters refuse their stages, may surely find a welcome at Antoine's *Théâtre-Libre*.

Zola's reply in the *Figaro* of the following day has been reprinted in the volume *Mélanges, Préfaces et Discours* of LES ŒUVRES COMPLÈTES (the second article on *Germinal*, pp. 143-147). Zola was angered by Wolff's accusation that he concealed himself behind Busnach, and in this reply, declared himself the sole author of the play :

D'abord, je déclare que le drame est entièrement de moi, que Busnach n'en a pas écrit une seule ligne. Entendons-nous : Busnach et moi avons discuté et arrêté le plan ensemble ; mais, pour cette fois, pour ce sujet spécial, j'ai tenu à tout écrire...

De mes cinq œuvres, adaptées par Busnach, celle-ci est celle qui a été la plus respectée. Malgré ce qu'on en a dit, pas une des situations, pas un des personnages employés n'a été changé dans son ensemble.

J'ai écrit la pièce, je l'ai prise dans le roman, et, si on la trouve mal écrite, c'est moi le coupable, c'est le roman qui a tort.

However, the press announcements of the play, as in the case of the other adaptations, listed Busnach as sole author (1), and Busnach's correspondence indicates that he had worked on the dialogue as well as Zola. It is probable that Zola exaggerated his part in the writing of the play for the sake of rebutting the presumption that he permitted Busnach to be the " whipping-boy " for hostile criticism. Zola is probably justified in stating that the stage adaptation of *Germinal* followed the original novel more closely than in the case of the other adaptations (although *Pot-Bouille*, too, had been followed closely), but his conclusion that the critics had erred in praising the novel and condemning the play is scarcely tenable.

Germinal has been revived occasionally. The *Collection Rondel* (2) contains programs of three revivals, for which the number of *tableaux* had been reduced from twelve to ten : 1) at the *Bouffes du Nord*, undated, listing both Zola and Busnach as authors ; 2) at the *Folies-Dramatiques*, in the fall of 1927, listing

(1) " Courrier des théâtres ", *le Figaro*, 21 April 1888.
(2) *Collection théâtrale Auguste Rondel*, RF 49154, Bibliothèque de l'Arsenal.

Busnach as sole author — an important revival on the occasion
of the 25th anniversary of Zola's death ; 3) at the *Bouffes du
Nord*, 3 June to 9 June 1932, listing Busnach as author.
Busnach made some changes in the play after its first production at the *Châtelet*, and it is probably his later version, in ten
tableaux, which has been revived. In an interview dated
3 November 1900, Busnach, after giving some details of the
productions of *l'Assommoir*, *Nana*, *Pot-Bouille*, *le Ventre de
Paris*, and *Germinal*, is reported to have said :

> A toutes ces pièces, Émile Zola a collaboré avec moi.
> Nous avons aussi tiré un drame de *la Bête humaine* qui n'a encore
> jamais été présenté.
> Seul *Germinal* fut un insuccès. C'était un ouvrage trop sombre.
> Je l'ai modifié un peu et depuis il a été joué avec succès dans des théâtres
> de quartier (1).

« La Bête humaine »

Busnach's correspondence indicates that he and Zola contemplated adaptation of *la Bête humaine* for the stage soon after
publication of the novel in 1890. That the resultant script was
unsatisfactory to Zola is evident from a letter of Busnach four
years later :

> Voulant savoir si votre si noire opinion sur *la Bête humaine* était
> fondée, j'ai porté la pièce à Floury. Il l'a lue. Hier il m'a dit textuelle-
> ment : « Cette pièce est impossible au Châtelet. Mais je la trouve superbe
> et intéressante au possible. Je vous donne ma parole d'honneur que si
> j'étais directeur de la Porte-Martin ou de l'Ambigu je la jouerais immé-
> diatement. »
> Donc... le moment venu, s'il vient, nous en causerons et je compte
> sur quinze jours de vous pour la mise au point de la pièce (2).

Busnach's subsequent letters reveal that his health and
finances were declining seriously, but that he still held hopes,
which turned out to be illusory, of sharing another theatrical
enterprise with Zola. He continued to write Zola about *la Bête*

---

(1) *Ibid.*, RF 49094 contains a newspaper clipping of this interview of
Busnach, signed " Frontin " and dated 3 November 1900. The newspaper is
not identified.
(2) *Correspondance Emile Zola*, t. IV, feuillets 356-357. letter dated 8 september 1894.

humaine for another six years, suggesting in January 1900 that Zola could, if he would, persuade Antoine to produce the play (1). Zola, however, had lost interest in his old collaborator. He gave the stage rights to *Une page d'amour, Au Bonheur des Dames* and *la Terre* to other adapters. The naturalist drama, moreover, was no longer his primary interest in the theater. In the last decade of his life, he became increasingly absorbed in the operatic form and in the creation of librettos for the musical talent of Alfred Bruneau. *La Bête humaine* remained unproduced (2).

Adaptations without Zola's active collaboration

In addition to the plays with Busnach, a number of other stage adaptations were made from Zola's novels and stories during his lifetime, as to which there is no evidence that Zola himself collaborated in any real sense. Since Zola did not participate substantially in the writing, it will be sufficient to make only brief comments on them.

Jacques Damour, a play in one act adapted by Léon Hennique from Zola's short story bearing the same title (3), was produced 30 March 1887 as one of the four plays chosen by Antoine for the inauguration of his *Théâtre-Libre*. The success of this short play, based on an Enoch Arden situation, was responsible for the favorable reception accorded to Antoine's first production (4). On 22 September of the same year, the play was produced at the *Odéon*. Zola's correspondence offers little evidence of his participation in the stage adaptation. A letter from Hennique to Zola, dated only " Vendredi soir ", alludes to the possibility of a production at the *Vaudeville* (5), while a letter from Zola to

(1) *Ibid.*, feuillets 378-379, letter dated 30 January 1900. For other letters of Busnach relating to *la Bête humaine*, see *ibid.*, t. IV, feuillets 318-324, 365-367, 371-372, 377, 478-479, 485-486, 495-496, 518, 542, 550-551, 569-570, 611-612, 622-623, 630-631, 643-644, 665-666 ; t. V, feuillet 1.

(2) A list of the tableaux for *la Bête humaine* which Busnach submitted to Zola in 1890, together with a list of the tableaux for Zola's own dossier of the novel, and a comparison of the lists, is to be found in the article by KANES in *PLMA*, LXVII, No. 1 (March 1962) at p. 114.

(3) Léon HENNIQUE, *Jacques Damour* (Paris, 1887). ZOLA's story upon which it is based is in LES ŒUVRES COMPLÈTES, *Contes et nouvelles*, II, pp. 405-440.

(4) See " Notes et commentaires ", in LES ŒUVRES COMPLÈTES, *Contes et nouvelles*, II, pp. 664-665.

(5) *Correspondance Emile Zola*, t. XI, feuillets 176-177.

Céard speaks of " la petite retouche " which he has made in the play for its production at the Odéon (1).

Tout pour l'honneur, a play in one act adapted by Henry Céard from Zola's short story le Capitaine Burle, was produced by Antoine's Théâtre-Libre at the Théâtre-Montparnasse on 23 December 1887 (2). Two letters from Céard show that he sought Zola's advice in making the adaptation, but do not establish the existence of a real collaboration. In the first of these, on 3 December 1886, he wrote Zola :

J'ai achevé le Capitaine Burle que je vous lirai sitôt qu'un moment de tranquillité me permettra d'aller à Médan. Les uniformes français contemporains rendent la pièce à peu près inadmissible. Ils feront hurler les patriotes sans rien ajouter d'essentiel au drame. Qu'est-ce que vous pensez de l'idée suivante : si on mettait l'action sous la Restauration. Les costumes de ce temps-là sont quasi préhistoriques et aussi impersonnels que les uniformes des Pharaons. Ils n'éveilleraient je crois aucune susceptibilité et il suffirait de huit jours d'études pour donner à la pièce quelque chose de la couleur intellectuelle et morale du temps... les choses ainsi orchestrées effraieraient peut-être moins les directeurs (3).

On 1 October 1887, he suggests that Zola look over the finished manuscript of the play :

Pour le Théâtre-Libre, j'ai retouché Tout pour l'honneur : l'acte est maintenant aussi au point que je puis le mettre. Toutefois à votre retour à Paris, il sera bon que vous y jetiez un coup d'œil (4).

Une page d'amour, adapted from Zola's novel by Charles Samson, was produced at the Odéon on 11 March 1893 (5). In a letter to de Goncourt prior to the opening, Zola disclaims having any knowledge of the play (6). There is no letter from Charles Samson among the Zola manuscripts at the Bibliothèque Nationale.

Au Bonheur des Dames, a play in six tableaux, adapted from Zola's novel by Charles Hugot and Raoul de Saint-Arroman, was

(1) Letter dated 15 August 1887, in LES ŒUVRES COMPLÈTES, Correspondance (1872-1902), p. 680.
(2) Henry CÉARD, Tout pour l'honneur (Paris, 1890). Zola's short story, le Capitaine Burle, upon which it is based is to be found in LES ŒUVRES COMPLÈTES, Contes et nouvelles, II, pp. 369-401. See ibid., " Notes et commentaires ", p. 664, for a short note concerning the stage adaptation.
(3) Correspondance Emile Zola, t. VII, feuillets 296-297.
(4) Ibid., feuillet 314.
(5) This play does not appear to have been published. For a brief note concerning the stage adaptation, see LES ŒUVRES COMPLÈTES, Une page d'amour," Notes et commentaires ", p. 356.
(6) LES ŒUVRES COMPLÈTES, Correspondance (1872-1902), pp. 756-757.

produced at the *Gymnase* on 4 June 1896 (1). A letter from Saint-Arroman dated 27 February 1895 reveals the essential terms of his agreement with Zola :

Mon cher Maître, encore merci et mille fois merci. Il est bien entendu que vous ne serez pas de la pièce, que je ne la ferai pas jouer sur un théâtre, sans que vous ayez accepté ce théâtre, et que vous rentrerez dans la propriété du sujet si, dans trois ans, la pièce tirée de *Au Bonheur des Dames* n'était pas jouée (2).

There is nothing to show that Zola assisted in the adaptation. Saint-Arroman's next letter, in November, advises him that the play has been completed and requests a short interview with him before submitting it to a manager (3). The play failed, and Saint-Arroman left explanation of the disaster to his colleague, Hugot, who wrote to Zola, attributing the failure to the producer's interference with the script (4). Zola apparently responded with great sympathy, and Hugot's next letter to him reveals the eminent writer's kindness to struggling young authors :

Mon cher Maître, quelle belle et bonne lettre vous m'avez écrite ! A la suite de la première représentation du *Bonheur des Dames* j'avais un peu perdu les étriers, votre indulgence m'a remis en selle et me voilà au travail de nouveau, grâce à vous. Il n'y a que les hommes de grand talent, comme vous, mon cher Maître, pour être si doux aux petits et pour trouver les mots qui consolent et qui encouragent (5).

Pour une nuit d'amour!, a play in one act adapted by Jane de La Vaudère from Zola's short story of the same title (without the exclamation mark), was produced, according to the title-page of the published play, at the *Grand-Guignol* on 16 May 1898 (6). No reference to this play has been found in Zola's correspondence.

La Terre, a play in five acts and ten *tableaux* adapted from Zola's novel by Raoul de Saint-Arroman and Charles Hugot,

---

(1) The adaptation of *Au Bonheur des Dames* does not appear to have been published. A program giving a summary of the six *tableaux* and biographical sketch of the authors may be found in the *Collection théâtrale Auguste Rondel*, RF 49132, Bibliothèque de l'Arsenal.
(2) *Correspondance Emile Zola*, t. XIV, feuillet 350.
(3) *Ibid.*, feuillet 351. Letter dated 4 November 1895.
(4) *Ibid.*, t. XI, feuillet 312, dated 6 June 1896.
(5) *Ibid.*, feuillets 313-314, dated 17 June 1896.
(6) Jane de LA VAUDÈRE, *Pour une nuit d'amour!* (Paris, 1898). ZOLA's story upon which it is based is to be found in LES ŒUVRES COMPLÈTES, *Contes et nouvelles*, I, pp. 253-287. In " Notes et commentaires ", vol. II, p. 659, it is stated that an American film has been made from this story.

was produced 21 January 1902 at the *Théâtre Antoine*, with Antoine in the rôle of the Père Fouan (1). The correspondence indicates that Zola furnished a certain amount of help to the adaptors, although it is probable that his assistance was limited to suggestions. On 12 March 1898, Saint-Arroman wrote him :

> Nous avons terminé hier le second acte de *la Terre*. Arrivés à ce point nous serions heureux de prendre vos avis... (2).

In November of that year, he wrote to Zola — then exiled in England as a result of the Dreyfus Case — that as a matter of courtesy he had shown the play to Coquelin, who had refused it, and that it had been accepted by Antoine (3). In June of the following year, he wrote :

> ... si vous avez le temps de lire notre manuscrit, ne pensez-vous pas qu'il serait utile d'en parler (4) ?

And in November :

> Puisque nous devons parler de *la Terre*, je convoque Hugot pour la seconde partie de notre entretien (5).

A letter written to Zola in May 1900 complains of Antoine's apparent reluctance to produce the play (6), and it seems probable from the subsequent correspondence that Zola intervened with some assistance of his own in order to assure the production. On 5 January 1901, Saint-Arroman wrote :

> Je viens de voir Antoine. Il est entendu que, *mercredi prochain*, à 2 heures précises, nous frapperons à votre porte. Vous mettriez le comble à votre bonté en lisant d'ici là les deux derniers actes de *la Terre*. De notre côté, nous vous apporterions et vous soumettrions quelques idées nouvelles (7).

And in August of that year :

> Bien cher Maître, Les modifications apportées à *la Terre* seront terminées dans le courant de la semaine prochaine. Je crois que vous

---

(1) The stage adaptation of *la Terre* has not been published. A program giving a summary of the play may be found in the *Collection théâtrale Auguste Rondel*, RF 49128, Bibliothèque de l'Arsenal. The bibliographical index of LES ŒUVRES COMPLÈTES for *la Terre*, p. 552, gives the date of the production as 22 January 1902, but the opening was announced for 21 January in the *Figaro* of that date.
(2) *Correspondance Emile Zola*, t. XIV, feuillet 359.
(3) *Ibid.*, feuillet 365, dated 24 November 1898.
(4) *Ibid.*, feuillet 367, dated 23 June 1899.
(5) *Ibid.*, feuillet 370, dated 20 November 1899.
(6) *Ibid.*, feuillet 373, dated 14 May 1900.
(7) *Ibid.*, feuillet 375.

en serez satisfait. Pour en être certain, je vous demande, au nom d'Hugot et au mien, de nous sacrifier deux ou trois heures, à partir du 9 7bre, le matin ou l'après-midi. Nous vous lirons ce qui est nouveau et forts de votre approbation, nous remettrons entre les mains d'Antoine notre nouveau manuscrit... (1).

The play achieved a certain success, but Antoine soon alternated his performance with another play, to which he gave greater publicity than to *la Terre*, and in later letters, Saint-Arroman wrote with some bitterness of " l'abandon inexplicable de *la Terre* " and of " l'inconcevable lâchage d'Antoine " (2).

Conclusions

The five Zola-Busnach adaptations have either been disregarded as unauthentic Zola, or, when his collaboration has been recognized, there has been a tendency to consider them ignoble alloys sullied by the plodding mercantile spirit of Busnach. Certainly they are unauthentic, in the sense that one cannot be sure which individual scenes were written principally by Zola, and which by Busnach. Zola, however, was an active participant in planning the scenario of all five of these plays, and in writing the dialogue of the last four (excluding *l'Assommoir*). His wishes prevailed in establishing the action, the number and nature of the settings, and the general spirit of all five plays. As to the last four, there was a continuing exchange of manuscripts between him and Busnach, each amending and rewriting the work of the other until the play was mutually considered complete. These circumstances alone would justify giving a place in Zola's career to his adaptations with Busnach. But his interest was not confined to collaborating on the plays. Each production aroused critical controversies to which Zola contributed with his customary vigor. And *Germinal* in particular raised important problems of censorship, which afforded him the opportunity of giving further expression to his ideas on the relation between government and literature.

(1) *Ibid.*, feuillet 378, 31 August 1901.
(2) *Ibid.*, feuillets 396 and 399-400, dated 20 February and 29 April 1902. For Antoine's opinion of Saint-Arroman and Hugot, see *infra*, Chapter V : " Antoine and the Théâtre-Libre. "

The adaptations, with their melodramatic action, inadequate characterization and reliance upon superficially spectacular settings, are inconsistent with Zola's expressed ideals of theatrical art (1). But they should not on that account be considered an inglorious chapter in Zola's career. While advocating methods of raising theatrical art to a higher level, he had often expressed his appreciation of purely popular plays provided that they were offered without artistic pretentions. In his own plays (excepting *le Bouton de Rose*), he had aspired to the highest level of which he was capable, and had failed to win either critical or public recognition. Now, in his collaborations with Busnach, he sought, without artistic pretentions, to make a tentative effort towards stage naturalism by adapting his novels, even though, in making concessions to public taste in the interest of success, the victory would not be complete. *L'Assommoir* was a phenomenal success on the stage, and the adaptation was perhaps even more instrumental than the novel in planting the idea of naturalism in the public mind. It is regrettable that the association of Zola and Busnach, which had begun so auspiciously, should have resulted in plays of progressively declining merit. The next three adaptations were based upon much weaker novels than *l'Assommoir*, and it is perhaps not surprising that the authors failed to reach with them the level of their first collaboration. The novel *Germinal*, however, ranks with or surpasses *l'Assommoir*, and the absolute disaster of their adaptation of this masterpiece, for which the censorship cannot justly be blamed, is the most disappointing aspect of the association. It should be said in behalf of the collaborators that there was probably no contemporary French playwright capable of adapting *Germinal* to the stage.

---

(1) Except in the matter of stage décor. Martin KANES (in *PMLA*, LXVII, No. 1, March 1962, p. 110) says, in reference to the lists of " tableaux " which were the starting-point of each of Busnach's adaptations, that " These lists reflect the capital fact that the plays were conceived from the very beginning *as a series of décors* ". (Italics are Kanes'.)

He points out, further, several specific criteria toward which Zola was aiming : realistic décor and stage effects, the elimination of painted canvas except for backdrops, the use of moving masses of supporting actors (pp. 112-113). Here is a particularly valuable observation : " And the ' optique ' of the theater, its essential condition, as Zola conceived it, was *the elimination of its formal characteristics as art*. It had to be more ' real ' than real, in a way the novel never could be. In this sense, the theater was for Zola the point of arrival of the novel, and this attitude goes far toward explaining his repeated returns to the theater after many disappointments and failures, and despite his awareness of the great problems involved. " (P. 115. Italics are Kanes'.)

The positive contribution of these adaptations to theatrical art was limited to the realistic settings and to a few isolated scenes. The bar-room scene of *l'Assommoir* is a good example of the slice of life technique and would be a creditable accomplishment in a modern naturalist play. The scene in the country between Nana and the adolescent Georges, probably written by Zola alone, shows a certain depth of feeling, although the effectiveness of the scene is destroyed by mechanical stage effects. In *Germinal*, Zola wanted to experiment with crowd scenes, and did in fact devote more time to rehearsals of this play than to the others, but the value of the experiment was lost in the failure of the play (1). Zola carried his experiments in scenery to extraordinary lengths, as in the use of real water in the laundry scene of *l'Assommoir* and the brook scene in *Nana*, but aside from a few such extravagances, his realistic settings were a credit to the stage. Unfortunately, the wealth of scenic detail presented an unhappy contrast with the poverty of dramatic inspiration. As Sarcey observed in his review of *Nana*, Zola's collaborations with Busnach presented only the superficial aspects of naturalism.

---

(1) In 1888, Antoine wrote a letter to SARCEY published in *le Temps*, in which he refers to the crowd scenes in *Germinal*. The letter is quoted by WAXMAN in his *Antoine and the Théâtre-Libre*, pp. 95-96, and reads in part (translation by Waxman) : " ... I have been told that in certain operas Wagner divided the choruses into several parts, and that each group of singers personified a distinct element of the crowd, which fused into a perfect ensemble. Why shouldn't we do that on the speaking stage ? M. Zola wanted to do it in *Germinal*, but could not because the directors objected on financial grounds. His idea was to have several rehearsals of ensembles led by actors who should take the parts of supernumeraries " (p. 96.)

As a matter of fact, the production of *Germinal* employed vast crowds of actors. " Un monsieur de l'orchestre " states that in the fourth *tableau* (" la ducasse ") he counted 300 actors on the stage (*le Figaro*, 22 April 1888). The critics do not comment, however, upon whether or not the crowd was divided into separate groups.

CHAPTER V

NEW TRENDS AND NEW INTERESTS

Introduction. — Becque. — Antoine and the *Théâtre-Libre*. — Alfred
Bruneau. — *Le Rêve*. — *L'Attaque du moulin*. — *Messidor*. —
L'Ouragan. — *L'Enfant-Roi*. — *Lazare*. — *Violaine la Chevelue*. —
Sylvanire ou *Paris en amour*. — An unrealised project.

Introduction

Two important talents emerged in the French theater during
the decade which followed Zola's five-year campaign of dramatic
and literary criticism. Henry Becque (1) presented the two
plays (*les Corbeaux* in 1882 and *la Parisienne* in 1885) which
entitle him to a rank in the forefront of French dramatists (2).
André Antoine (3), in 1887, inaugurated his *Théâtre-Libre*, which
offered a convention-free stage to the coming generation of
playwrights and provided the stimulus for a theatrical renaissance such as Zola had imagined. Becque, three years older
than Zola, kept aloof from the naturalist orbit, and it does not
appear that he was directly influenced by the latter's dramatic
principles. He benefited indirectly, however, from the liberalization of the theater which had been induced by Zola's theatrical
campaign. Antoine owed a far greater debt to Zola. Zola's
interest and patronage were instrumental in the initial success
of the *Théâtre-Libre* and were a continuing source of inspiration
to Antoine in subsequent years.

During Zola's last decade, up to his death in 1902, he became

(1) Henry Becque, 1837-1899.
(2) Eric DAWSON states in the conclusion of his *Henry Becque, sa vie et
son théâtre* (Paris, 1923) : " Excepté Alfred de Musset, Henry Becque ne trouve
personne qui lui soit comparable parmi les dramaturges du xixe siècle. Dès
aujourd'hui le nom de Henry Becque apparaît comme l'un des points culmi-
nants de l'évolution du théâtre français " (p. 231).
(3) André Antoine, 1857-1943.

increasingly interested in symbolic works and correspondingly less interested in the naturalist method. The completion of the *Rougon-Macquart* in 1893 was the end of an epoch in his life. Without becoming actually an apostate of naturalism, he turned increasingly in his last six novels (the *Trois villes* and the three " *Évangiles* ") to the expression of visionary ideas. A corresponding change took place in his theatrical interests. Stimulated by the composer, Alfred Bruneau, he developed an ardent attachment to the operatic form. Bruneau's first compositions in association with Zola were based upon adaptations of *le Rêve* and *l'Attaque du moulin*, for which the librettos were written by Louis Gallet with some assistance from Zola. Subsequently, Zola as sole author wrote six lyric dramas, of which three, with music by Bruneau, have been performed on the operatic stage in Paris.

Henry Becque

While Zola was denouncing the current state of the drama and proclaiming the need of a theatrical renaissance, Becque was unostentatiously preparing for the production of his two master-pieces — *les Corbeaux* and *la Parisienne* — which brought the ideal of a comparatively convention-free theater out of the limbo of theory into the realm of accomplished fact. Neither Becque nor Zola, however, sought to establish a mutual community of interest, and it seems clear that a certain coolness existed between the two writers, both of whom were later recognized by Antoine as the principal progenitors of the *Théâtre-Libre*. Zola, during his tenure as dramatic critic of the *Voltaire*, had defended Becque's one-act gem, *la Navette*, against the " pudibonderie stupéfiante " of the contemporary audience, and approved the moral lesson to be drawn from this comedy of a promiscuous woman :

> Je ne veux point donner à *la Navette* une importance qu'elle ne saurait avoir. M. Henri Becque y a pourtant mis une idée très juste, l'amour des filles pour qui les gruge et les bat. J'ajouterai que rien n'est plus moral que cette petite comédie : si tous les sots qui se ruinent pour les filles la voyaient jouer et réfléchissaient, quelques-uns peut-être s'arrêteraient sur la pente où ils roulent. La vérité n'est jamais dangereuse. Il n'y a que le mensonge qui pousse au mal (1).

(1) *Le Voltaire*, 26 November 1878. Not reprinted.

Three years later, Becque, who was then writing a series of dramatic criticisms for the *Union républicaine*, spoke somewhat caustically of *l'Assommoir* during a revival of the play at the *Ambigu*, with particular reference to Zola's preface. Zola, he finds, is correct in saying that *l'Assommoir* differs from preceding popular melodramas, in that it displays no dukes, marquis, lost children nor stolen papers. Zola is right, too, in speaking of the moral lesson to be derived from the work, although Becque makes the reservation : " La leçon pourrait être excellente sans que le spectacle fût bien sain. " And Becque agrees with Zola that the adaptors, Busnach and Gastineau, have employed considerable skill and produced some excellent scenes. " Il s'en faut cependant ", he adds, " que je sois d'accord avec M. Zola sur tous les points de sa préface, et surtout dans ce qu'il dit du naturalisme ". Becque cites the laundry scene of *l'Assommoir* as a particular example of the unwarranted pretensions of the naturalists. The laundry and the real hot water are merely spectacular, and the climax of the scene — the spanking administered by Gervaise to Virginie — is hidden from the audience. " Est-ce qu'une scène compte au théâtre ", he complains, " lorsqu'elle est cachée expressément par un rideau de figurants ". Becque raises a more fundamental objection to naturalism in reproaching Zola for confining his analysis to the evil aspects of life and ignoring what is good and generous :

Pourquoi, dirai-je à M. Zola, dans l'honneur et le devoir, ne voyez-vous que des tirades ? Pourquoi ce qui est bon et généreux vous paraît-il en même temps poncif ? Pourquoi n'apportez-vous pas dans des personnages moraux notre analyse ordinaire et un langage original ? Le tort ne vient pas de ces personnages ni du public, il vient de vous.

And, continuing the deflation of Zola's pretensions, he concludes :

Je m'arrête. Si je me laissais aller à parler d'Hamlet et de Coupeau que M. Zola a rapprochés l'un de l'autre, je ne pourrais pas m'empêcher de rire (1).

One cannot be certain that Zola read this criticism by Becque. However, when *les Corbeaux* opened at the *Comédie-Française* a year later (2), Zola maintained an absolute silence upon the merits of the work. He had ceased to write weekly

---

(1) Henry BECQUE, *Œuvres complètes*, V : *Querelles littéraires* (Paris, 1925), pp. 94-96, reprinted from *l'Union républicaine*, 27 September 1881.
(2) *Les Corbeaux* opened on 14 September 1882.

articles in the press, and was of course under no contractual obligation to report on the play. But it was the sort of work which he might have been expected to defend. Its somber quality aroused the hostility of the critics, who associated it with the naturalist movement, and the play was withdrawn after it had played 18 performances during the season (1). Zola, at the time, was at his home in Médan, near Paris, and was surely aware of the criticism which the play had evoked. His failure to support *les Corbeaux* was perhaps due to Becque's caustic criticism of Zola's ideas expressed in the preface to *l'Assommoir*.

Arnaoutovitch suggests, in his monumental work on Becque, that the playwright may have resented Zola's abstention from the controversy :

Il nous paraît que le silence de Zola sur la première représentation des *Corbeaux* a vexé Henry Becque. Le comité-directeur du groupe naturaliste n'a mis ni son autorité ni son empressement à défendre notre auteur ; il a observé une neutralité étonnante aussi bien envers *les Corbeaux* qu'envers *la Parisienne*. Leur armée est entrée en action mais sans ses généraux (2).

Certainly the acrimony of Becque's comments upon Zola and the naturalists increased in the next few years. For example, in 1884 he stated :

Mais vraiment M. Zola et ses amis, les doctrinaires du parti naturaliste, se moquent de nous, et nous le leur rendons bien. Ils sont là, trois ou quatre romanciers, mettons-en cinq, mettons-en six, qui n'ont jamais rêvé que des planches et qui y ont échoué misérablement. Ils y ont échoué sans originalité, sans hardiesse, sans maladresse même. Ils ont eu toutes les scènes à leur disposition, depuis le Théâtre-Français jusqu'au théâtre Cluny ; ils les ont eues sans débats et sans conditions ; *Henriette Maréchal, le Candidat, Bouton de Rose*, voilà les noms bien connus de leurs ridicules défaites. Après de pareilles platitudes, les dédains et les fanfaronnades ne trompent plus personne. On se tait, on se juge, on se limite, et on se renferme dans l'art où l'on excelle. Mais il y a des gens, lorsqu'ils se sont étalés au coin d'une rue, qui y repassent continuellement ; les romanciers naturalistes sont ainsi (3).

During a lecture in Milan in 1893, he said :

... nous avions avec les romanciers naturalistes les alliés les plus dangereux. Tous ces messieurs, Goncourt, Flaubert, Zola, s'étaient

(1) According to Alexandre ARNAOUTOVITCH, *Henry Becque* (Paris, 1927), vol. III, p. 51.
(2) *Ibid.*, p. 436.
(3) *Querelles littéraires*, p. 118, reprinted from *le Matin* 11 April 1884.

promis de révolutionner le théâtre. Ils faisaient des théories magnifiques et des ouvrages bien médiocres (1).

And he wrote to the same effect in 1887 :

L'École nouvelle, il faut bien le reconnaître, a quelque chose contre elle, quelque chose de très fâcheux. Elle n'a rien produit. Elle a eu ses docteurs et ses apôtres ; ils n'ont rien produit. M. Zola, toujours si convaincu dans ses programmes et ses réclames, n'a encore rien écrit pour le théâtre. M. de Goncourt pareillement. M. de Goncourt a joué pendant trente ans à l'auteur sifflé, sans raisons, sans titres, pour cette panade d'*Henriette Maréchal*. Un autre, M. Henry Céard, est un homme très fort, très sûr de lui ; on attend toujours qu'il éclate. Si on avait écouté ces messieurs, ils devaient briser des portes, escalader des murs, planter des drapeaux. Finalement ils n'ont réussi qu'à ridiculiser leurs théories et à laisser à leurs successeurs une partie fort compromise (2).

In only one respect — the censorship — do Becque's opinions appear identical to Zola's. " Tout le monde est libre ", he writes, " excepté les auteurs dramatiques " (3). The censorship of *Germinal* inspired him to write sympathetically of Zola :

Quand M. Zola, avec son talent admirable, étudie une classe spéciale de travailleurs ; qu'il nous montre leurs poignantes misères, la barbarie qui les opprime et la répression qui les attend, il est en pleine donnée démocratique et sociale ; il fait une pièce, bonne ou mauvaise, peu importe ici, que la république devrait récompenser, et si la république l'interdit, quel gouvernement la permettra (4) ?

Becque's consummate artistry rendered him impatient with Zola's comparative clumsiness on the stage, and scornful of theoreticians who failed to practise as well as they preached. Although he satisfied the naturalist program of opening the theater to harsh reality, his approach to the stage was different. As Arnaoutovitch points out, he wrote with the curiosity of an artist, rather than with the quasi-scientific preoccupations of Zola. " Je ne copie pas. Je n'ai jamais pris une note ", he said in alluding to the method of extensive documentation employed by the naturalist school (5). *La Parisienne* is evangelical compared

---

(1) BECQUE, *Œuvres complètes*, VII : *Conférences*, etc., pp. 63-64. Lecture at Milan, 22 May 1893, reprinted in *le Journal*, 20 June 1893.
(2) Henry BECQUE, *Souvenirs d'un auteur dramatique* (Paris, 1895), " Deux préfaces, 1887 ", pp. 223-224.
For some other comments by Becque upon Zola and the naturalists, see ARNAOUTOVITCH, *ibid.*, vol. III, pp. 434-441.
(3) *Querelles littéraires*, " la Censure ", p. 253, reprinted from *le Figaro*, 17 November 1888.
(4) *Ibid.*, p. 257.
(5) ARNAOUTOVITCH, *ibid.*, vol. III, p. 442.

to *Thérèse Raquin.* Becque is interested in bourgeois society rather than in the lower depths. He portrays meanness rather than ugliness, and makes no effort to compete with the pathologists. Human bestiality is absent from his theater. He probed ulcers of the mind, heart and soul, not of the flesh. Arnaoutovitch concludes :

Il faudrait oublier toutes ces différences aussi bien que celles qui se dégagent — nous nous plaisons à le croire — de notre étude, pour assigner à Becque une place soit à la tête du théâtre naturaliste, soit même parmi les naturalistes (1).

Notwithstanding this judgment, there would seem to be no objection to classifying Becque, with suitable reservations, as an independent naturalist. Certainly he regenerated the theater, and followed naturalist principles in creating a greater illusion of reality without flinching at unpleasant or daring subjects. Rejecting the scientific pretensions and the more repugnant aspects of naturalism, he succeeded in bringing the movement within artistic bounds.

It does not appear that Zola exercised any creative influence upon Becque, but it is possible that Zola's dramatic criticisms during 1876-1881 affected Becque's theatrical fortunes in creating an atmosphere receptive to the production of so unconventional a play as *les Corbeaux.* Becque had determined his course before Zola began his campaign in the press. His *Michel Pauper,* produced in 1870, had been described by critics as " d'un réalisme qui soulève le cœur et donne des nausées " and as " un art grossier, tout fait de violences et du plus brutal réalisme " (2). This play contains a scene with manual workers and a few words of workers' dialect ; its protagonist, an educated workman who has risen from the ranks, dies of alcoholism at the end of the play. It has, accordingly, sometimes been considered a precursor of *l'Assommoir.* There is, however, no real similarity between the two works. Four of the five acts take place in drawing room settings (the fifth in a laboratory), the workers' scene is short, the dialect used only occasionally, and the aspect of alcoholism enters only briefly at the beginning and end of the play, which is far inferior to Becque's later work. Although *Michel Pauper* foreshadowed *l'Assommoir* but slightly, it does show that Becque was interested in somber aspects of realism

(1) *Ibid.,* p. 443.
(2) Quoted in Becque, *Œuvres complètes,* I, preface by Jean Robaglia, p. 15.

before Zola's campaign of 1876-1881. *Les Corbeaux* was produced in 1882, but had been completed by 1877. Becque had spent five years attempting to have it produced. There is no reason to believe that Becque derived any inspiration from Zola's works or theories in writing it, but it is significant that during the five years in which this masterpiece remained unproduced, Zola was undermining the strength of theatrical conventions through his weekly denunciations in the press. Although Zola's own plays were failures, his ideas were gradually taking root. Becque's play, which was unacceptable when Zola began his campaign, found a stage only after the campaign was concluded. Zola's struggle for a new theater may have aided Becque more than Becque himself realized. Conversely, Becque fulfilled the prophecies of the naturalists more completely than Zola was ever willing to admit. Each in his way inspired Antoine. Becque's artistry and Zola's prolific force coalesced into a common ideal for the *Théâtre-Libre*.

Antoine and the Théâtre-Libre

The influence and prestige of Zola were instrumental in launching Antoine's career. In his souvenirs, Antoine describes his exultation at the opportunity of associating, first, with Zola's intimate friends, Alexis and Hennique, and finally with Zola himself. Speaking of Alexis, he wrote, " Ce contact entrevu avec de pareils milieux me donna la fièvre " (1), and he describes himself at their first meeting as being " fort intimidé d'abord près d'un homme qui est l'intime de Zola " (2). Alexis was able to give him publicity through his theatrical column, written in *argot* under the pseudonym " Trublot " in *le Cri du Peuple* (3). But the most valuable publicity of all was attained with the inclusion on the opening night program, 30 March 1887, of a play adapted from a work of Zola (Hennique's, *Jacques Damour*). Antoine describes his first meeting with Zola following a rehearsal two nights before the opening :

Comme nous terminons *Jacques Damour*, le maître, monté sur la scène, conduit par Hennique, m'accule dans un angle sous un bec de

(1) ANTOINE, *Mes souvenirs sur le Théâtre-Libre* (Paris, 1921), p. 17.
(2) *Ibid.*, p. 19, diary entry dated 16 January 1887.
(3) *Ibid.*, pp. 18 and 20.

gaz ; je suis ému à défaillir tandis que ses yeux me détaillent ; il y a sur sa figure un étonnement, et il me dit assez brusquement : « Qu'est-ce que vous êtes, vous ? » Je balbutie, il me laisse barboter sous son regard fouilleur et ajoute : « C'est très bien, c'est très beau, hein ! Hennique, n'est-ce pas que c'est très bien ! Nous reviendrons demain (1). »

Zola, who had brought some friends with him to the tiny theater in the *passage de l'Élysée-des-Beaux-Arts* near the *place Pigalle*, returned for the final rehearsal on the following night with a number of influential writers and critics. Although another production opened at one of the popular theaters on the same night and drew many critics away from Antoine, Zola's interest sufficed to give him the publicity which he needed to carry on his work. As Antoine's production was for one performance only, the influence which Zola exerted in drawing attention to this single performance cannot be overestimated. Had it not been for Zola's intervention at this critical moment, Antoine's experiment might have fallen into the limbo of forgotten dreams, and his name be unknown today.

The *Théâtre-Libre* was on a subscription basis, exempt from censorship regulations, and in the beginning gave performances at very infrequent intervals (2). Another Zola adaptation, Céard's *Tout pour l'honneur*, was given as part of the fifth production of the *Théâtre-Libre* on 23 December 1887, and Zola's early play, *Madeleine*, was presented at the sixteenth production on 1 May 1889. Antoine described the latter as merely a literary curiosity (3). Zola made no effort to impose his views upon Antoine, for whom Zola's continuing support and friendship were in no way conditioned upon Antoine's choice of plays. As the latter related in his souvenirs :

Zola, qui sait l'énorme ascendant qu'il pourrait exercer sur moi, évite toujours soigneusement d'intervenir, et pourtant il est en ce temps, où je suis entouré d'écrivains et d'hommes considérables, le seul que je sente le plus grand et le plus clairvoyant (4).

Thus Antoine did not confine his productions to the works of naturalist writers. Commenting on a statement by the critic

(1) *Ibid.*, p. 29, diary entry dated 28 March 1887.
(2) See Adolphe THALASSO, *le Théâtre-Libre* (Paris, 2e éd., 1909) for a chronological list of productions of the organization, as well as for other data. See also Samuel Montefiore WAXMAN, *Antoine and the Théâtre-Libre* (Harvard University Press, 1926).
(3) ANTOINE, *Mes souvenirs sur le Théâtre-Libre*, p. 149.
(4) *Ibid.*, p. 144, diary entry dated 6 May 1889.

NEW TRENDS AND NEW INTERESTS 165

Harry Bauer — " S'il veut continuer à prospérer, le Théâtre-Libre sera naturaliste ou ne sera pas " — Antoine wrote :

Je ne suis pas tout à fait de cet avis. Je pense qu'une formule trop étroite serait la mort, et que, au contraire, il faut nous tenir prêts à accueillir largement tout le monde (1).

On one occasion, for his seventh production on 23 March 1888, he even presented, with Zola's permission (2), three short plays by young writers known to be hostile to Zola. These included four of the signatories to the " Manifeste des Cinq ", a denunciatory article which appeared in the *Figaro* on 18 August 1887 in protest against the indecencies of Zola's novel, *la Terre* (3). Antoine, in his diary entry of 30 March 1888, gives Zola's comment upon this production :

Zola, que l'on est allé interviewer sur la soirée des Cinq, comme toujours, plein de bon sens et de raison, dit avoir assisté au spectacle et trouvé la tentative intéressante ; cependant, pour lui, elle n'a pas révélé la nouvelle forme théâtrale qu'il attendait d'eux après leur récent éclat (4).

Zola was interested in the work of the Scandinavian dramatists, Strindberg and Ibsen. A French translation of Strindberg's *The Father* (translated by the Swedish dramatist himself) (5), was published in 1888 with a letter-preface by Zola. The preface betrayed the uneasy and somewhat confused admiration which this compact, powerful work aroused in the French writer. The criticism which he directed against one aspect of Strindberg's drama is typical of a novelist's point of view :

Pour être franc, des raccourcis d'analyse m'y gênent un peu. Vous savez peut-être que je ne suis pas pour l'abstraction. J'aime que les personnages aient un état civil complet, qu'on les coudoie, qu'ils trempent dans notre air. Et votre capitaine qui n'a pas même de nom, vos autres personnages qui sont presque des êtres de raison, ne me donnent pas de la vie la sensation complète que je demande. Mais il y a

(1) *Ibid.*, pp. 143-144.
(2) " Zola m'a tout le premier vivement encouragé à réserver une soirée complète à ses cinq adversaires et le monde littéraire s'apprête curieusement à juger l'effort des dissidents " (*ibid.*, p. 86, diary entry dated 15 February 1888).
(3) For details of this controversy, see the recent biography by Alexandre ZÉVAÈS, *Zola* (Paris, 1946), pp. 145-150, and the account in LES ŒUVRES COMPLÈTES, *la Terre*, " le Manifeste des Cinq et la Terre ", pp. 523-528.
(4) ANTOINE, *Mes souvenirs sur le Théâtre-Libre*, p. 91.
(5) According to A. Dikka REQUE, *Trois auteurs dramatiques scandinaves, Ibsen, Björnsen, Strindberg, devant la critique française, 1889-1901* (Paris, 1930), p. 17.

certainement là, entre vous et moi, une question de race. Telle qu'elle est, je le répète, votre pièce est une des rares œuvres dramatiques qui m'aient profondément remué (1).

In the novel, Zola was free to re-create reality out of masses of detail. Attempting to bring his talent as novelist to the stage, he was inclined, as in his recent failure, *Renée*, to dissipate the essence of his drama in awkward and unnecessary explanations. A less patronizing attitude to Strindberg might have improved immeasurably his own work in the theater.

As to Ibsen, Zola is entitled to share with Antoine in the credit for introducing the Norwegian dramatist to the French stage. An entry in Antoine's souvenirs reads :

Zola, que je vois ce soir, attire mon attention sur un article de Jacques Saint-Cère, au sujet d'un auteur scandinave dont on vient de représenter en Allemagne une œuvre dont l'effet a été énorme (2).

The date of 12 January 1890 which Antoine gives to this entry is probably in error. There is reason to believe that this conversation with Zola took place a year — or more probably two years — earlier (3).

Further entries among Antoine's souvenirs reveal that Zola strongly urged Antoine to produce *Ghosts* and that he even provided Antoine with a translator. Under the date of 5 February 1890 (which should probably be earlier), Antoine wrote :

Zola, a qui j'ai fait part de ce que j'ai pu apprendre sur cet Ibsen et ses *Revenants*, m'engage vivement à le jouer au Théâtre-Libre. Et il me

---

(1) This letter-preface to Strindberg, dated 14 December 1887, is published in Zola's Les Œuvres complètes, *Mélanges, Préfaces et Discours*, p. 240.

(2) Antoine, *Mes souvenirs sur le Théâtre-Libre*, p. 160.

(3) The article in question by Jacques Saint-Cère is " Un poète du Nord ", in *Revue d'Art dramatique*, t. V, janvier-mars 1887, pp. 277-282 and t. VI, avril-juin 1887, pp. 20-24. It is unlikely that nearly three years would have elapsed before Zola spoke of it to Antoine.

Further evidence in support of the belief that this conversation with Zola took place in 1888 may be found in a letter written by Ibsen to Antoine, published among Antoine's souvenirs under the diary date of 20 April 1890 (*Mes souvenirs sur le Théâtre-Libre*, p. 160). Ibsen's letter reads, in part : " Aussi éprouvai-je une grande satisfaction lorsque j'appris, il y a deux ans, que vous aviez conçu le dessein de faire représenter ma pièce *les Revenants* sur cette scène dirigée par vous. " Ibsen goes on to authorize the translation which Antoine planned to use, and says that he is awaiting the result of Antoine's endeavors with great interest. Since Ibsen's letter was written prior to Antoine's production of *Ghosts* (Which took place on 30 May 1890), it is clear from internal evidence in the letter that Antoine had been thinking of *Ghosts* at least two years before the actual production.

promet de trouver parmi les étrangers qui le visitent sans cesse un homme capable de me traduire la pièce (1).

And, in his entry dated 15 February 1890, he printed a letter from Zola introducing a translator, Louis de Hessem (2). Hessem's translation was inadequate, and the translation actually used, and approved by Ibsen, was that of Rodolphe Darzens (3). Antoine's presentation of *Ghosts* in 1890 and of *The Wild Duck* in the following year were the first productions of Ibsen in France. The importance of Zola's recommendation to Antoine may be judged by the fact that, during the next six years, thirteen other Ibsen plays were produced at various theaters in Paris (4). At a revival of *An Enemy of the People* in 1898, shortly after Zola's conviction in a criminal court on account of his letter *J'accuse*, it is reported that Zola was identified in the public mind with Dr. Stockmann, amid cries of " Vive l'anarchie ! " (5). Zola in 1894 considered Ibsen to be strongly influenced by French romanticism (6). Three years later, he summarized his opinions of Scandinavian literature, finding that it was derived from both French romanticism and naturalism, and questioning its importance in relation to French letters :

Je m'entête à être convaincu, malgré les plaidoyers contraires et malgré les démentis, que les œuvres scandinaves, récemment introduites en France, sont nées sous l'influence des idées françaises, romantiques et naturalistes. Et la question intéressante à se poser serait de se demander quand et comment cette influence indéniable a pu se produire et agir si puissamment.

Maintenant, de même que notre vin de Bordeaux, dit-on, gagne à faire le voyage des Indes, il est certain que quelques-unes de nos idées, en passant par le génie du Nord, ont pris une ampleur et une intensité admirables. Mais comment ces idées pourraient-elles influer sur notre littérature, puisqu'elles y existent toutes déjà, exprimées dans des œuvres, dont l'action, pour quelques-unes, est dans son plein développement, tandis que l'action des autres est même épuisée ? Toutes ces semences ont germé dans notre vieille terre de France, et nous n'avons plus à attendre des moissons, dont nos granges sont pleines.

Et, d'ailleurs, pour savoir qui a raison, il faut attendre. Dix années

---

(1) ANTOINE, *Mes souvenirs sur le Théâtre-Libre*, p. 162.
(2) *Ibid.*, p. 163.
(3) A further report of ANTOINE's production of *Ghosts* may be found in ANTOINE, *le Théâtre* (Paris, 1932), pp. 247-250.
(4) According to REQUE, *Trois auteurs dramatiques scandinaves*, p. 213.
(5) *Ibid.*, p. 191.
(6) According to *Journal des Goncourt*, t. IX, entry dated 6 May 1894.

sont au moins nécessaires avant d'établir ce qu'a pu rapporter une littérature étrangère à notre littérature nationale. Dans dix ans, on verra que, de même que Tolstoï, Ibsen et Bjoernson ne nous ont rien appris, s'ils nous ont émus et charmés (1).

Although Zola appears to have been moved only superficially by the work of the Scandinavian dramatists, his recommendation to Antoine undoubtedly hastened Ibsen's arrival before a French audience.

For the adaptation of *la Terre* by Hugot and St. Arroman, Antoine relied strongly upon Zola's revisions, as may be seen from his letter to Zola written upon the latter's return in 1899 from exile in England :

Vous savez sans doute que Hugot et St. Arroman m'ont apporté *la Terre* il y a déjà presque une année ? on avait tout remis à votre retour. Les trois premiers actes que vous avez surveillés sont d'une grande venue. Tout se gâte vers la fin et c'est, je crois, la partie de l'œuvre qui reste à vous soumettre — avant de les voir, je souhaiterais vivement savoir votre sentiment et en causer avec vous, de façon à ce que ce grand projet fût réalisable l'hiver prochain.

Comment pourrais-je sans risquer de vous importuner savoir ce que vous en pensez ?

Enfin, vous voici revenu !

Votre A. Antoine (2).

The play did not open until January, 1902, with Antoine in the rôle of the *père* Fouan. According to Antoine's souvenirs, Zola was pleased with the production, and particularly with Antoine's acting :

On a soupé hier soir en tout petit comité, après *la Terre*. Je sens chez Zola un contentement de moi qui m'emplit le cœur. Il me parle de *l'Abbé Mouret*. « Après ce que vous venez de faire, dit-il, avec la promenade du père Fouan, il n'y a que vous qui puissiez nous arranger le *Paradou*. Vous êtes décidément mon homme. Massenet fera la musique et nous travaillerons à ça tous les deux (3). »

However, the production was not financially successful.

(1) " Enquête sur l'influence des lettres scandinaves ", in *la Revue blanche,* 15 February 1897, t. XII, pp. 153-166, at p. 166. Zola was one of 25 writers whose opinions were sought on the question.
(2) *Correspondance Émile Zola,* t. I, feuillets 606-607.
(3) ANTOINE, *Mes souvenirs sur le Théâtre Antoine et sur l'Odéon (Première Direction),* Paris, 1928. P. 190, diary entry dated 22 January 1902.
Zola had originally assigned the musical rights to *la Faute de l'abbé Mouret* to MASSENET. The composition was eventually written by Alfred Bruneau and produced by Antoine at the *Odéon* in 1907.

Passions were still engaged in memories of the Dreyfus Case, as is evident from the next diary entries in Antoine's souvenirs :

26 janvier 1902. — Nos représentations de *la Terre* sont souvent troublées. On crie : « A bas Zola ! » à l'orchestre et : « Vive Zola ! » aux galeries supérieures...

30 janvier 1902. — Toujours des incidents. Ce soir, à l'orchestre, un spectateur en gifle un autre qui lui casse sa canne sur la figure.

2 février 1902. — A la matinée, il y a encore eu une manifestation assez sérieuse après le quatrième acte de *la Terre*. Les saint-cyriens et les polytechniciens, toujours très nombreux à nos matinées dominicales, s'abstiennent de prendre part au tapage.

2 février 1902. — Zola est venu ce soir voir la pièce, qui a très bien marché. Heureusement, sa présence n'a pas été connue, car nous aurions eu du grabuge...

10 février 1902. — Nous baissons beaucoup ; incontestablement, le public bien pensant, celui des loges, n'aime pas *la Terre* ; nous sommes soutenus par les petites places qui, elles, sont combles et manifestent bruyamment.

Finally, Antoine is obliged to record :

13 février 1902. — *La Terre* ne fait plus ses frais, et j'en suis bien contrarié à cause de Zola. Les deux adaptateurs, qui ne songent qu'à eux, s'étonnent qu'il soit question de changer l'affiche, et, n'osant pas me présenter directement leurs doléances, se sont adressés à Zola pour le faire agir sur moi. Heureusement, le maître est aussi un brave homme, plein de bon sens, et après mes explications, il m'a donné raison (1).

On several occasions, Antoine publicly acknowledged his indebtedness to Zola as a source of inspiration. At a dinner given in Antoine's honor in December 1896, at which Zola presided, Antoine made the following tribute :

Et d'abord, je désire saluer en votre présence, puisque l'occasion m'en est donnée, deux maîtres, Émile Zola et Henry Becque, à qui je dois toutes les convictions et toutes les clartés qui ont guidé ma route (2).

Writing of *Thérèse Raquin*, Antoine describes it as " une œuvre-type, une de ces pièces-mères préparant une nouvelle formule ", and concludes :

... si les maîtres du roman naturaliste ne parvinrent pas à s'emparer définitivement du théâtre, ils déblayèrent la route et préparèrent l'avenir avec des œuvres comme celle-ci, bousculant les formules surannées (3).

---

(1) *Ibid.*, pp. 190-191.
(2) *Ibid.*, pp. 102-103, diary entry dated 9 December 1896.
(3) Quotation from *l'Information*, 4 August 1924, as reprinted in LES ŒUVRES COMPLÈTES, *Théâtre II*, " Thérèse Raquin et la critique ", pp. 691-692.

And in his address on the occasion of the annual pilgrimage
to Médan of the *Société des Amis de Zola* in October, 1922, he
said :

Je témoigne ici que tout le mouvement du Théâtre-Libre fut déclen-
ché par son geste de puissant animateur. Pendant quinze années de
luttes il n'y eut pour nous d'autre certitude et d'autre réconfort que
son approbation. Cette formule du naturalisme qu'il venait de créer
était, pour nous, nous le voyons à présent, un simple retour à la tradition
pure de la race, la liaison, par-dessus notre xviie siècle, avec le génie
du Moyen Age. La vie, l'observation de l'homme dans son milieu, dont
le sens s'était obscurci avec l'évolution classique, il les faisait reparaître...
Par lui, nous avons conquis la liberté du théâtre, la liberté d'y porter
tous les sujets, tous les milieux, le peuple, les ouvriers, les soldats, les
paysans, toute la foule tumultueuse et magnifique. Si Georges de Porto-
Riche peut magistralement y analyser l'amour, si François de Curel
confesse les détresses d'un autre enfant du siècle, si Henry Bataille,
en dix-neuf chefs-d'œuvre, peut audacieusement fouiller les âmes, si
Mirbeau a porté jusque sur notre première scène ces cinglantes et venge-
resses satires, si Brieux a pu livrer et gagner dans d'utiles batailles contre
la routine, les abus et les préjugés, si Henri Bernstein put déchaîner ses
monstres, c'est qu'Émile Zola avait préparé, éduqué et affranchi le
grand public (1).

Antoine was speaking before a special group devoted to
the memory of Zola, twenty years after the writer's death.　The
occasion called for a panegyric rather than a critical judgment.
Yet there is a great measure of truth in Antoine's praise.　He
was not referring to Zola's influence as a dramatist, but to the
intangible spirit of freedom which Zola infused into the theater
in urging the adaptation to the stage of those principles by
which he had liberalized the novel.

Alfred Bruneau

Alfred Bruneau (1857-1934) relates in his biography of Zola,
A l'ombre d'un grand cœur (Paris, 1932), that he secured an
introduction to Zola in 1888 through their mutual friend Frantz
Jourdain, in hope of obtaining the musical rights to *la Faute de
l'abbé Mouret*, the fifth novel in the *Rougon-Macquart* series.
Zola had already disposed of the rights to Massenet, of whom

---

(1) LES ŒUVRES COMPLÈTES, *Théâtre II*, " Notes et commentaires ",
p. 677 ; reprinted from *Bulletin de la Société des Amis de Zola*, 1923, no. 2.

young Bruneau had been a pupil, and suggested that he might be interested in making a lyrical adaptation of *le Rêve*, Zola's forthcoming novel upon which he was still at work. Bruneau accepted the offer with enthusiasm, and thus began a collaboration which endured throughout the remainder of Zola's life. The first two operas based upon Zola's works — *le Rêve* and *l'Attaque du moulin* — were composed to librettos, in verse, by Louis Gallet, who received some assistance from Zola. They do not appear in LES ŒUVRES COMPLÈTES, which comprise only those works written by Zola alone. Subsequently, Zola unassisted wrote six operatic librettos in lyric prose, three of which — *Messidor*, *l'Ouragan*, and *l'Enfant-Roi* — were produced in Paris with music by Bruneau. These six librettos were published by Fasquelle in 1921 under the title *Poèmes lyriques*, and appear in LES ŒUVRES COMPLÈTES, *Théâtre II*. After Zola's death in 1902, Bruneau produced three additional operas, for which he wrote both the book and music, based upon Zola's works : *Naïs Micoulin* (at the *Théâtre de Monte-Carlo*, 1907), *la Faute de l'abbé Mouret*, the rights to which had been given up by Massenet (at the *Odéon*, 1907), and *les Quatre Journées* (at the *Opéra-Comique*, 1916). Since Zola did not participate either in the writing or the production of the three last-named works, no further mention of them need be made.

Bruneau became a close friend, as well as a literary associate, of Zola. It was through Zola's influence that he became music critic of the *Gil Blas*, Zola having agreed to give serial publication rights of his novel *Lourdes* to this journal in exchange for their employment of Bruneau. As Bruneau relates the incident :

Il télégraphia immédiatement à Guérin [of the *Gil Blas* staff] :
« Prenez Bruneau. »
On lui répondit :
« Prendrons Bruneau si donnez *Lourdes*. »
Et il donna *Lourdes* et l'on prit Bruneau et voilà comment je devins critique musical du *Gil Blas* (1).

Later, when Zola resumed for a brief period a series of regular contributions to the *Figaro* (2), he arranged that Bruneau join the *Figaro* staff with him, and when Zola resigned because of a disagreement with the editor, he sent Bruneau the following

---

(1) Alfred BRUNEAU, *A l'ombre d'un grand cœur, Souvenirs d'une collaboration* (Paris, 1932), p. 48.
(2) See *supra*, Chapter III.

letter of advice so that his young associate would not rashly jeopardize a situation he could ill afford to lose :

Médan, 22 juin 1896. Mon cher Ami, l'affaire est finie, j'arrête ma campagne au *Figaro*. Et je vous en préviens parce que des inquiétudes me viennent sur la solidité de la situation que vous y occupez. Certainement les audaces, les opinions braves et révolutionnaires ne sont pas aimées dans la maison. Je vous conseille donc d'être très prudent, car il serait désastreux pour vous que ma chute pût avoir un contrecoup qui vous atteindrait. Nous causerons de cela. Peut-être l'affection que j'ai pour vous me cause-t-elle là une inquiétude vaine. Et j'espère bien qu'elle est vaine. N'importe. Soyez prudent dans vos prochains articles, soyez vieille France et sans coups d'ailes.

Bien affectueusement à vous et aux vôtres de notre part à tous deux. Émile Zola (1).

Bruneau was a constant companion of Zola during his trial before the *Cours d'assises* in 1898, following publication of Zola's *J'accuse* (2), and, as one of Zola's most intimate friends, was one of the eight pall-bearers at his funeral four years later (3).

Zola's association with Bruneau began at a time when French literature was experiencing a growing idealist reaction against naturalism. The " Manifeste des Cinq " in 1887 (4) and Jules Huret's, *Enquête sur l'Évolution littéraire* in 1891 (5) were symptoms of the new trend. Huret classified the sixty-four writers whom he interviewed into eight categories — " psycho-

---

(1) BRUNEAU, *A l'ombre d'un grand cœur*, p. 83. This letter does not appear in LES ŒUVRES COMPLÈTES. Notwithstanding ZOLA's dispute with the *Figaro* in 1896, this paper opened its columns to him in November and December 1897 for three articles on the Dreyfus Case, reprinted in LES ŒUVRES COMPLÈTES, *la Vérité en marche*, pp. 3-29.

ZOLA's letter, *J'accuse*, addressed to the President of the French Republic, appeared in *l'Aurore* on 13 January 1898. As a result of it, he was brought to trial on 7 February charged with having libeled the members of the court martial which had recently acquitted Esterhazy. Zola was found guilty by the jury and sentenced to serve one year in prison and to pay a fine of 3 000 francs. The conviction was reversed on appeal. Zola was brought before a new court on 23 May and 18 July. Protesting the court's jurisdiction and procedure, Zola of his own accord refused a new jury trial and he was resentenced on the latter date to the same punishment as before. Zola left forthwith for England, where he remained in exile until 5 June 1899. By this time, the innocence of Dreyfus was sufficiently clear to permit Zola's return to France.

(2) *Ibid.*, pp. 119-121.
(3) *Ibid.*, p. 193.
(4) See *supra*, p. 165, note 3.
(5) A series of interviews with 64 writers, first published in *l'Echo de Paris* between March and July, 1891. Subsequently published in volume : Jules HURET, *Enquête sur l'évolution littéraire* (Paris, 1894). The interview with Zola is at pp. 169-176.

logues ", " mages ", " symbolistes et décadents ", " naturalistes ", " néo-réalistes ", " parnassiens ", " indépendants ", and
" théoriciens et philosophes " — with Zola, of course, among the
naturalists. Zola admits in his interview that naturalism is
waning :

> Le naturalisme est fini ! Qu'est-ce à dire ? Que le mouvement
> commencé avec Balzac, Flaubert et Goncourt, continué ensuite par
> Daudet et moi, et d'autres que je ne nomme pas, tire à sa fin ? C'est
> possible.

It is true, Zola suggests, that the adversaries of naturalism
have a case against it. He sums up the case which might be
made as follows :

> Vous avez abusé du fait positif, de la réalité apparente des choses,
> du document palpable ; de complicité avec la science et la philosophie,
> vous avez promis aux êtres le bonheur dans la vérité tangible, dans
> l'anatomie, dans la négation de l'idéal et vous les avez trompés ! Voyez,
> déjà l'ouvrier regrette presque les jurandes et maudit les machines,
> l'artiste remonte aux balbutiements de l'art, le poète rêve au Moyen
> Age... Donc, sectaires, vous avez fini, il faut autre chose, et nous, voilà
> ce que nous faisons !

To this hypothetical case against naturalism, Zola gives his
reply, in which he distinguishes between the moribund and the
enduring aspects of naturalism :

> On pourrait à la vérité répondre : Cette impatience est légitime,
> mais la science marche à pas lents et peut-être conviendrait-il de lui
> faire crédit. Pourtant cette réaction est logique, et, pendant dix ans,
> pendant quinze ans, elle peut triompher, si un homme paraît, qui résume
> puissamment en lui cette plainte du siècle, ce recul devant la science.
> Voilà comment le naturalisme peut être mort ; mais ce qui ne peut pas
> mourir, c'est la forme de l'esprit humain qui, fatalement, le pousse à
> l'enquête universelle, c'est ce besoin de rechercher la vérité où qu'elle
> soit, que le naturalisme a satisfait pour sa part.

Then he ridicules the pretensions of the symbolists in seeking
to replace fifty years of solid, positivist endeavor with their
gim-crack verses (" vers de pacotille "), and compares them to
nut-shells dancing over Niagara Falls. But he specifically
exempts Mallarmé (1) — " un esprit distingué, qui a écrit de fort

---

(1) Mallarmé was an ardent admirer both of Zola's novels and of his plays.
See *Dix-neuf lettres de Stéphane Mallarmé à Emile Zola* with introduction by
Léon Deffoux and commentary by Jean Royère (Paris, 1929) ; and Sté-

beaux vers et dont on peut attendre l'œuvre définitive " — and Verlaine — " incontestablement un très grand poète ". Naturalism, however, will not outlive its practitioners, nor will it be revived in its former shape :

> Donc, c'est entendu, le naturalisme finira quand ceux qui l'incarnent auront disparu. On ne revient pas sur un mouvement, et ce qui lui succédera sera différent, je vous l'ai dit. La matière du roman est un peu épuisée, et pour le ranimer il faudrait un bonhomme !

As to the theater, Zola replies vaguely that one can only wait :

> Rien ne s'est fait du jour au lendemain. On arrive à mettre peu à peu sur la scène des œuvres de vérité de plus en plus grande. Attendons. Le théâtre est toujours en retard sur le reste de la littérature.

At about this time, Zola wrote to André Maurel :

> Maintenant, il est bien certain qu'on me fait un peu trop enterrer le naturalisme. Je n'ai jamais accepté ni pronostiqué si allègrement sa mort. Ce que je crois, c'est que les procédés que j'ai apportés mourront avec moi. Mais quant à la méthode expérimentale, quant à l'évolution scientifique contemporaine, elle est plus vivace que jamais ; et je défie bien un écrivain, s'il la néglige, de rien bâtir actuellement de durable (1).

During this last decade of his life, Zola was torn between, on the one hand, his own profound faith in science and, on the other, the growing idealism reflected around him in the minds of those for whom science had failed to satisfy their early hopes. The last novel of the *Rougon-Macquart* — *le Docteur Pascal* — portrays the moral struggle between the scientific faith of an elderly doctor and the Christian faith of a young woman, and the struggle is continued in Zola's next novel, *Lourdes*, where the protagonists are a devout woman and a doubting priest. Science is the implied victor in both cases, but only after defensive battles in which victory is no longer taken for granted. Naturalism, as Zola conceived it, was the method of science applied to literature. The general weakening of faith in the value of science itself brought with it an antipathy to its literary counter-

phane MALLARMÉ, *Œuvres complètes* (Paris, 1945, Bibliothèque de la Pléiade) : " le Genre ou des Modernes ", pp. 320-321 ; " Notes sur le théâtre ", pp. 344-345 ; " Sur l'évolution littéraire (enquête de Jules Huret) ", p. 87ʌ (Published also in Huret's volume cited above).

(1) Letter dated 30 June 1891, in LES ŒUVRES COMPLÈTES, *Correspondance (1872-1902)*, p. 734.

part, naturalism.   Zola struggled against the tide.   In one of his later *Figaro* articles, entitled " A la Jeunesse ", he wrote defiantly in 1896 :

Rompons d'abord sur le besoin de clarté qui me dévore et sur le goût de l'obscur où vous plongez...
Rompons ensuite sur l'amour que je garde à mon temps... J'ai la faiblesse de n'être pas pour les cités de brume et de songe, les peuples de fantômes errant par les brouillards, tout ce que le vent de l'imagination apporte et emporte...
Et rompons enfin sur mon entêtée croyance au vrai, à la vieille nature, à la jeune science. Tout en elle, rien en dehors d'elle. Ce qu'elle ne sait pas, elle le saura, et ce qu'elle ne saura pas, nous tâcherons que cela reste de l'inconnu, sans devenir de l'erreur. J'ai mis ma foi en la vie, je la crois l'éternellement bonne, l'unique-ouvrière de la santé et de la force. Elle seule est féconde, elle seule travaille à la Cité de demain.
Si je m'entête dans la règle étroite du positivisme, c'est qu'elle est le garde-fou de la démence des esprits, de cet idéalisme qui verse si aisément aux pires perversions, aux plus mortels dangers sociaux. Vous en êtes déjà au mysticisme, au satanisme, à l'occultisme, à la religion qui vit du diable, à l'amour qui ne fait pas d'enfants. Les peuples meurent, quand ils n'aiment plus la vie, quand ils vont par les ténèbres, hurlant à la mort, dans l'affolement du mystère. Seuls, les braves gens font le plus de vérité qu'ils peuvent, donnent leur effort jusqu'au bout, comme les arbres donnent les fruits sains et naturels de la terre ; et il n'est pas de meilleurs citoyens. Nous n'avons donc plus rien de commun, rompons, jeunes gens, rompons au grand jour (1).

He admits, in this same article, that the search for truth has been pushed to an extreme, away from which the trend of literature is now swinging, but predicts that literature will swing back like a pendulum from the opposite extreme of idealism :

Admettons que, pour un moment, la passion du vrai s'atténue. Ne savez-vous pas que le jeu de bascule, dans la littérature, est éternel, que trop de vérité mène à trop de rêve, et que trop de rêve ramène à trop de vérité ?

And he re-affirms his belief in the survival of naturalism :

Il est toujours debout, le fameux naturalisme, le naturalisme que vous dites chaque jour dans la tombe, pour bien vous convaincre qu'il y est. Et la raison de sa vitalité vigoureuse est fort simple, c'est qu'il est la

(1) " A la jeunesse ", in *le Figaro*, 7 February 1896, reprinted in LES ŒUVRES COMPLÈTES, *Nouvelle campagne*, pp. 32-34.

floraison même de l'époque, c'est que lui seul peut pousser dans notre
sol de démocratie et de science...
Quelle revanche vous nous préparez, mes petits ! Si votre moisson
de lis, seule cause des migraines contemporaines, dure quelques années
encore, le naturalisme, ce vilain naturalisme que vous avez mis en terre,
va repousser dru comme les grands blés, nourrisseurs des hommes.

This was still Zola's theory, but even as he was writing these
words, he was in fact and in practice leaving the naturalist
technique aside, both in the novel and in the theater. His faith
in science was as robust as ever, but he was no longer attempting
to apply scientific methods to literature. Naturalism had
ceased to be adequate to express the thought of his maturity.
He resorted increasingly to symbolism and his own brand of
idealism. As Martino states in reference to his last novels :

Et si, après le *Docteur Pascal,* Zola se libéra de la formule naturaliste,
ce fut pour s'obliger aussitôt à une autre formule. *Les Trois Villes* et
les Quatre Évangiles sont des romans de propagande et de foi ; les intentions documentaires y diminuent peu à peu jusqu'à disparaître presque
complètement, à la fin ; l'intention sociale y prend toute la place.
Ç'a été là une des façons dont le naturalisme est mort, une des raisons
de sa fin. Le rêve d'impartialité et d'enquête scientifiques, que compor-
tait la théorie du roman naturaliste, était une gageure impossible.
Documentaire ou non, le roman n'avait rien à faire avec la science (1).

Martino's statement applies equally well to Zola's six final
plays, beginning with *Messidor.* The inception of this trend
may be observed in the first two operas which Bruneau composed
upon his works, *le Rêve* and *l'Attaque du moulin.* Zola did not
participate, except informally, in these first two librettos, but
they served to introduce him to the symbolic and idealist
possibilities of the musical form.

« Le Rêve. » « L'Attaque du Moulin »

Le Rêve, with libretto by Louis Gallet and music by Bruneau,
opened at the *Opéra-Comique* on 18 June 1891, and was an
immediate success. Bruneau's music provoked some discussion,
but the production as a whole was acclaimed as an important
event in the history of French opera. Henry Bauer, commenting

(1) MARTINO, *le Naturalisme français,* p. 88.

on the critical reviews, found that " les plus réservés ne pouvaient se défendre contre l'admiration et avouaient que la représentation du *Rêve* marquait une date " (1). The libretto was described by Charles Darcours as " d'un saisissant intérêt dans sa simplicité, et une émotion croissante s'y développe par l'habile gradation des situations " (2). Auguste Vitu found it " plein de grâce et de fraîcheur " (3). The novel, published in 1888, upon which the opera is based was of course an unexpectedly charming story from Zola's pen. As " Un Monsieur de l'orchestre " points out :

Le *Rêve* est le premier livre d'Émile Zola dont les mères aient pu sans danger permettre la lecture à leurs filles. C'est aussi la première pièce tirée de l'œuvre du maître qu'elles leur permettraient d'aller applaudir (4).

A particular novelty of the work was the modern dress of the actors. According to " Un Monsieur de l'orchestre ", this was only the second production of a musical drama in modern dress, the first having occurred in 1877. But, he goes on to say, the modernity of the costumes was offset by the legendary quality of the work :

Ce qu'il pourrait y avoir de trop moderne, au point de vue musical, dans le *Rêve*, est atténué par le côté légendaire de l'œuvre. Les héros en sont vêtus comme nous, mais ils sont d'une autre chair et d'un autre sang. Ce sont des personnages de missel... On sort de ce spectacle... avec l'impression d'un mystère.

Le *Rêve* was Zola's first attempt to blend reality with idealism. As Henry Bauer stated :

Le drame lyrique de M. Alfred Bruneau marquera date, non seule-

---

(1) In *l'Echo de Paris*, quoted in LES ŒUVRES COMPLÈTES, le *Rêve* (the novel), " Notes et commentaires ", p. 256.
(2) *Ibid.*, p. 257, quoting from the *Figaro*.
(3) *Le Figaro*, 19 June 1891.
(4) *Le Figaro*, 19 June 1891. The " wholesomeness " of le *Rêve* is of course not necessarily a measure of its literary worth. Angus WILSON in his *Emile Zola, an Introductory Study of his Novels*, writes of it at p. 77 : " Le *Rêve*, the novel of purity and beauty, is a forerunner of the novels of his last years with their elevated positive messages and their debased literary worth " ; and at p. 100 : " It is interesting, however, to note how often this novel is selected for special praise by those to whom Zola's work is repugnant, but who yet feel the need to acknowledge his greatness. "
F. W. J. HEMMINGS in *Emile Zola*, pp. 222-223, observes that le *Rêve* is " a product of the same sweetish sentimentality as had dictated the *Contes* and the *Nouveaux Contes à Ninon* ; it was thus not written against the grain of his temperament, but in obedience to a primitive tendency which had long lain neglected ".

ment dans le progrès de la musique, mais pour le mouvement des idées contemporaines. Nulle œuvre récente n'affirme pareil effort vers la parfaite beauté esthétique, par la réunion de deux termes d'apparence contradictoire, la fusion de l'idéal avec la réalité (1).

The novel, *Le Rêve*, was for Zola a significant departure from naturalism. Although he returned to naturalism in completing the *Rougon-Macquart*, there is no doubt that the success of the musical adaptation of this novel encouraged him to attempt further idealist works. As to Zola's own participation in the production, he wrote to J. Van Santen Kolff :

Vous me demandez si j'ai réellement collaboré au livret que Louis Gallet a tiré de mon roman. Je n'aime guère répondre à ces questions-là. Mettez que le plan m'a été soumis et que j'ai donné quelques conseils (2).

Bruneau's biography confirms the fact of Zola's participation. Speaking of his collaboration with Gallet, he writes : " Nous établîmes ensemble, sur les indications précises de Zola, le scénario du *Rêve* (3). " Zola made some minor changes in the final text, " avec une adresse délicate destinée à ménager la susceptibilité de Gallet " (4). He made sketches of the scenery for the designers and attended rehearsals (5). Further confirmation may be found in several letters which Bruneau wrote to Zola in 1888 and 1889 (6).

Following its success at the *Opéra-Comique*, le *Rêve* was produced in a number of European centers, and has been revived from time to time in Paris (7).

The adaptation of Zola's celebrated short story, *l'Attaque du moulin*, opened at the *Opéra-Comique* on 23 November 1893, with book by Gallet and music by Bruneau. Zola assisted again with the libretto, perhaps still more than in the case of le *Rêve*. In June of 1892, he wrote to Bruneau :

Je vous envoie enfin les quelques vers que je vous ai fait attendre.

(1) *L'Echo de Paris*, quoted in LES ŒUVRES COMPLÈTES, le *Rêve*, " Notes et commentaires ", p. 257.
(2) In *Emile Zola's Letters to J. Van Santen Kolff*, edited by Robert Judson NIESS (Saint-Louis, 1940). The quoted portion of this letter does not appear in LES ŒUVRES COMPLÈTES, which gives only a fragment of the letter.
(3) BRUNEAU, *A l'ombre d'un grand cœur*, p. 20.
(4) *Ibid.*, p. 21.
(5) *Ibid.*, p. 32. As to Zola's attendance at rehearsals, see the account of Un monsieur de l'orchestre, in le *Figaro*, 19 June 1891.
(6) *Correspondance Emile Zola*, t. II, feuillets 162, 164, 165.
(7) Programs of several revivals are to be found in the *Collection théâtrale Auguste Rondel*, RF 49125, Bibliothèque de l'Arsenal.

Pour les strophes sur le couteau, j'ai cru devoir briser le rythme et affecter un peu de prosaïsme, de façon à éviter la romance. Il m'a semblé que de la netteté et de la vigueur suffisaient. Au contraire, pour les adieux à la forêt, j'ai élargi le ton jusqu'au lyrisme. C'était ce que vous désiriez, n'est-ce pas ? Dites-le moi franchement, si vous désiriez autre chose. Je n'ai que l'envie de vous contenter, avec mes mauvais vers de mirliton.

J'envoie une copie des deux morceaux à Gallet, en le prévenant que, pour gagner du temps, je vous les adresse directement. Je pense qu'il ne se blessera pas. Je lui dis aussi que vous êtes pressé et que j'attends les troisième et quatrième actes (1).

And a month later :

Je vous envoie le troisième acte. J'ai eu simplement à modifier certains vers. Il me paraît bien, toujours un peu court, un peu sec. Mais cela vaut peut-être mieux pour la rapidité, la netteté de l'œuvre. Seulement, je vous conseille fort d'élargir tout cela par des flots de musique. Il faut que vous mettiez là-dedans toute la puissance, toute l'envolée qui n'y est pas ; autrement, nous aurons une œuvre bien étroite. — Quelques petites observations : le cri des sentinelles doit être un *oh ! oh !* modulé et repris ; les chœurs des jeunes filles m'effrayent un peu et vous devriez en donner chaque phrase, sinon à des voix différentes, au moins à des groupes différents ; enfin, je voudrais beaucoup de mimique, avec de la belle musique par-dessous, entre les scènes proprement dites, et au lever du rideau, et pendant le travail des moissonneuses, et avant et après la scène de la sentinelle, et surtout pendant ce qui précède et ce qui suit le meurtre. De la musique, beaucoup de musique (2) !

Bruneau quotes these two letters in his biography : " Afin de renseigner ceux à qui des gens mal documentés glissèrent dans l'oreille que Zola fut insensible aux arts de la mélodie et de la polyphonie (3). " Letters from Bruneau and Gallet to Zola confirm the latter's participation in the musical drama (4). According to Le Blond, editor of LES ŒUVRES COMPLÈTES, the words of the song, " Les adieux à la forêt ", were written entirely by Zola (5).

For the musical adaptation, an important new character was introduced who did not appear in the original story — an old

---

(1) Letter dated 6 June 1892, in LES ŒUVRES COMPLÈTES, *Correspondance (1872-1902)*, pp. 746-747.
(2) Letter dated 8 July 1892, *ibid.*, pp. 748-749.
(3) BRUNEAU, *A l'ombre d'un grand cœur*, pp. 49-51.
(4) *Correspondance Emile Zola*, t. III, feuillets 180, 189, 192, 193, 195, 197-198 ; t. X, feuillets 255, 256-257, 260-261, 278-279.
(5) LES ŒUVRES COMPLÈTES, *le Rêve* (the novel), " la Collaboration avec Alfred Bruneau ", p. 260.

family servant, Marcelline, personifying, somewhat in the manner
of a Greek chorus, woman's hatred of war. This character, in
the words of " Un Monsieur de l'orchestre ", " éclaire tout le
drame, en résume admirablement la philosophie " (1). The
ending of the story was altered for the play. The Père Merlier
of the drama sacrifices himself for his daughter's fiancé, Domi-
nique, and the latter, unaware of the sacrifice, does not lose his
life. The change mitigates only slightly the tragic mood of the
opera, which, like the story terminates with the French captain's
ironic cry of " Victoire ! ". It was deemed prudent not to show
Prussian uniforms on the stage, and the time of the story was
accordingly set back to the revolutionary period of the preceding
century, with the hostile soldiers designated simply as the
" enemy ".

While this opera was far more dramatic than *le Rêve*, the
critics in general showed themselves less favorably disposed
to it (2). However, the production evoked some extremely
favorable comments, as, for example, that by Charles Darcours :

> On demandait le « drame lyrique » : le voilà dans tout son réalisme,
> et son apparition a valu, hier, à l'Opéra-Comique, une sensationnelle
> soirée et une éclatante réussite...
> Tel est le drame saisissant que M. Louis Gallet a tiré de la nouvelle
> de M. Zola, drame développé avec une science remarquable du théâtre,
> et qui impressionnera jusqu'aux intelligences les plus primitives, car il
> est établi sur des sentiments profondément humains (3).

Immediately prior to the opening night, *le Journal* printed a
long article by Zola (published in LES ŒUVRES COMPLÈTES in the
volume *Mélanges, Préfaces et Discours* under the title, " Le
drame lyrique "), in which Zola advocates the improvement of
operatic librettos. The article begins with a tribute to Bruneau :

> Sur le tard de ma vie, je me suis intéressé à la musique, ayant fait
> la rencontre heureuse d'Alfred Bruneau, une des intelligences les plus
> vives, un des passionnés et des tendres les plus pénétrants que j'ai
> connus.

The new form of the " drame lyrique " has replaced the old-
fashioned grand opera, and for this new form, the musical

---

(1) *Le Figaro*, 24 November 1893.
(2) According to LE BLOND, LES ŒUVRES COMPLÈTES, *le Rêve, ibid.*,
p. 260. Some extracts from the critics' reviews are given at pp. 265-267.
(3) *Le Figaro*, 24 November 1893.

composer must be able to rely upon a good libretto, in which Zola believes :

... il doit y avoir un milieu nettement indiqué et des personnages vivants, en un mot, une action humaine que le rôle du musicien est uniquement de commenter et de développer.

Wagner weighs upon the spirits of contemporary musicians, who may despair of surpassing him, and Wagner cannot be ignored. His renovation of musical drama must be assimilated, but instead of containing themselves within his discoveries, composers should seek to go forward. Zola indicates the path of progression :

Je vois un drame plus directement humain non pas dans le vague des mythologies du Nord, mais éclatant entre nous, pauvres hommes, dans la réalité de nos misères et de nos joies. Je ne suis pas à demander l'opéra en redingote ou même en blouse. Non ! il me suffirait qu'au lieu de antoches, au lieu d'abstractions descendues de la légende, on nous donnât des êtres vivants, s'égayant de nos gaietés, souffrant de nos souffrances. Et je voudrais encore que tout poème intéressât par lui-même comme une histoire passionnante qu'on nous raconterait. On peut l'habiller de velours, si l'on veut ; mais qu'il y ait des hommes dedans, et que de toute l'œuvre sorte un cri profond d'humanité.

Voilà le mot lâché. Je rêve que le drame lyrique soit humain, sans répudier ni la fantaisie, ni le caprice, ni le mystère. Toute notre race est là, je le répète, dans cette humanité frémissante dont je voudrais que la musique traduisît les passions, les douleurs et les joies (1).

The enterprising Huret — " notre subtil Jules Huret ", as Bruneau describes him (2) — remembered that Zola's *l'Attaque du moulin* had appeared in 1880 in the volume *les Soirées de Médan* along with short stories by five younger writers who were then devoted to him — Maupassant, Huysmans, Hennique, Céard and Alexis. On the day after the opening of *l'Attaque du moulin* at the *Opéra-Comique*, Huret published interviews with the surviving members of this group (Maupassant having died), of whom he had somewhat maliciously enquired :

... s'ils ne se trouvent pas un peu peinés, un peu humiliés, peut-être, de voir la nouvelle qui a servi de drapeau, de manifeste à l'École réaliste, réduite jusqu'à entrer dans le moule de l'Opéra-Comique, qui, dans la

(1) This article is in LES ŒUVRES COMPLÈTES, *Mélanges, Préfaces et Discours*, " le Drame lyrique ", pp. 148-154. The quotations are at pp. 148, 149 and 152.
(2) BRUNEAU, *A l'ombre d'un grand cœur*, p. 66.

convention, semble une formule inférieure de l'adaptation littéraire ?
En même temps il pouvait être curieux de questionner les hommes
qui, il y a treize ans, livrèrent la même bataille, sur leur désillusion
devant la séparation dans la vie et la variation esthétique et philosophique de certains d'entre eux ; par la même occasion, de savoir comment
ils jugent la nouvelle attitude de leur ancien maître, ses manifestations
officielles, ses présidences, sa candidature à l'Académie, etc. (1).

To Huysmans, the theater is the lowest of all the arts, and he
finds it curious that, in his words : " Zola meurt d'envie de ne
plus s'occuper que de théâtre. " He is astonished, too, that
Zola should seek entrance to the French Academy, after having
been scornful of it for so long. Nevertheless, he concludes :

N'importe, en somme, l'œuvre de Zola reste au-dessus de ces petites
choses-là, et lui, personnellement, demeure un brave homme.

Hennique, having attended a rehearsal of *l'Attaque du moulin*,
describes it as a mediocre, unrecognizable adaptation — " un
mélo quelconque " — which left him absolutely cold. He, too,
is surprised that Zola should want to be an academician.

As to Céard, nothing which Zola does can surprise him.
Zola's driving force is the will to conquer. " Voyez toute son
œuvre ; le mot CONQUÊTE y est répété sans cesse, et s'il est allé à
l'Opéra-Comique, croyez-le bien, c'est pour *conquérir* encore. "

Only Alexis, the most faithful of Zola's friends, gives full
approval to his artistic and honorific aspirations. " Liberté
pour tous, même pour Zola ! "

On the following day, the *Figaro* published Zola's reply,
which the editor of the newspaper described as " pleine d'habile
et charmante mélancolie " :

Mon cher Confrère, Répondre, grand Dieu ! Fouiller dans le tiroir
aux vieilles lettres d'amour, remuer la poussière sacrée des tombes !
Ah ! non ! Mon cœur saignerait trop ! Mes vieux amis des *Soirées de
Médan* ont tous un très grand talent que j'admire. Je les ai beaucoup
aimés, et je les aime beaucoup (2).

---

(1) These interviews by HURET appeared in *le Figaro*, 24 November 1893,
and are reprinted in his book : Jules HURET, *Tout yeux, tout oreilles* (Paris, 1901),
pp. 173-181.
    Huret's mention of Zola's " nouvelle attitude " refers to Zola's apparent
aspirations to respectability. In 1891, he was made president of the *Société
des Gens de Lettres*, and beginning in 1890, he presented himself repeatedly
and unsuccessfully as a candidate before the French Academy, failing of
election in 1890, 1891, 1892, 1894, 1896 and 1897.
    (2) *Le Figaro*, 25 November 1893.

L'Attaque du moulin was played in Brussels and London (1), and has been revived with the 1870 setting of the story. According to Le Blond, these revivals were more poignant and more successful than the original Paris production (2).

« Messidor »

Messidor, for which Zola alone wrote the libretto, opened at the *Opéra* on 19 February 1897 (3). The event was so important that the *Figaro* allotted nearly four columns of its front page to separate articles by Zola and Bruneau, in which each explained what he sought to accomplish (4). Zola's opening statement explains the theme of the play :

Ce que j'ai voulu faire ?

Donner le poème du travail, la nécessité et la beauté de l'effort, la foi en la vie, en la fécondité de la terre, l'espoir aux justes moissons de demain. Imaginez, dans notre pays d e France, un village, des montagnes où les ruisseaux roulent d e l'or et dont les habitants ont vécu jusqu'à ce jour de la récolte de cet or ; et, là, faire qu'un d'eux ait capté tout l'or, en détournant les ruisseaux, ce qui a ruiné le village entier ; et, dans une catastrophe, anéantir l'or, rendre l'eau à la moisson du blé, lorsque, de laveurs d'or qu'ils étaient, les hommes sont devenus des laboureurs.

Then, after a detailed summary of the action, he concludes :

Le symbole ici, est d'une telle clarté, que les enfants le comprendront. Je crois que le rôle du poète est de don ner au musicien un large thème où se développent les idées générales, les grands sentiments humains. J'ai pris un sujet brûlant, tout actuel, je l'ai traité dans un milieu simple et coloré, et, bien que le faisant se passer d e nos jours, j'ai cru devoir y faire la part de la légende. Véronique, c'est l'antique foi, si grande encore, et qui attend d'être remplacée par la foi nouvelle. Au dénouement, quand elle chante la vie et sa fécondité, elle indique elle-même où va la

(1) BRUNEAU, *A l'ombre d'un grand cœur,* pp. 69, 88.
(2) LES ŒUVRES COMPLÈTES, *le Rêve,* " la Collaboration avec Alfred Bruneau ", p. 260.
(3) By some writers, the date of the opening is erroneously given as 15 February.
(4) " Messidor appliqué par les auteurs " (" le Poème ", by ZOLA ; " la Musique ", by BRUNEAU), in *le Figaro,* 20 February 1897. Zola's article is reproduced in full in BRUNEAU, *A l'ombre d'un grand cœur,* pp. 92-99. A short fragment from each of these articles is given in LES ŒUVRES COMPLÈTES, *le Rêve,* " la Collaboration avec Alfred Bruneau ", pp. 261-262.

croyance. C'est le laboureur Guillaume qui triomphe, c'est Hélène l'aimée, la nécessaire, qui enfantera demain. Et, après la mort du destructeur Mathias, après la grande poésie noire du néant, c'est le berger qui retourne là-haut, dans la lumière, pour conduire les hommes au grand air pur de la santé et de la joie.

Je serai simplement heureux, si j'ai donné au musicien l'occasion d'affirmer cette joie, cette santé, l'éternelle fertilité heureuse, le grand soleil clair et puissant de notre vieille terre de France.

At the time of *l'Attaque du moulin*, Zola had acknowledged the importance of Wagner's revolution in lyric drama, but had recommended that it be a point of departure for greater humanization of the characters. Wagner should not be slavishly imitated by French composers, he repeated in an interview in connection with *Messidor*, but should serve as a model for the expression of the national temperament :

La formule wagnérienne, est, je le répète, la meilleure qui soit ; elle est, de beaucoup, supérieure à celles qui l'ont précédée. Mais elle correspond à un tempérament particulier. Nous avons notre tempérament, nous aussi, les Latins. Est-ce que nous ne pouvons pas tirer de la formule wagnérienne, ce qui en fait l'incontestable supériorité, et la transformer, la modifier, l'améliorer dans le sens de notre génie national (1) ?

The legendary elements of *Messidor* were undoubtedly inspired by Wagner. As the critic Fourcaud observed in a letter to Zola published in *le Gaulois* : " ... sans la révolution qu'il a faite vous n'eussiez jamais conçu votre *Messidor* dans sa forme légendaire... " (2).

All six of Zola's librettos are in lyric prose. *Messidor*, one of the first operas based on a prose libretto (3), set loose an extensive controversy as to the relative merits of prose and verse in operatic works. Among other musicians, Widor and d'Indy pleaded in favor of prose, Saint-Saëns against it (4). It is not certain whether the choice of prose was at Zola's or at Bruneau's behest. On the one hand, Zola stated in an interview :

Mon opinion est moins arrêtée en ce qui concerne la substitution de la prose au vers, pour l'écriture du livret. *Messidor* est en prose. Bruneau

---

(1) Quoted in LES ŒUVRES COMPLÈTES, *le Rêve, ibid.*, p. 261, from an interview in *le Temps*, February 1897.
(2) " Réponse à M. Emile Zola ", in *le Gaulois*, 25 February 1897.
(3) Other early prose librettos are listed by Etienne DESTRANGES in his *Messidor d'A. Bruneau, étude analytique et critique* (Paris, 1897), pp. 12-13.
(4) According to BRUNEAU, *A l'ombre d'un grand cœur*, p. 102.

estime que le vers a le tort d'introduire un rythme particulier dans un autre rythme. Il s'y connaît mieux que moi (1).

Bruneau, on the other hand, implies in his biography that the choice was Zola's :

> Depuis l'achèvement de *l'Attaque du moulin*, nous n'avions cessé de songer à d'autres pièces qui, signées de Zola seul, resserreraient encore davantage notre collaboration déjà si intime. Mais il nous fallait substituer aux vers, usuels alors en matière de livret, la prose, qui était considérée généralement comme l'ennemie barbare de la musique, *et que Zola entendait uniquement employer* [italics ours] (2).

In any case, the collaborators were in perfect agreement. Bruneau goes on to explain that he was willing to use prose on the authority of Gounod :

> Moi, je ne partageais point ces préventions et je me rappelais la page où, à propos de *Georges Dandin*, Gounod — l'opposé d'un sot, n'est-ce pas ? — avait dit, très sensément, je crois, que « la variété infinie des périodes en prose ouvre devant le musicien un horizon tout neuf qui le délivre de la monotonie et de l'uniformité, qu'avec le vers — espèce de *dada* qui, une fois parti, emmène le compositeur, lequel se laisse conduire nonchalamment et finit par s'endormir dans une négligence déplorable — le musicien devient en quelque sorte l'esclave du dialogue au lieu d'en rester le maître, et que la vérité de l'expression disparaît sous l'entraînement banal de la routine ; que la prose, au contraire, est une mine féconde, inépuisable de variété dans l'intonation chantée ou déclamée, dans la durée et dans l'intensité de l'accent, dans la proportion et le développement de la période... ». Nous n'hésitâmes point à adopter désormais le principe de la prose, à braver les disputes qu'allait provoquer notre tentative (3).

Messidor is unlike anything which Zola had written theretofore, and foreshadows his novel *Fécondité* (published in 1899). In his work notes to *Fécondité*, he wrote :

> Je puis contenter mon lyrisme, me jeter dans la fantaisie, me permettre tous les sauts d'imagination dans le rêve et l'espoir. Je voudrais un optimisme éclatant. C'est la conclusion naturelle de toute mon œuvre : après la longue constatation de la réalité, une prolongation sans demain, et d'une façon logique, mon amour de la force et de la santé, de la fécondité et du travail. Je suis content surtout de pouvoir changer

---

(1) Interview in *le Temps*, quoted in LES ŒUVRES COMPLÈTES, *le Rêve*, *ibid.*, p. 261.
(2) BRUNEAU, *A l'ombre d'un grand cœur*, pp. 71-72.
(3) *Ibid.*, p. 72.

ma manière, de pouvoir me livrer à tout mon lyrisme et à toute mon imagination (1).

Messidor was undertaken in this spirit. It is a drama of pronounced social meaning, based on the theme of fertility, human and terrestrial, and ending in a mood of optimism with the rogation blessing of the fertile wheat fields. The principal characters are the old mother Véronique, symbol of superstition and fatalism, her son Guillaume, the laborer, her nihilist nephew, Mathias (the " villain " of the drama), the rich man, Gaspard, and his daughter, Hélène. The opera has four acts, representing the four seasons, and a separate ballet entitled " La Légende de l'or ". The locale is a village in the Pyrenees, whose inhabitants formerly made a living by washing gold from the river sands. The first act takes place in a summer of drought and famine. The scene is Véronique's house. Véronique reminds her son of the happy days of hand-labor, before the advent of the machine. Then she explains to him :

Il a fallu qu'un des nôtres, notre ancien voisin Gaspard, mordu par l'enragé désir des richesses, ne se contentant pas de l'antique lavage à la main, eût l'idée d'établir une usine, en amont du torrent. Et il a tari nos ruisseaux, et il n'y a plus de l'or que pour lui... Ah ! qu'il soit damné, lui qui nous a ruinés tous !

But Guillaume proudly answers that he has become a tiller of the soil :

Oui, le laveur d'or que j'étais est devenu le laboureur. Le lit desséché du torrent est aujourd'hui le champ que j'ensemence, et j'attends que mon travail obstiné fasse du sable une terre nourricière... Puisque la moisson d'or a disparu, que pousse donc un jour la grande moisson du blé !

(Act I, scene II.)

Mathias arrives from the city, filled with nihilist ideas of vengeance and total destruction. Véronique, with her antique sense of fate, feels that destruction is useless : " A quoi bon ? Ce ne sont pas les hommes qui font la justice, c'est le destin. " Here, legend and superstition enter the play, as she describes the mythical cathedral of gold :

Ne savez-vous donc pas, tous deux, d'où vient cet or qui roule dans

(1) Quoted in ZÉVAÈS, *Zola*, p. 220.

les eaux ? Là-bas, parmi les grands rocs écroulés, au bout d'un long couloir que nul ne connaît, il est une salle immense, une cathédrale d'or,
où jamais vivant n'est entré.
Et là, sur les genoux de la Vierge, l'Enfant Jésus est assis. Et,
c'est lui, avec un rire de gamin joueur, qui, prenant à poignées le sable
le laisse retomber de ses petites mains divines, dans l'eau claire de la
source, éternellement. Et le sable, toujours, se change en une poudre
d'or, qui s'en va au fil de l'eau, charriée dans tous les ruisseaux de nos
montagnes.
Mais, si quelqu'un trouvait le couloir, si jamais quelqu'un pénétrait
dans la cathédrale d'or, tout disparaîtrait, s'écroulerait au fond de la
terre ; et il n'y aurait plus d'or, et nos ruisseaux ne rouleraient plus d'or.

Véronique alone believes in the myth. But this is not the
only legendary aspect of the play. There is also a magic gold
necklace, which she describes as follows :

Est-ce donc aussi un conte que le collier d'or qui me reste ; l'or
unique que j'ai gardé dans notre misère est un collier magique, donnant
la joie et la beauté aux êtres purs, forçant les coupables à se livrer ?
(Elle va chercher le collier et le montre.)
J'en ai fermé moi-même les chaînons, en disant, sous la pleine lune
de Noël, les paroles secrètes que ma mère m'a transmises.

(Act I, scene iii.)

Gaspard, whose factory has brought destitution to the village,
enters with Hélène, fainting from thirst, and begs a glass of water
for his daughter. Guillaume, against his mother's command,
offers her the precious water, symbolic of the life-giving and
fertilizing force of nature, more divine than gold. After they
have gone, he sings of his love for the young girl in terms which
reveal Zola's theme of fertility :

Non, non ! la maison est vide et sans enfants, le blé refuse de pousser
dans la terre stérile, notre solitude n'a pour hôtesse que la misère. Et je
l'aime, et je l'attends, et elle est la seule qui fécondera le travail, qui
fera pousser les grands blés, qui emplira la vieille maison de beaux
enfants rieurs... Oh ! ma mère, c'est l'amour qui fait la vie, l'amour qui
embrase tout, sans lequel rien ne se crée. Je l'aime, elle est ma joie,
ma force et ma fécondité !

(Act I, scene v.)

But his mother points out that there is an impediment to
their marriage. Guillaume's father was found dead at the foot
of a precipice under circumstances which indicated that he was
murdered by Hélène's father. However, the audience is given a

clue that the murderer may have been Mathias, as, indeed, turns
out to be the case.
The theme of fertility returns at the beginning of the second
act, season of the autumn planting.

GUILLAUME

... Ah ! si la pluie tombait, si la terre enfin, épaissie et forte, se gonflait
de vie !
Demain, au lever du soleil, je serai là, j'ensemencerai une fois encore
ce champ de cailloux, cette terre stérile que mon travail s'entête à
féconder... Et que de peine toujours ! et quel besoin d'éternel espoir !

And in a scene between the lovers :

HÉLÈNE

Toi seul feras de moi l'épouse heureuse, la mère féconde.

GUILLAUME

Oui, cela doit être pour que l'éternelle vie triomphe.

HÉLÈNE

Et pour que l'amour donne sa vivante moisson de bonheur.

(Act II, scene III.)

Hélène's wealth is a further impediment to their love : " Cet
or maudit, qui me gâte jusqu'à mon amour ! " But she devotes
herself as much as possible to works of charity : " L'or n'a que
cette divine consolation, il fait de la bonté, il soulage " (Act II,
scene IV).
Mathias has called a meeting of the villagers to discuss an
attack upon the factory. The Shepherd tries to quiet the
crowd :

Je suis le gardien solitaire. Je redescends de très loin, de très haut,
avec mes bêtes. Et je ne comprends pas, et je redoute la colère brusque
qui vous emporte... La souffrance, ah ! grand Dieu ! elle est éternelle
comme le monde, et il faut la combattre d'un cœur vaillant d'homme
juste... *(Montrant Mathias.)* Mais pourquoi donc écoutez-vous celui-ci,
qui n'est plus des nôtres, qui nous rapporte des villes lointaines d'abo-
minables rancunes ?

Guillaume, however, has gone over temporarily to Mathias'
side, and denounces the love of gold in an impassioned appeal :

C'est la passion de l'or qui nous a tous changés en loups, les dévorants,

les affamés, les misérables gens que nous sommes... Rappelez-vous,
le pays vivait dans le travail, dans la tendresse et dans la joie ; et,
depuis que Gaspard a voulu être le plus riche, le seul riche, il n'y a que
haine, que souffrances et que larmes... Prenez donc des bâtons, et que
l'usine soit détruite, et que la poussière en soit semée aux quatre vents
du ciel !

(Act II, scene v.)

Véronique tries to restrain the crowd — " le destin seul est le
maître " — and announces that she will look for the cathedral
of gold (in which she alone believes), and by the act of finding it,
destroy gold forever. The crowd disperses, leaving Guillaume
alone. He resumes his sowing, and the act ends upon the theme
of fertility :

Semence auguste, blé nourrisseur, va, va, vole de mes mains, et
couvre la terre. Comme la poussière même de la vie, vole, vole, emplis
le sillon de ta fécondité. Tu es l'inconnu de demain ; qui sait le triomphe
que tu réserves à l'effort de mon travail ? Pendant tout un hiver, la
terre froide dormira. Et elle couvera ton inconnu, ô divine semence,
blé qui nourris les hommes ! Et peut-être pousseras-tu en une moisson
débordante, au soleil d'avril, dans le printemps triomphal.

The next scene, in the intention of the authors, was that
of the ballet, " La Légende de l'or ", in the legendary cathedral
of gold. However, scenic difficulties induced the directors of
the *Opéra* to play it as a prologue preceding Act I, a decision
which Bruneau described as " détestable " (1). For the revival
of *Messidor* in 1917, the ballet was restored to its proper position
following Act II.

The scene of the ballet suggests the nave of a Gothic cathedral
hewn in a great rock of gold. In the apse is a large statue of the
Virgin bearing the Christ-Child on her lap, from whose outstret-
ched hands flow two streams of golden dust. The curtain rises
upon two groups of dancers, one led by the Queen — " une
danseuse noble, altière, souveraine, qui incarne le désir humain
du pouvoir et de la domination " — the other by " l'Amante "
— " une danseuse belle, désirable, voluptueuse, qui incarne le
désir humain de la possession et de toutes les jouissances char-
nelles ". Then Gold is born, personified by a ballerina. Gold
is wooed in turn by the leader of each of the two groups. " L'humanité entière est là, le désir du pouvoir et le désir de l'amour ;
et l'un et l'autre, pour se contenter, ont besoin de l'or. " As

(1) BRUNEAU, *A l'ombre d'un grand cœur*, p. 90.

to the Queen : " Si elle avait l'or, elle achèterait tous les hommes, elle serait la maîtresse du monde. " As to " l'Amante " ; " ... c'est avec l'or qu'on satisfait tous les appétits, qu'on goûte toutes les jouissances. Si elle avait l'or, elle achèterait tous les baisers, elle ferait du monde un brûlant et unique baiser ".

Gold is indifferent to both groups, who engage in mutual combat until the Queen and " l'Amante " fall exhausted at her feet. She then becomes the Gold of Charity and the Gold of Beauty. Here Zola has expressed his idea of the highest uses of gold :

L'or a ce privilège sacré de pouvoir secourir, de faire des heureux, en soulageant la misère... il s'arrête à la fin devant la reine et devant l'amante ; et il les relève, il leur explique qu'il est l'or de charité, que son plus beau titre est le bien qu'il permet de faire, ce qui est son excuse de toutes les folies qu'il éveille et de tous les crimes dont il est la cause.

Puis, il leur enseigne aussi qu'il est l'or de beauté, et c'est comme or de beauté qu'il veut être adoré. L'or qui flambe au soleil et qui embellit, le métal précieux dont sont faits les bijoux des femmes et les couronnes des rois. L'or esthétique, image de la splendeur et de la richesse, symbole de toute beauté et de toute puissance.

Véronique enters : " Enfin, je te vois, ô splendeur de l'or. Et que tout s'écroule ! " With a clap of thunder, the vision disappears.

The third act is in Gaspard's factory during a winter storm. An enormous wheel actually turns on the stage. Guillaume at first sides with the crowd who have come to destroy the factory :

GASPARD

Que voulez-vous ?

GUILLAUME

Nous voulons qu'un seul n'ait pas le droit de prendre aux autres la fortune de la terre, qui est notre mère à tous.

GASPARD, *gaiement*

Eh ! mon ami, est-il défendu d'avoir plus d'intelligence et d'activité que les autres ?

GUILLAUME

Il est défendu de prendre à son voisin l'eau qui passe et qui fait vivre.

GASPARD

Mais c'est l'eau qui, d'elle-même, est venue à moi, pareille à la femme désirée, qui va au plus fort, à celui qui la fécondera.

GUILLAUME

Vous l'avez retenue, vous nous l'avez volée.

Hélène persuades Guillaume to restrain the crowd, which turns for leadership to Mathias. Before they can begin their attack, the storm culminates in an avalanche which destroys the factory. Legend and reality join as Véronique enters and exclaims : " Dieu a fait justice ! " The final act is a paean to fertility, set in late spring. Guillaume exults over the bountiful crop of wheat :

Ah ! oui, le travail a vaincu, mon dur travail qui s'obstinait à féconder le sol ingrat... Mais l'eau a fait le prodige. Depuis que le torrent s'est abîmé en terre, l'eau cachée ruisselle sous les champs de ce vallon ; elle trempe, elle baigne les germes, et de là naît cette fécondité formidable... L'eau en emportant l'or maudit, nous a donné le blé, le blé auguste, le blé nourrisseur des hommes !

(Act IV, scene i.)

The evil of Mathias is recognized. With a cry of hatred, the destroyer throws himself from the precipice, and his passing brings joy and relief to the villagers. Gold has disappeared, except for the magic necklace, symbolizing the Gold of Beauty and of Tenderness. There is no further obstacle to the young lovers. The opera ends with their betrothal and with the blessing of the wheat by the priest, accompanied by the rogation procession :

Véronique

Cher fils, chère fille, c'est l'amour qui fait la vie, lui seul est la sève du monde. Aimez-vous, soyez la joie, la force et la fécondité.

La procession, *en scène*

Ut fructus terrae dare et conservare digneris, te rogamus, audi nos.

Le prêtre, *bénissant les blés*

Domine, exaudi orationem meam.

La procession et toute la foule

Et clamor meus ad te veniat.

(Tous sont à genoux, et le prêtre achève de bénir les blés, d'un geste large, qui emplit l'horizon.)

Bruneau's music was widely praised while the libretto, which Zola had published prior to the opening and which critics were able to study in detail, evoked mixed reactions. A typical criticism was that by Fourcaud, who objected to Zola's mixture of incompatible elements (legend and reality), to his misuse of symbolism, and to the falsity of the dialogue with respect to characters speaking Zola's language rather than their own (1). Zola replied, denying that his characters spoke his own language, and insisting that, in any case, his drama was lyric and symbolic, and not intended as realism :

> Il n'est pas exact que tous mes personnages parlent ma langue. Je me suis efforcé, au contraire, de donner à chaque personnage sa langue propre. Et vous l'auriez sans doute vu si vous ne vous étiez pas forgé je ne sais quelle idée préconcue d'un poème réaliste. Pourquoi réaliste ? Qui vous a parlé de cela ? C'est un poème lyrique, et très lyrique, des personnages d'épopée, que j'ai voulus aussi grands que ceux d'Homère, une action très haute, très générale, exaltée en plein symbole. Vous me jugez donc bien sot, si vous vous imaginez que j'ai fait parler là des paysans (2).

And he suggests that Fourcaud dislikes his libretto because, from a social and philosophical point of view, it is the negation of Wagner's mysticism. He continues :

> Le mysticisme wagnérien, nous y voilà donc ! La légende nécessaire, les dieux d'un olympe quelconque, le salut par l'au-delà, dans la défaite de la bonne nature ! Ce sont toutes les perversions fatales, l'amour aboutissant à la mort, les sexes eux-mêmes inutiles et inféconds, la religion du renoncement poussée jusqu'à ce point louche où la virginité devient le crime humain, l'assassinat même de la vie.
>
> Et vous avez raison alors de ne pas m'admettre dans votre formule, car j'ai horreur de ce mysticisme wagnérien. Dites-le, soyez franc, vous ne voulez pas de moi dans le temple de Parsifal, et vous avez raison. Car je suis pour l'amour qui enfante, pour la mère et non pour la vierge ; car je ne crois qu'à la santé, qu'à la vie et qu'à la joie ; car je n'ai mis mon espérance que dans notre travail humain, dans l'antique effort des peuples qui labourent la bonne terre et qui en tireront les futures moissons du bonheur ; car tout mon sang de Latin se révolte contre ces brumes perverses du Nord et ne veut que des héros humains de lumière et de vérité.

Fourcaud's reply a few days later (3) missed the point of Zola's explanation. The characters do not, as Fourcaud observed, speak according to their condition in life, as real peasants — but they each have their " langue propre " in the sense that each expresses his own aspirations, elevated to the level of poetry.

Admirers of Zola's prior works were unprepared for so

---

(1) In *le Gaulois*, 20 February 1897.
(2) " Une lettre de M. Emile Zola ", in *le Gaulois*, 23 February 1897. This letter is reproduced, except for an unimportant first paragraph, in BRUNEAU's, *A l'ombre d'un grand cœur*, pp. 99-102.
(3) " Réponse à M. Emile Zola ", *le Gaulois*, 25 February 1897.

extreme a departure from naturalism. As one of them complained : " Comment surtout l'admirable auteur de *Germinal* et de *la Terre* n'a-t-il fait de ses personnages que des entités symboliques, confusément raisonnantes, au lieu de leur insuffler la simple vie dont il s'est montré dans ses romans si large et si puissant dispensateur (1) ? " *Messidor* defies analysis in terms of realism. The settings, the characters, the incidents, the language and the legends all have symbolic values, resulting in a work intended to be larger than life, soaring on the wings of music above the plane of real existence. Thus many of the criticisms directed at *Messidor* as though it were a realistic work are frivolous in the light of its symbolic character.

Messidor was played in Brussels and Munich (2), and revived at the *Opéra* in February 1917. Following publication in *l'Aurore* of Zola's letter *J'accuse* (13 January 1898), riots outside of the opera-house at each performance of *Messidor* caused the work to be withdrawn (3).

« L'Ouragan »

L'Ouragan, a lyric drama in four acts with libretto by Zola and music by Bruneau, opened at the *Opéra-Comique* on 29 April 1901. The authors expressed their intentions in a program note, in which they said, in part :

... C'est l'ouragan de nos passions qui, tout d'un coup, sans raison, souffle dans notre ciel bleu, dans le train ordinaire de notre vie, qui saccage et emporte tout, jusqu'au retour du joyeux soleil, nous laissant dévastés, saignants, devant l'existence qui recommence. L'horizon de nouveau se déroule, le voyageur se remet en marche pour l'infini, pour l'inconnu des vastes mers.

L'action se passe, dit le poème, « dans l'île de Goël ». Il est inutile de chercher cette île sur la carte, on ne l'y trouverait pas. Elle est partout et nulle part, l'intention des auteurs a été de la situer dans le temps et dans l'espace pour qu'elle soit de toutes les nations et de toutes les époques. Il leur a semblé que leur drame humain gagnerait en simplicité, en clarté et en force, à rester de l'humanité pure, qu'aucune contingence ne complique ni ne date. Leur île est là-bas, où des couples aiment, souffrent, pleurent et espèrent, dans la tourmente de leurs cœurs et des

(1) Georges HARTMANN, in *l'Illustration*, quoted in Les Œuvres complètes, *le Rêve, ibid.*, pp. 267-268.
(2) BRUNEAU, *A l'ombre d'un grand cœur*, pp. 120, 206.
(3) According to BRUNEAU, *ibid.*, p. 114.

éléments. Cela ne suffit-il pas à l'envolée lyrique, cette continuelle bataille
où nous laissons tout notre sang et d'où nous repartons sans cesse avec
un nouveau chant d'espérance (1) ?

True to his intentions, Zola created a drama in classic form,
with an action beginning near its climactic point and driving
to its conclusion within 24 hours. The four principal characters
are caught in a mesh of love, jealousy and vengeance which in
one or two respects is reminiscent of Racine's *Andromaque*.
Two sisters — Marianne and Jeanine — and two brothers
— Richard and Landry — are the surviving property-holders
on the remote fishing island of Goël. Both sisters love the older
brother, Richard ; both brothers love the younger sister, Jeanine.
Richard has left the island, vowing never to return, in order to
sacrifice his love in favor of his younger brother. After an
absence of three years, a hurricane has forced him to seek refuge
on the island. He finds that his younger brother is mistreating
Jeanine. He learns that she has always loved him, and that his
self-sacrifice has resulted in her unhappiness. They decide to
leave the island together. But Marianne's jealousy has been
awakened. She reveals their love to Landry, who is then
determined to kill his brother. Marianne, like Hermione, is
torn between love and vengeance. She makes a final effort to
win Richard, but is repulsed and permits Landry to challenge
Richard to a duel. As Richard refuses to fight his brother,
Landry prepares to stab him, but at the last moment, Marianne
herself takes a dagger and kills Landry. " Il l'a voulu.
Comment a-t-il pu croire que je lui laisserais tuer l'homme que
j'aime ? " In the last act, the three survivors are filled with
remorse. But Hope (personified by a 15-year old girl named
" Lulu ", whom Richard brought with him) entreats Richard
to set forth again " vers les îles fortunées et lointaines, dans
l'inconnu toujours rêvé, toujours fuyant ". He bids both sisters
farewell, and, alone with Hope, embarks on " l'éternel voyage,
par l'infini des mers ".
    While the drama is classic in form, its language and thought
are symbolic. The two sisters are repetitions of the rival
dancers in the ballet of *Messidor* — the Queen and " l'Amante ".
Marianne's passion is to conquer and reign. " Tu es l'orgueil ",
her sister tells her, " l'éternel besoin de domination ; et, quand tu
aimes, c'est la jalousie qui ravage et qui tue ". Jeanine hungers

(1) Program of *l'Opéra-Comique*, 29 April 1901, reprinted in LES ŒUVRES
COMPLÈTES, *le Rêve, ibid.*, pp. 262-263.

for love : " Tu es le désir, la femme qui perd le monde, qui sème
la démence et les catastrophes " (Act I, scene IV). Richard is
the eternal seeker : " L'espérance n'est que dans le départ "
(Act IV, scene II). Lulu is " l'inconnu, le continuel départ pour
des cieux ignorés " (Act I, scene v), " l'espérance, l'âme errante
des eaux qui n'a d'autre joie que d'aller sans cesse devant elle,
d'épuiser l'infini, l'au-delà de tout ce qu'on désire et de tout ce
qu'on cherche, éternellement. ... ta passion des mers sans
bornes, du monde sans limites... la fille de ton rêve, passionnée,
très chaste, très pure " (Act IV, scene IV).

The settings, too, are symbolic. Act II is along the shore
of the " baie de Grâce ", a fertile spot dominated by the great,
singing tree of Love, reminiscent of the symbolic tree in the
" Paradou " of Zola's novel, *la Faute de l'abbé Mouret*. Under
this tree, the lovers sit and tell their love :

JEANINE

Viens, viens nous abriter sous l'arbre tutélaire. Il est l'asile inexpu-
gnable... Entends-tu la divine musique ?

RICHARD

Oui, j'entends un concert délicieux, qui m'enveloppe et me pénètre.

JEANINE

Il chante, il chante sous la brise, l'arbre d'amour. Il chante pour nous
et veut que nous nous aimions.

RICHARD

Son tronc énorme chante, ses branches légères chantent, ses feuilles
sans nombre chantent, chantent ta beauté et mon désir.

JEANINE

A son ombre, des milliers d'oiseaux chantent notre ravissement, les
mousses se réjouissent, les herbes nous caressent, tandis que ses rameaux
supportent sur nos têtes la tente nuptiale.

RICHARD

Les oiseaux chantent, les insectes chantent, l'arbre géant chante,
toute la forêt et toute la terre chantent, le concert de l'éternelle vie
chante, nous unit et nous emporte.

(Act II, scene IV.)

The four acts have contrasting moods, as the movements
of a symphony. The first is menacing, with the imminent
approach of the storm ; the second, by the Bay of Grace, is
radiant with the song of love ; the third exhibits the full fury of
the storm ; the fourth is calm, with the peace of passion spent
and the rebirth of hope.

Lingering enmities aroused by the Dreyfus Case prevented the work from attaining the wide-spread popularity which it would seem to have merited (1). Among the favorable criticisms is that of Gustave Charpentier, who, after highly praising Bruneau's score, wrote of Zola :

Il faut être reconnaissant à M. Émile Zola d'avoir apporté au drame musical, l'autorité, le prestige, les ressources d'un talent que — à part M. Catulle Mendès et quelques rares contemporains — les musiciens ont rarement rencontré chez leurs collaborateurs.

L'école française, l'école du bon sens, de la vérité, de la vie — qui n'exclut pas la pensée ni le symbole — a triomphé une fois de plus sous ses auspices (2).

« L'Enfant-Roi »

A letter to Bruneau in 1899 reveals that Zola's first intention was to place *l'Enfant-Roi* in " le monde légendaire " (3). All trace of legend disappeared, however, in the writing, and the work emerged as a real-life story of a small Parisian household told with warmth, tenderness and mellow humor. Zola has returned in this libretto to scenes of every-day life and to generally prosaic dialogue. As Le Blond states in his commentary : " On sent chez les deux auteurs la volonté de montrer que la musique peut être apte à commenter les aventures les plus ordinaires de l'existence quotidienne... (4). " A letter from Zola, written four days before his death, shows that both the libretto and the score were then complete, and that the work had been accepted for a subsequent season by the *Opéra-Comique* (5). It was not played, however, until 3 March 1905.

The theme of this " comédie lyrique " is the aspiration to paternity — a corollary to the theme of *Messidor* and of the novel, *Fertilité*. François, proprietor of a small bakery, is childless after fourteen years of marriage. Unknown to him, his wife, Madeleine, had given birth to an illegitimate child two years before their marriage. The youthful father died in

(1) See BRUNEAU, *ibid.*, p. 177 ; LES ŒUVRES COMPLÈTES, *le Rêve, ibid.*, p. 263.
(2) *Le Figaro*, 30 April 1901. BRUNEAU was the regular music critic for the *Figaro*. Charpentier took his place on this occasion.
(3) Letter dated 26 July 1899, in LES ŒUVRES COMPLÈTES, *Correspondance (1872-1902)*, pp. 845-846.
(4) LES ŒUVRES COMPLÈTES, *le Rêve, ibid.*, p. 263.
(5) Letter to BRUNEAU dated 25 September 1902, reproduced by him in *A l'ombre d'un grand cœur*, pp. 182-183. This letter does not appear in LES ŒUVRES COMPLÈTES.

military service before the birth, and the child, Georget — now a boy of sixteen — has been brought up secretly by a grandmother. The childless couple are tenderly attached to each other until the day that François, having followed his wife upon one of her surreptitious visits, learns of the child's existence. He is willing to forgive Madeleine, provided that she prove her love for him by giving up the child. The child is the stranger, the interloper out of the past who, in a sense, has robbed François of his own paternity. (It will be recalled that the heroine of Zola's first play, whose happiness, too, was marred by a sinful past, was named also after the Mary Magdalena of the Gospel.) If Madeleine chooses to return to him, she must vow never to see her child again. At first, mother-love is uppermost. She stays with Georget during a fortnight, during which the grief-stricken François allows production at the bakery to decline. Two of his employees, a conniving young man and young woman, plan to gain control of the business. Through them, Zola shows his contempt for the type of younger generation which declines to embrace the joys and responsibilities of parenthood :

AUGUSTE, *goguenard*

Un enfant ! c'est pour un enfant qu'ils se font un mauvais sang pareil ! Alors, ils sont plus bêtes encore que je ne croyais. Mais ça ne compte pas, un enfant ! ça s'accroche quelque part et ça s'oublie !

PAULINE, *gaiement*

Vous n'êtes pas pour les enfants, vous ?

AUGUSTE

Fichtre non ! L'enfant, ça n'est pas dans mon idée. N'en faut pas, jamais ! Pas un fil à la patte qui vous embarrasse dans l'existence. Et l'on est libre comme l'air, on a le plaisir sans la peine...

PAULINE

C'est bien sûr que les mioches, ça pousse toujours trop vite. Ça n'embellit pas une femme, ça la cloue chez elle, plus de liberté ni d'amusements... Enfin, nous recauserons de ça, quand nous serons les maîtres...

(Act IV, scene II.)

Their egocentric cynicism is in contrast to the sincerity of François' lament :

Jaloux d'un enfant, je suis jaloux d'un enfant ! Est-ce possible d'être tombé à cette misère ? Moi qui en souhaitais un de tout mon désir éperdu, moi qui l'aurais adoré de tout mon cœur attendri ! L'enfant, c'est la joie et le bonheur nécessaire, c'est l'âme sans laquelle la maison ne peut vivre !

Mais l'enfant d'un autre, non, non ! cela me déchire. Si je suis jaloux, c'est que l'autre est toujours là, c'est que cet enfant d'un autre m'a volé mon enfant à moi, l'enfant que j'attendais de ma femme tant aimée. Et ma maison est à jamais vide, jamais je n'y verrai l'enfant naître et grandir !

                                                    (Act IV, scene III.)

Madeleine leaves Georget and returns to her husband. The household is happy once more, until Georget comes to bid his mother farewell. He has decided to seek his fortune overseas, so as to relieve his mother of any impediment which might stand in the way of her marital happiness. The problem arises again. But François' burning desire for a child gives him the strength to rise above jealousy :

GEORGET

Et qu'on laisse donc partir l'enfant d'amertume et de querelle, qui fait saigner tous les cœurs, et dont la disparition ramènera la paix !

FRANÇOIS, *dans un dernier éclat*

Non ! ce n'est pas vrai, l'enfant emportera tous les cœurs, l'enfant laissera un tel vide, une blessure si inguérissable, que nous en souffririons tous à jamais !...
Qu'il reste et qu'il nous réunisse !

                                                    (Act V, scene II.)

And the play ends happily in the household which at last is alive and fertile. The bakers set joyfully to work : " Paris s'éveille, il faut que Paris ait du pain, pour la besogne géante de son enfantement ! "

In *l'Enfant-Roi*, Zola has freed himself from legendary symbolism inspired by Wagner, and has, instead, adorned his theme of fertility with symbols carefully chosen to blend with an atmosphere of reality. As rarely in Zola's theater, *l'Enfant-Roi* contains an art which conceals art. The trade which Zola chose for his protagonist has a particular bearing upon the theme of fertility. *Messidor* was a hymn glorifying the virtue of wheat-bearing soil. The bakery of *l'Enfant-Roi* represents the final stage in the process of soil fertility before the life-giving wheat is distributed throughout the hungry city — a theme suggestive, moreover, of Zola's early novel, *le Ventre de Paris*. The second act is set in the toy shop where the little Georget has been brought up — a locale chosen for its connotation of childhood. The third act takes place in the outdoor flower market beside the church which bears the same name as the heroine, the Madeleine. For this act, Zola imagined a particularly felicitous symbol of fertility : a baptismal procession slowly crosses the stage and enters the church, and, at the end of the act, emerges joyfully as the happy parents of the infant buy white roses for all the members of the procession.

Zola attempted with *l'Enfant-Roi* to bring a greater degree of reality to the operatic stage. The characters are ordinary people, expressing themselves generally in the language of ordinary life. At least one critic — Gabriel Faure — was troubled by the translation into song of the prosaic speech of common-place reality :

> Cependant, si le poème de *l'Enfant-Roi* me paraît musical par l'humanité qu'il dégage, par la puissance des sentiments qu'il exprime, je ne puis pas dire que la forme littéraire qu'il revêt ne m'ait semblé, en plus d'un endroit, défier la musique plutôt que l'appeler. Sans doute l'emploi d'un langage aussi extraordinairement familier que celui qu'on rencontre parfois dans *l'Enfant-Roi* est-il nécessaire à la réalité des personnages et du milieu. Mais n'est-ce pas s'éloigner prodigieusement de la réalité que de faire chanter ces personnages, que de traduire musicalement ces milieux (1) ?

Other critics praised the production unreservedly, among them Catulle Mendès, who wrote :

> Un succès, un grand, incontestable, unanime et juste succès. Combien je me réjouis de la chaleureuse estime témoignée à la mémoire d'un illustre écrivain ; combien je suis heureux des enthousiasmes qui ont acclamé l'effort neuf et sincère de M. Alfred Bruneau (2) !

Unproduced Librettos : « Lazare », « Violaine la chevelue », « Sylvanire ou Paris en amour »

Lazare, Violaine la chevelue and *Sylvanire* ou *Paris en amour* remain unproduced, although a musical score was composed for *Lazare* by Alfred Bruneau, and incidental music for *Sylvanire* ou *Paris en amour* by Robert Le Grand.

According to a letter to Bruneau, Zola completed *Lazare* by the end of 1893 (3). The work, in a single act, portrays the miracle of the resurrection of Lazarus, with the difference that

---

(1) Gabriel Faure, in *le Figaro*, quoted in Les Œuvres complètes, *le Rêve, ibid.*, pp. 270-271.
(2) *Ibid.*, p. 270, quoting Catulle Mendès in *le Journal*.
(3) Letter dated 31 December 1893, quoted by Bruneau in *A l'ombre d'un grand cœur*, p. 71. It is not in Les Œuvres complètes.

in Zola's conception Lazarus prefers the peace of death to the
suffering of life. Appearing with the Christ are Lazarus' mother,
his wife and his child. Each pleads with him to be willing to
resume his life. To each he replies that eternal sleep is a happier
state than life. They join with him then in entreating the
Christ to let him return to the grave, and Jesus, in pity, consents.

JÉSUS

Ah ! pauvre créature humaine, créature de souffrance et de misère,
dors, dors maintenant, à jamais heureuse, pour l'éternité.

TOUS

Ah ! Pauvre Lazare, pauvre homme las, brisé de misère et dè souffrance, dors, dors maintenant, heureux à jamais, pour l'éternité.

The play is an amplification of two pages of Zola's novel,
Lourdes, where the doubting priest, Pierre Froment, reflects upon
Lazarus in connection with the failure of an attempted resuscitation (1). Since Zola was still working upon *Lourdes* after
having finished *Lazare*, it is not possible to say whether this
particular passage of the novel preceded the play, or *vice versa*.
Lazare was the first libretto which Zola wrote for Bruneau,
ante-dating *Messidor*. Bruneau recognized at once the difficulty
of finding a producer receptive to a work of this nature — although
Zola, as Bruneau writes in his biography, " " n'avait pas réfléchi
à cette question secondaire et néanmoins importante " (2) —
and the matter was deferred for several years. A letter from
Zola in 1899 shows that he was particularly anxious that the
rôle and theme of Christ be conceived in beauty :

Et, puisque vous me parlez de vous mettre à *Lazare*, je veux vous
dire qu'il sera bon que je relise ces pages avant tout. Je crois me rappeler
que nous avons causé un soir du personnage du Christ, et qu'il nous a
semblé un peu vague, illogique. Il faut revoir cela, il faut en causer,
car vous avez besoin d'un Christ nettement défini, que vous sentiez
bien, si vous voulez le camper en beauté (3).

Bruneau did not compose the score until after Zola's death,
when, as he writes, " Je songeai alors au magnifique *Lazare* que
Zola m'avait offert en 1894 et je pensai que mon douloureux état
d'esprit s'accordait particulièrement avec le caractère saisissant

    (1) LES ŒUVRES COMPLÈTES, *Lourdes*, " Deuxième Journée, IV ", pp. 189-
190.
    (2) BRUNEAU, *A l'ombre d'un grand cœur*, pp. 74-75.
    (3) *Ibid.*, pp. 152-153, letter dated 16 April 1899, not in LES ŒUVRES
COMPLÈTES.

de cette œuvre exceptionnelle " (1).   The score was completed
in a few months, and, at one time, a production was contemplated
in the ancient Roman theater at Orange in the south of France.
Bruneau mentions *Violaine la chevelue* only once in his
biography.   Referring to the period following Zola's death when
he was reviewing the surviving manuscripts of Zola's librettos,
he writes :

> J'avais bien, depuis assez longtemps, une autre pièce de Zola, écrite
> pour moi avant *l'Ouragan* : *Violaine la chevelue*, somptueuse féerie
> lyrique, mais son auteur s'était aperçu, après l'avoir achevée, qu'elle
> transposait dans le domaine du surnaturel l'idée réaliste de *Messidor*
> et nous avions décidé de ne pas la mettre en musique sans qu'il l'eût
> revue et métamorphosée (2).

Zola's death intervened before the accomplishment of this
purpose.   In this play, Zola used the " féerie " form as a vehicle
for poetic fancy.   As in *A Midsummer-Night's Dream*, three
groups of characters are interwoven in the action — fairies,
royalty and common people — but unlike Shakespeare, Zola has
intentionally kept all three groups far above the earth in the
stratosphere of fantasy.   His courtiers are stylised parodies of
lust and insatiable appetite : " A l'ivresse, à l'amour, qui clame
et qui consume !   Que les torches flambent, que les vins coulent !
Et que notre désir monte jamais rassasié, dans la nuit noire et
brûlante " (Act III, scene I).   They worship the evil princess,
Faustine — the dominating, power-hungry type of woman, of
which examples have been seen in *l'Ouragan* and the ballet of
Messidor.   Only the young king, Sylvère, and his sardonic fool
are righteous.   Sylvère hopes to restore the Golden Age of joy
and fraternity, and goes down among his people to find the lass
with the magic tresses who alone can save the kingdom, according
to the ancient prophecy :

> Quand le royaume craquera,
> Une chevelure y naîtra,
> Qui l'âge d'or y refera,
> Dès que sa chevelure descendra,
> Jusqu'à la terre, et fleurira.
>
> (Act I, scene I.)

The people have the task of making flowers for the springtime,
but, discouraged by the indifference of the evil court, they

(1) *Ibid.*, p. 202.
(2) *Ibid.*, p. 201.

neglect their duty of embellishing the earth and frolic idly in the fields. The King falls in love with Violaine of the long tresses, and upon returning to court, tries to persuade the nobles to his own belief that work alone can liberate the kingdom from corruption and restore the Golden Age. Faustine triumphs for a time : the King is imprisoned as mad, and Violaine shorn of her locks. But the fairies give her a new set of tresses, and, as the marriage of the King and Violaine is celebrated at the end, the Golden Age has finally arrived. " Plus de chômage, tous au travail ! Et que la terre enfin fleurisse, dans la joie et dans la fraternité ! "

This allegory, with a title as odd as the tale itself, was of course inspired by utopian aspirations. Its theme — joy, beauty and fraternity through work — is not quite the same as that of *Messidor*, where the emphasis is upon work in its relation to the life-giving fertility of the soil. Indeed, throughout his association with Bruneau, Zola was experimenting with different styles and moods in constructing his librettos. No one of them is like the others. *Violaine la chevelue* is the most fantastic of them all, and in writing it, Zola was undoubtedly satisfying a long-standing ambition to compose a " féerie ". *Violaine la chevelue* was written between *Messidor* and *l'Ouragan*. Zola himself must have recognized that he had permitted his fancy to soar too far above the earth, as his later librettos were founded upon human realities.

Sylvanire ou *Paris en amour*, a tale of artists' life, was the last work to come from Zola's pen. He was still engaged upon it at the time of his death (29 September 1902), and had not yet decided upon the title, as is indicated by his letter to Bruneau written four days earlier :

Sylvanire, ou plutôt *Paris en amour*, titre que je préfère pour plusieurs raisons, avance. J'aurai certainement fini dès les premiers jours d'octobre. Je suis content de ce qui est fait. Mais quand je travaille pour vous, vous savez mes scrupules. Et je me tourmente beaucoup, hanté d'idées pratiques, me demandant comment nous allons pouvoir décider Gailhard à passer un traité avec nous. Dès que vous serez là, nous lirons d'abord la pièce, vous me direz franchement ce que vous en pensez, au point de vue musical et au point de vue de la réception plus ou moins possible à l'Opéra. Et puis, nous causerons de la façon de la soumettre à Gailhard. Je n'ai pas trop chargé le rôle de Sylvanire, qui irait très bien à Mlle Ackté, je crois. Les rôles des deux barytons ne sont également pas trop lourds. Je crains que le rôle du ténor ne soit le plus dur. Beaucoup de mouvement et même de légèreté, une variété très grande et des choses très poignantes vers la fin. Mais cela ne ressemble à rien, tout y

est nouveau comme drame lyrique, et j'ai la terreur de Gailhard (1).
[*Gailhard was manager of the* Opéra.]

This work, as Zola had previously told Bruneau, " exigeait
impérieusement le théâtre de l'Opéra ", inasmuch as three of its
five acts take place in or adjacent to the opera house, and as the
work includes a ballet intended to renovate the operatic dance (2).
The difficulties of production to which Zola alludes in his letter
discouraged Bruneau from ever composing a score. Incidental
music was written for the work by Robert Le Grand.

The libretto, as it appears in *Théâtre II*, of LES ŒUVRES
COMPLÈTES, is complete, although Zola wrote four days before his
death in late September that he did not intend to have the
script finished until the first days of October. It is possible that
Zola completed the script himself earlier than he expected, that
the work remaining to be done consisted only of minor revisions,
or that final touches were added by another hand.

The story is that of a young sculpter, Gilbert, who falls in
love with Sylvanire, a celebrated ballerina. Sylvanire, tender
and warm-hearted, leaves the ballet to hide with him in a
secluded corner of Paris. After seeing her rival triumph in a
starring role, she returns to her former life. " Elle n'est pas que
l'amour ", Gilbert's old tutor explains to him, " elle est aussi
l'art, l'art immortel " (Act IV, scene II). Gilbert, unable to
understand the dual nature of a primadonna's love, stabs
himself, and dies in her arms in the final act. " Ah ! Paris qui
mange les cerveaux et les cœurs ", the old tutor concludes,
" Paris qui tue et qui enfante " !

Paris, city of love and heartbreak, is the theme of the work,
expressed spectacularly in the ballet at the end of the third act,
in which four groups of singers — the Old, the Poets and Sages,
the Workers, and the Young — exalt Paris for its liberty, its
master-pieces, its labor, and its love, while the ballet executes
symbolic dances. The division of stage crowds into separate
groups each representing a segment of society was an idea which
Zola had held as far back as the stage adaptation of *Germinal*.
In *Sylvanire*, the romantic idyll of the two lovers was not
sufficient to support the grandiose conception of ballet which
Zola incorporated into the story, and the work remained
unproduced.

---

(1) *Ibid.*, pp. 182-183, letter dated 25 September 1902, not in LES ŒUVRES
COMPLÈTES.
(2) *Ibid.*, p. 201.

An Unrealized Project

Found among Zola's papers was the preliminary outline in some 1 200 words of a vast cycle of dramas, through which Zola proposed to present on the stage the " natural and social history " of the Third Republic — a project analogous to his study of the Second Empire in the *Rougon-Macquart*, but utilizing the theater instead of the novel. The outline was published in 1927 by Maurice Le Blond in the *Mercure de France* (1). Although it is undated, internal evidence (mention of the Dreyfus Case, and a statement attributing an age of 30 years to the Republic) shows that it was written in or about 1900. As the project was conceived so close to Zola's death, it is unlikely that he had abandoned it. It seems reasonable to suppose, on the contrary, that after writing the fourth novel of his " *Évangiles* " (2), he intended to give his major effort to the stage in the accomplishment of a theatrical counterpart to the *Rougon-Macquart*. Although unrealized projects are necessarily matters of conjecture, Zola's design for a vast cycle of dramas is particularly interesting as revealing his final thoughts upon the theater.

The outline, entitled " La France en marche ", begins :

Je veux faire pour la IIIᵉ République ce que j'ai fait pour le Second Empire : une série d'œuvres, où se retrouvera l'histoire naturelle et sociale de l'époque. Seulement, ces œuvres, au lieu d'être des romans, seront des drames (p. 21).

Zola sees France democratic in form but not in spirit, torn between the long tradition of her clerical and monarchical past, and the new forces of progress striving towards liberty, truth and justice. He describes the opposing forces as :

D'une part, les forces du passé, l'esprit monarchique, l'esprit clérical, agissant, profitant de la liberté républicaine pour revenir en arrière. De l'autre, toutes les forces du progrès. C'est toute la bataille, c'est tout l'intérêt de la France en marche. Avancera-t-elle ? Reculera-t-elle ? Et tout est là (pp. 21-22).

Around this conflict between tradition and innovation (or, to use Zola's word " progress ") which is to be the core of the entire

---

(1) Maurice LE BLOND, " les Projets littéraires d'Emile Zola au moment de sa mort, d'après des documents et manuscrits inédits ", in *Mercure de France*, vol. 199, 1 October 1927, pp. 5-25, at pp. 20-23.

(2) Death prevented ZOLA from beginning *Justice*, intended to be the fourth novel of the " *Evangiles* ". As to his projects for *Justice*, see LE BLOND's article, *ibid.*, pp. 7-20.

work, Zola will build dramas treating specific problems of current interest, which he describes in some detail :

En outre, je pourrai chercher un lien commun littéraire par les sujets, par les cadres, etc. Ainsi, tout de suite, comme sujet, je vois : la question du féminisme, l'affranchissement de la femme, la question de l'instruction (très importante), l'enfant restera-t-il au dogme ou ira-t-il à l'affranchissement ; la politique avec ses arrivistes, ses modérés, ses pêcheurs en eau trouble ; la liberté de conscience par l'antisémitisme ; la pourriture de l'armée, tout le militarisme traité avec son idolâtrie du sabre, son armée permanente, son corps d'officiers, organisation incompatible avec une démocratie, la science qu'on accuse de faire faillite, la science la seule révolutionnaire ; la littérature allant au plus grand nombre, les tours d'ivoire, les annonciateurs nouveaux de la bonne parole ; le socialisme, la lutte des écoles, les sectaires se dévorant, la question de la réorganisation du travail se posant d'abord ; la magis-trature, tout le problème nouveau, la question de savoir si le prêtre régnera, si Rome confisquera la France à son profit, tout le lent complot qui est parti de l'esprit nouveau pour éclater lors de l'Affaire Dreyfus, la bataille suprême où la France peut rester, le commerce tel qu'il est aujourd'hui avec ses tendances, etc. Et, dès lors, je m'aperçois que chaque drame peut s'incarner dans un type : *l'Instituteur, le Prêtre, le Magistrat, le Savant, le Militaire, la Femme, l'Enfant, le Gouvernement politique, l'Écrivain, l'Ouvrier, le Paysan, le Commerçant.* Ces titres sont naturellement provisoires. D'autres sujets plus typiques peuvent être trouvés ; et deux des types indiqués plus haut peuvent être fondus en un seul (p. 22).

Zola was clearly intent upon promulgating utopian theories. He recognized that one of his problems would be to conceal his propaganda in the interests of art :

Des drames de progrès, de délivrance. Et surtout des drames d'ensei-gnement, écrits pour servir à la propagande, sans cesser d'être des œuvres purement littéraires, très hautes, très simples, d'une beauté pure... La leçon, et sans qu'on la sente (pp. 22-23).

He hoped to create a people's theater :

On se plaint qu'il n'y ait pas de théâtre pour le peuple. Le créer. Être compris de tous. Pouvoir être joué partout... La puissance du théâtre sur les foules. S'en servir (pp. 22-23).

But he did not intend to limit his plays to any one type of audience :

Varier pourtant, avec les milieux. Avoir des drames intimes et des drames de foules. Des comédies, des idylles, des tragédies. Des décors

très variés. Tout mettre dans la passion, revenir à la simplicité classique...
Aller jusqu'au bout de ma pensée, sans m'inquiéter de la représentation (p. 23).

And finally, he would not remain a prisoner of this theory, but would, as with his novels, descend to the arena of life for his action and characters :

Quant à chaque fable, il faudra la créer dans l'action, dans la passion et non pas dans la théorie. Chercher le général, ce qui se passe le plus ordinairement sous nos yeux, dans la catégorie indiquée. Composer les drames, comme je compose mes romans, en partant du général pour arriver à la vie. Et arriver aux personnages vivants, à l'action très vraie et très intense, dans des décors réels (p. 23).

Zola was 62, in unimpaired mental and physical health, at the time of his fatal accident. He had learned much of theatrical art in the 30 years or more during which he had been passionately interested in the stage. It is unlikely that in his maturity he would have repeated the melodramatic crudities of *Thérèse Raquin*, the callow satire of *les Héritiers Rabourdin*, the twisted reasoning of *Renée*, or that he would have resorted to thesis argumentation *à la Dumas*. His association with Bruneau had inspired him to the beautiful lyric symbolism of *Messidor* and of *l'Ouragan*, and to the mellow charm of *l'Enfant-Roi*. Notwithstanding the propaganda nature of his new program, it is not impossible to believe that Zola might have descended sufficiently from his utopian dais to embrace humanity in the warmth of his genius and to create, out of this ambitious, unrealized project, some fine plays of deep human feeling.

SUMMARY

Zola's life-long courtship of the stage was inspired by motives which varied with the changes in his literary stature and personal ambitions. After some youthful, tentative exercises in play-writing, of which only *Madeleine* has survived, financial necessity obliged him to approach the theater as an empty-handed adventurer in whom the commercial instinct was uppermost. In this spirit was conceived his first produced play, the hackneyed *Mystères de Marseille* written in collaboration with Marius Roux. The failure of the venture taught him to treat the theater with greater respect and originality, and his next plays, *Thérèse Raquin* and *les Héritiers Rabourdin*, were real efforts to enlarge the horizons of the stage. The inability of critics and public alike to appreciate their worth induced a shift in his perspective. His literary stature was growing with the first novels of the *Rougon-Macquart*, and he was now armed with the powerful weapon of naturalism, derived from his assimilation of scientific methods to literature. As if determined to avenge his own defeats by destroying the forces which had operated against him and to conquer by force of argument a medium which had resisted his creative efforts, Zola began a series of weekly articles in the press, in which for more than four years he laid vigorous siege to theatrical conventions. Early in this campaign, the astounding success of his novel *l'Assommoir* brought him renown and independence, and caused a further shift in his perspective. While continuing to denounce the contemporary theater in a voice resonant with his success as a novelist, he poured all of his naturalist philosophy into his novels, and, for a time, contented himself in the theater with somewhat cynical concessions to the box office. His farce of *le Bouton de Rose*, unobjectionable for a hack writer, was on Zola's part a contemptuous gesture to the theater. His collaborations with Busnach were intended for the most part as popular melodramas, exhibiting some aspects of naturalism in their scenes of every-day life, but generally impregnated with commercial considerations. In refusing to allow his name to appear as co-author of the Busnach adaptations, Zola in effect served notice on the public that he considered them unworthy of his talent, although he defended them stoutly against hostile criticism. He was willing to acknowledge authorship to only one other play of his naturalist period, but *Renée*, built on the most implausible of foundations, was inadequate as a demonstration of his theories, in spite of its well-projected characters. Zola was not seriously affected by the lukewarm reception given to *Renée*. His interest in the theater increased, and he was concerned more and more with enlarging the capacities of the stage. He was the most influential of Antoine's early supporters, lending the prestige of his name in authorizing productions of *Jacques Damour* (adapted by Hennique), of *Tout pour l'honneur* (adapted by Céard), and of his own early play, *Madeleine*. He took vicarious pleasure in recommending the first production of Ibsen in France. Of Busnach's five adaptations of his novels, it was *Germinal*, with its social purpose, in which Zola put his greatest personal effort. After *Germinal*, he dissociated himself from the commercially-minded Busnach and entered into an informal partnership with the composer, Alfred Bruneau. Bruneau brought out Zola's latent lyricism and inspired him to perhaps his finest writing for the stage. Their association co-incided with the termination of the *Rougon-Macquart*, with the general reaction against naturalism, and with the growing idealist and utopian tendencies of Zola's later novels. The six librettos which represent his final work for the stage reveal a new Zola, a Zola who, in keeping with his epoch, turned from an objective and scientific examination of life to a symbolic and lyric interpretation of what life is and of what it may be. His unrealized project for a vast cycle of dramas demonstrates that at the time of his death, far from discouraged at his many past frustrations in the theater, he was determined to devote his major effort to this form of expression, and to repeat on the stage his triumphs in the novel.

As a liberating force, Zola exercised considerable influence on the contemporary stage, even though in large measure the influence was intangible. His program of theatrical reform, as to both subject matter and technique, did in fact come to pass, stripped, however, of his scientific pretensions. The scope of the stage was in fact enlarged to include the frank and objective portrayal of disagreeable subjects, of unsympathetic characters, and of all classes of society engaged in scenes of every-day life. Dialogue, stage movement and scenery became more faithful to the speech, gestures and settings of real life, so that actors were increasingly able to convey the illusion of " living ", rather than of " play-acting ", their rôles. But the ranks of Zola's disciples did not include any major playwright. His elders — Augier, Dumas *fils* and Sardou — had produced the major portion of their work by the time of his reforming campaign, and refused to be frightened by Zola's denunciations into changing their style. Becque, his contemporary, pursued an independent course. The failure of Zola's own plays detracted from his reputation as a critic. *Thérèse Raquin* appears in retrospect as a minor theatrical landmark, but it aroused no interest comparable to that accorded a decade later to Becque's *les Corbeaux*. Zola's subsequent plays offered examples of dramatic art which no playwright of genuine talent would have wanted to emulate. In his collaborations with Busnach, particularly in the adaptation of *l'Assommoir*, Zola was able to present successfully some elements of naturalism on the stage, but the value of these contributions was limited to superficial matters of setting and of costume, and to a few isolated scenes foreshadowing the " slice of life " technique. Essentially, however, the Busnach collaborations were so tainted with time-worn theatrical clichés as to disqualify them as models of a new art.

Although Zola's failure in the theater impaired his reputation as critic, his prestige as novelist gave amplitude to his voice. Specially privileged by success to speak of the novel, he cannily extended this privilege into the domain of the theater by drawing a parallel between the two forms. Why, he enquired, did the novel enjoy greater freedom than the stage ? The force of his dramatic criticism was derived from this parallel. The indisputable success of the naturalist novel, with its freedom to reveal festering sores of humanity, was a reproach to the theater. Zola's complaint could not be ignored, and the theatrical climate of the 1880s did in fact become more favorable to shocking or repellant plays than it had been before his campaign of reform. Becque's *les Corbeaux* was finally produced after a wait of five years. Antoine, aided and inspired by Zola, was able to win a place for his *Théâtre-Libre* and to launch a movement which extended into the Twentieth Century. It is justifiable to believe that Zola's dramatic criticism was instrumental in creating an atmosphere receptive to new ferments in the theater.

The weakness of Zola's criticism, corroborated by the weakness of his own plays, lay in his inability or unwillingness to distinguish between freedom of subject matter and freedom of technique. He never acknowledged that the stage had a discipline of its own. In his enthusiasm to rid the theater of conventions which hampered a candid portrayal of life, he failed to recognize the necessity of other conventions to replace them. Expert in the free manipulation of prose narrative, he was a theatrical anarchist, hoping to make the stage over into a utopia for novelists. But, as in the case of the social utopias of his last novels, he was unable or unwilling to supply workable disciplines in exchange for those which he sought to destroy. The task of carrying on the theatrical evolution fell to other minds, more sensitive than Zola's to the subtle currents of the stage. Nevertheless, his insensitivity was redeemed by his force. The strident tone of his criticism tolled the knell of outworn theatrical methods. The seeds of his discontent were fertile, and yielded a harvest which, insofar as the theater is concerned, was left for others to gather.

BIBLIOGRAPHY

A) WORKS BY ZOLA

I. — LES ŒUVRES COMPLÈTES

Notes et commentaires de Maurice Le Blond, Texte de l'édition Eugène Fasquelle, 50 volumes. Printed by François Bernouard, Paris, 1927-1929. (At the time of this edition, Eugène Fasquelle was the head of the Bibliothèque Charpentier, the firm which has published Zola's works subsequent to 1873.)

1. Plays

Théâtre I : Madeleine, Thérèse Raquin (with preface by ZOLA) ; *les Héritiers Rabourdin* (with preface by ZOLA) ; *le Bouton de Rose* (with preface by ZOLA).

Théâtre II : Renée (with preface by ZOLA), *Messidor, l'Ouragan, l'Enfant-Roi, Violaine la chevelue, Sylvanire ou Paris en amour, Lazare.*

2. Dramatic and literary criticism

Mes haines (first published by Faure in 1866).
Le Roman expérimental (first published by Charpentier in 1880).
Le Naturalisme au théâtre (first published by Charpentier in 1881).
Nos auteurs dramatiques (first published by Charpentier in 1881).
Les Romanciers naturalistes (first published by Charpentier in 1881).
Documents littéraires (first published by Charpentier in 1881).
Une campagne (first published by Charpentier in 1882).
Nouvelle campagne (first published by Charpentier in 1897).
Mélanges, Préfaces et Discours (first edition of this volume).

3. Poetry

Mélanges, Préfaces et Discours, « les Poèmes de jeunesse » (first published by Paul Alexis in his biography, *Émile Zola, notes d'un ami, avec des vers inédits de Émile Zola*, Charpentier, Paris, 1882).

4. Correspondence

Correspondance (1858-1871).
Correspondance (1872-1902).

Zola's correspondence was first published by Charpentier in 1907 and 1908 in two volumes entitled : *Correspondance : Lettres de jeunesse ;* and *Correspondance : les Lettres et les Arts.* Some additional correspondence, not included in the Charpentier or Le Blond editions, is to be found in the following :

Lettres de Émile Zola à Messieurs de Goncourt, avec préface de M. Maurice LE BLOND. Le Document autographe, collection publiée sous la direction de Mme Alice La Mazière, n° 1, Paul Catin, 1929.

Émile Zola's Letters to J. Van Santen Kolff, edited by Robert Judson Niess. Washington University Studies, New Series, Language and Literature No. 10. St. Louis, 1940.

Alfred BRUNEAU, *A l'ombre d'un grand cœur, souvenirs d'une collaboration, avec de nombreuses lettres inédites d'Émile Zola,* Bibliothèque Charpentier, Paris, 1932.

II. — DRAMATIC AND LITERARY CRITICISM NOT COLLECTED
IN " LES ŒUVRES COMPLÈTES "

The following articles by Zola, not collected in LES ŒUVRES COMPLÈTES have been mentioned in this dissertation :

1866

Articles in *l'Événement* :

30 avril. — " Mon salon " (Zola's comments upon each of the 21 members of the *salon* jury, omitted from *Mes haines*).
19 mai. — " Livres d'aujourd'hui et de demain. "
18 juin. — " Livres d'aujourd'hui et de demain. "
29 juin. — " Livres d'aujourd'hui et de demain. "
15 juillet. — " Livres d'aujourd'hui et de demain. "
25 juillet. — " Livres d'aujourd'hui et de demain. "
19 août. — " Marbres et plâtres : M. H. Taine. "

1867

In *l'Événement* :

9 février. — " Marbres et plâtres : M. Sainte-Beuve. "

1868

" Mon salon ", in *l'Événement illustré* :

2 mai. — " I. L'ouverture. "
10 mai. — " II. Édouard Manet. "
19 mai. — " III. Les naturalistes. "
24 mai. — " IV. Les actualistes. "
1er juin. — " V. Les paysagistes. "
9 juin. — " VI. Quelques bonnes toiles. "
16 juin. — " VII. La sculpture. "

In *la Tribune* :
14 juillet. — " M. Duruy et le rapport sur le progrès des lettres. "
27 septembre. — " Causerie. "
15 novembre. — " Causerie. "

1869

In *la Tribune* :
28 novembre. — " Causerie. "

In *le Gaulois* :
10 janvier. — " Livres d'aujourd'hui et de demain. "
19 janvier. — " Livres d'aujourd'hui et de demain. "

1872

In *le Corsaire* :
22 décembre. — " Le lendemain de la crise. "

1873

Dramatic and literary criticism in *l'Avenir national* :
25 février. — " Causerie dramatique et littéraire. "
4 mars. — " Causerie dramatique et littéraire. "
11 mars. — " Causerie dramatique et littéraire. "
18 mars. — " Causerie dramatique. "
21 mars. — " Causerie dramatique. "
25 mars. — " Causerie dramatique. "
1er avril. — " Causerie dramatique et littéraire. "
6 avril. — " Causerie littéraire. "
10 avril. — " Causerie dramatique. "
15 avril. — " Causerie dramatique. "
20 avril. — " Causerie dramatique. "
24 avril. — " Causerie dramatique. "
30 avril. — " Causerie dramatique. "
1er mai. — " Causerie dramatique. "
5 mai. — " Causerie dramatique. "
11 mai. — " Causerie dramatique. "
12 mai. — " Causerie dramatique. "
15 mai. — " Causerie dramatique. "
23 mai. — " Causerie dramatique. "
3 juin. — " Causerie dramatique. "
7 juin. — " Causerie dramatique. "
10 juin. — " Causerie dramatique. "

1876

Dramatic criticism in *le Bien public* :
5 juin.

1877

Short stories and reminiscences in his theatrical column of *le Bien public* :
6 août, 13 août, 20 août, 27 août, 3 septembre, 10 septembre, 17 septembre, 24 septembre.

Dramatic and literary criticism in *le Bien public* :
19 mars, 9 avril, 31 décembre.

1878

Dramatic and literary criticism in *le Voltaire* :
26 novembre, 3 décembre.

1879

Dramatic and literary criticism in *le Voltaire* :
28 janvier, 11 février, 1er avril, 2 juillet, 16 septembre, 28 octobre, 25 novembre, 30 décembre.

1880

Dramatic and literary criticism in *le Voltaire* :
23 janvier, 3 février, 23 mars, 20 juillet.

" Le Naturalisme au salon ", in *le Voltaire* :
18 juin, 19 juin, 21 juin, 22 juin.

1881

Articles in *le Figaro* :
24 janvier. — " Le marquis de Sade. "
23 mai. — " Après une promenade au salon. "

1885

In *le Figaro* :
28 octobre. — Letter to Francis Magnard, editor of the *Figaro*, concerning the censorship of *Germinal*.
7 novembre. — Article protesting the censorship of *Germinal*.
10 novembre. — Reply to Dumas, *fils*.

1891

In *le Figaro* :
12 mars. — Zola's testimony before a parliamentary commission investigating stage censorship.

1893

In *le Figaro* :
25 novembre. — Reply to Huysmans, Hennique, Céard and Alexis concerning *l'Attaque du moulin*.

1897

In *le Figaro* :
    20 février. — " Messidor expliqué par les auteurs : le poème. "
In *le Gaulois* :
    23 février. — " Une lettre de M. Émile Zola " (reply to Fourcaud concerning *Messidor*).
In *la Revue blanche* :
    15 février (t. XII, p. 166) : Zola's reply in " Enquête sur l'influence des lettres scandinaves ".

B) THEATRICAL PRODUCTIONS

I. — Zola's plays of the naturalist period

1. *Madeleine*
Drama in three acts. Written in 1865, first performed by the *Théâtre-Libre* on 1 May 1889. Published only in Les Œuvres complètes, *Théâtre I*.

2. *Thérèse Raquin*
Drama in four acts, adapted by Zola from his novel bearing the same title. First performed at the *théâtre de la Renaissance* on 11 July 1873. First published by Charpentier in 1873.

3. *Les Héritiers Rabourdin*
Comedy in three acts, first performed at the *théâtre de Cluny* on 3 November 1874. First published by Charpentier in 1874.

4. *Le Bouton de Rose*
Farce in three acts, first performed at the *Palais-Royal* on 7 May 1878. First published in Émile Zola, *Théâtre, Thérèse Raquin, les Héritiers Rabourdin, le Bouton de Rose* (Charpentier, Paris, 1878).

5. *Renée*
Drama in five acts, adapted by Zola from his novel, *la Curée* and from his story, *Nantas*. First performed at the *théâtre du Vaudeville* on 16 April 1887. First published by Charpentier in 1887.

II. — Zola's operatic librettos

1. *Messidor*
Lyric drama in four acts, first performed at the *théâtre de l'Académie nationale de Musique (l'Opéra)* on 19 February 1897, with musical score by Alfred Bruneau. First published by Fasquelle in 1897.

2. *L'Ouragan*

Lyric drama in four acts, first performed at the *Théâtre national de l'Opéra-Comique* on 29 April 1901, with musical score by Alfred Bruneau. First published by Fasquelle in 1901.

3. *L'Enfant-Roi*

Lyric comedy in five acts, first performed at the *Théâtre national de l'Opéra-Comique* on 3 March 1905, with musical score by Alfred Bruneau. First published by Fasquelle in 1905.

4. *Lazare*

Lyric drama in one act, first published, with Zola's five other librettos, in the volume *Poèmes lyriques* (Fasquelle, 1921). A musical score has been written for *Lazare* by Alfred Bruneau. It has not been performed.

5. *Violaine la chevelue*

Lyric fantasy in five acts, first published, with Zola's five other librettos, in *Poèmes lyriques* (Fasquelle, 1921). It has not been performed.

6. *Sylvanire* ou *Paris en amour*

Lyric drama in five acts, first published, with Zola's five other librettos, in *Poèmes lyriques* (Fasquelle, 1921). Incidental music has been composed for it by Robert Le Grand. It has not been performed.

III. — COLLABORATIONS AND ADAPTATIONS

1. *Les Mystères de Marseille*

Drama in five acts, adapted from Zola's novel of the same title by Zola and Marius Roux. First performed at the *théâtre du Gymnase*, in Marseille, on 6 October 1867. Not published.

2. *L'Assommoir*

Drama in five acts and nine *tableaux*, adapted from Zola's novel of the same title by William Busnach and Octave Gastineau. First performed in ten *tableaux* at the *théâtre de l'Ambigu* on 18 January 1879. First published by Charpentier in 1881, with a preface by Zola. Although Zola is not named as co-author, he collaborated to a considerable extent upon the plan of the play.

3. *Nana*

Drama in five acts, adapted by William Busnach from Zola's novel of the same title. First performed (in nine *tableaux*) at the *théâtre de l'Ambigu* on 29 January 1881. First published, with *l'Assommoir* and *Pot-Bouille* and prefaces by Zola to each play, in William BUSNACH, *Trois pièces* (Charpentier, 1885). Although Zola is not named as co-author, he collaborated actively upon both the plan and dialogue of the play.

4. *Pot-Bouille*

Drama in five acts, adapted by William Busnach from Zola's novel of the same title. First performed at the *théâtre de l'Ambigu* on 13 December 1883. First published, with *l'Assommoir* and *Nana* and prefaces by Zola, in William BUSNACH, *Trois pièces* (Charpentier, 1885). Although Zola is not named as co-author, he collaborated actively upon both the plan and dialogue of the play.

5. *Le Ventre de Paris*

Drama in five acts and seven *tableaux*, adapted by William Busnach from Zola's novel of the same title. First performed at the *Théâtre de Paris* on 18 February 1887. It has not been published, except for the sixth *tableau*, which appears over Zola's name in *le Figaro, Supplément littéraire* of 19 February 1887. Zola collaborated actively upon both the plan and dialogue of the play.

6. *Jacques Damour*

Drama in one act adapted by Léon Hennique from Zola's story of the same title. First performed at the inauguration of the *Théâtre-Libre* on 30 March 1887. Published by Charpentier in 1887.

7. *Tout pour l'honneur*

Drama in one act adapted by Henry Céard from Zola's story entitled *le Capitaine Burle*. First performed by the *Théâtre-Libre* on 23 December 1887. Published by Charpentier in 1890.

8. *Germinal*

Drama in five acts and twelve *tableaux* adapted by William Busnach from Zola's novel of the same title. It was banned by the censorship in 1885 and first performed in Paris at the *Châtelet* on 21 April 1888. Although Zola was not named as co-author, he collaborated actively on the plan and dialogue of the play. It has not been published.

9. *Le Rêve*

Lyric drama in four acts adapted by Louis Gallet from Zola's novel of the same title. First performed, with musical score by Alfred Bruneau, at the *Théâtre national de l'Opéra-Comique* on 18 June 1891. Published by Fasquelle in 1891.

10. *La Bête humaine*

Drama in five acts adapted by William Busnach from Zola's novel of the same title. It has not been performed nor published.

11. *Une Page d'amour*

Drama in five acts adapted by Charles Samson from Zola's novel of the same title. First performed at the *Odéon* on 11 March 1893. It has not been published.

12. *L'Attaque du moulin*

Lyric drama adapted by Louis Gallet from Zola's story of the same title. First performed, with musical score by Alfred Bruneau, at the *Théâtre national de l'Opéra-Comique* on 23 November 1893. Published by Fasquelle in 1893.

13. *Au Bonheur des Dames*

Drama in six *tableaux* adapted by Charles Hugot and Raoul de Saint-Arroman from Zola's novel of the same title. First performed at the *Gymnase* on 4 June 1896. It has not been published.

14. *Pour une nuit d'amour!*

Drama in one act adapted by Jane de La Vaudère from Zola's story, *Pour une nuit d'amour*. First performed at the *Grand-Guignol* on 16 May 1898. Published by Ollendorff in 1898.

15. *La Terre*

Drama in five acts and ten *tableaux* adapted by Charles Hugot and Raoul de Saint-Arroman from Zola's novel of the same title. First performed at the *théâtre Antoine* on 21 January 1902. It has not been published.

16. *Naïs Micoulin*

Lyric drama in two acts adapted by Alfred Bruneau from Zola's story of the same title. First performed, with musical score by Bruneau, at the *théâtre de Monte-Carlo* on 2 February 1907. Published by Fasquelle.

17. *La Faute de l'abbé Mouret*

Drama in four acts and fourteen *tableaux* adapted by Alfred Bruneau from Zola's novel of the same title. First performed, with incidental music by Bruneau, at the *Odéon* on 1 March 1907. Published by Fasquelle.

18. *Les Quatre Journées*

Lyric play in four acts adapted by Alfred Bruneau from Zola's story, *les Quatre Journées de Jean Gourdon*. First performed, with musical score by Bruneau, at the *Théâtre national de l'Opéra-Comique* on 19 February 1916. Published by Fasquelle.

C) MANUSCRIPT LETTERS TO ZOLA

CORRESPONDANCE ÉMILE ZOLA, t. I-XV

A collection of manuscript letters to Zola in the *Bibliothèque Nationale*, Paris, classified as *Nouvelles acquisitions françaises* 24510-24524. The following letters have been utilized in this dissertation :

In tome   I : Letters from Antoine.
In tome   III : Letters from Bruneau.

In tome   IV : Letters from Busnach.
In tome   V : Letters from Busnach.
In tome   VI : Letters from Busnach.
In tome VII : Letters from Céard.
In tome IX : Letters from Dumas *fils.*
In tome   X : Letters from Louis Gallet.
In tome XI : Letters from Ludovic Halévy, Charles Hugot.
In tome XIV : Letters from Raoul de Saint-Arroman, Sarcey, Sardou.

D) COLLECTION THÉATRALE AUGUSTE RONDEL

This theatrical collection, the largest in France, is in the *Bibliothèque de l'Arsenal,* Paris. The following files pertaining to Zola have been consulted :

RF 49070. — Fiches bibliographiques.
49078. — Recueil d'articles de presse sur *Thérèse Raquin.*
49094. — Recueil d'articles de presse et programmes sur *l'Assommoir,* pièce.
49096. — *L'Assommoir,* parodie-pantomime.
49097. — PERRINET et GALIPAUX, *En revenant de l'Assommoir.*
49098. — PERRINET et GALIPAUX, *En revenant de l'Assommoir.*
49099. — BLONDELET et BAUMOUNE, *l'Assommoir pour rire.*
49100. — LOUVET et SCHMALL, *le Petit Assommoir,* bouffonnerie.
49101. — LÉTRAZ, « Il n'y a pas loin de la coupe aux lèvres » (d'après *l'Assommoir*).
49107. — Recueil d'articles sur *Nana,* pièce.
49111. — BLONDELET et MAY, *Nana & Cie,* parodie-opérette.
49113. — Recueil d'articles de presse et programmes sur *Pot-Bouille.*
49115. — Recueil d'articles de presse sur *le Ventre de Paris,* pièce.
49117. — Recueil d'articles de presse et revues sur *Renée.*
49125. — Recueil d'articles et programmes sur *le Rêve.*
49128. — Articles de presse sur *Une page d'amour.*
49130. — Article de presse sur *l'Attaque du moulin.*
49132. — Recueil de programmes sur *Au Bonheur des Dames.*
49135. — Recueil de programmes et d'articles de presse sur *Messidor.*
49140. — Recueil d'articles et de programmes sur *l'Ouragan.*
49143. — Recueil d'articles et de programmes sur *la Terre,* drame.
49146. — Recueil d'articles de presse et programmes sur *l'Enfant-Roi.*
49151. — Recueil d'articles et de programmes sur *la Faute de l'abbé Mouret.*

49153. — Recueil d'articles de presse et programmes sur *les Quatre Journées*.
49154. — Recueil d'articles de presse et programmes sur *Germinal*, drame.
49167. — Recueil de nouvelles et d'articles parus dans la presse.
49168. — Recueil d'articles de presse sur diverses œuvres de Zola.
49172. — Recueil d'articles de presse sur le procès des lettres de Stéphane Mallarmé à Émile Zola.
49176. — Recueil d'articles de presse sur la *Correspondance* de ZOLA.
49184. — Recueil d'articles de presse biographiques sur Zola.
49185. — Recueil d'articles de presse sur les anniversaires de Zola.
49189. — ANTOINE, « Émile Zola et le théâtre », extrait fait de *l'Information*, août 1924.
49199. — GRAMONT, « le Théâtre de M. Zola », extrait de *la Revue d'Art dramatique*, 15 février-15 avril, pp. 66-73, 197-204.
49200. — Un autre exemplaire de Gramont.
49206. — LE BLOND, « Projets littéraires d'Émile Zola au moment de sa mort », extrait du *Mercure de France*, octobre 1927.
49224. — Recueil d'articles de presse sur Zola.

E) PRINCIPAL WORKS CONSULTED

ALEXIS (Paul), *Émile Zola, notes d'un ami avec des vers inédits de Émile Zola*, Charpentier, Paris, 1882, 336 pages (of which pp. 1-227 are biography ; pp. 231-233, a preface by Zola ; pp. 235-336, Zola's early poetry).

AMICIS (Edmondo de), *Souvenirs de Paris et Londres*, ouvrage traduit de l'italien avec l'autorisation de l'auteur par Mme J. COLOMB, Hachette & Cⁱᵉ, Paris, 1880, 314 pages (chapter on Zola, pp. 162-220).

ANTOINE (André), *Mes souvenirs sur le Théâtre-Libre*, Arthème Fayard & Cⁱᵉ, Paris, 1921, 324 pages.

— *Mes souvenirs sur le théâtre Antoine et sur l'Odéon (première direction)*, Bernard Grasset, Paris, 1928, 297 pages.

— *le Théâtre*, Les Éditions de France, Paris, 1932, 515 pages.

ARNAOUTOVITCH (Alexandre), *Henry Becque*, 3 vol., Presses Universitaires de France, Paris, 1927 : vol. I, 557 pages ; vol. II, 382 pages ; vol. III, 633 pages.

BARBUSSE (Henri), *Zola*, Gallimard, Paris, 1932, 296 pages.

BECQUE (Henry), *Œuvres complètes :* I. *Théâtre* (with preface by Jean ROBAGLIA) ; V. *Querelles littéraires* ; VII. *Conférences, Notes d'Album, Poésies, Correspondance*, Grès & Cⁱᵉ, Paris, 1925-1926.

— *Souvenirs d'un auteur dramatique*, Bibliothèque artistique et littéraire, Paris, 1895, 230 pages.

BERNARD (Claude), *Introduction à l'étude de la médecine expérimentale*, J.-B. Baillière & Fils, Paris, 1865, 400 pages.

BROWN (Calvin S.), *Repetition in Zola's Novels*, University of Georgia Press, Athens, 1952, 124 pages.

BRUNEAU (Alfred), *A l'ombre d'un grand cœur, Souvenirs d'une collaboration, avec de nombreuses lettres inédites d'Émile Zola*, Bibliothèque Charpentier, Paris, 1932, 235 pages.

BRUNETIÈRE (Ferdinand), *le Roman naturaliste*, nouv. éd., Calmann-Lévy, Paris, 1892, 421 pages.

CÉARD (Henry), *Lettres inédites à Émile Zola, publiées et annotées par C.-A. Burns avec une préface de René Dumesnil*, Librairie Nizet, Paris, 1958, 428 pages.

CÉZANNE (Paul), *Correspondance*, recueillie, annotée et préfacée par John REWALD, éd. Bernard Grasset, Paris, 1937, 319 pages.

DAWSON (Eric), *Henry Becque, sa vie et son théâtre*, Payot, Paris, 1923, 246 pages.

DEFFOUX (Léon), *le Naturalisme*, les Œuvres représentatives, Paris, 1929, 2ᵉ éd., 286 pages.

— *la Publication de l'Assommoir*, Société française d'Éditions littéraires et techniques, Paris, 1931, 152 pages.

DESPREZ (Louis), *l'Évolution naturaliste*, Tresse, Paris, 1884, 372 pages.

DESTRANGES (Étienne), *Messidor d'A. Bruneau, étude analytique et critique*, Librairie Fischbacker, Paris, 1897, 65 pages (of which pp. 1-38 refer to Zola's libretto).

DOUCET (Fernand), *l'Esthétique d'Émile Zola et son application à la critique*, The Hague, 1923, 360 pages.

DUMAS *fils* (Alexandre), *Entractes, deuxième série*, Calmann-Lévy, Paris, 1878.

— *Théâtre des autres*, t. I, Calmann-Lévy, Paris, 1894.

FEJÈS (André), *le Théâtre naturaliste en France*, thèse de doctorat présentée à la Faculté des Lettres de l'Université de Lausanne, 1925 (publisher not given), 163 pages.

FRÉVILLE (Jean), *Zola: semeur d'orages*, Éditions sociales, Paris, 1952.

GIRARDIN (Émile de), *le Supplice d'une femme*, drame en trois actes avec une préface, Michel Lévy Frères, Paris, 1865.

— *les Deux Sœurs*, drame en quatre actes avec une préface, Michel Lévy Frères, Paris, 1865.

GONCOURT (Edmond de), *Journal des Goncourt*, t. V (1872-1877), t. IX (1892-1895), Bibliothèque Charpentier, Paris, 1891 (t. V), 1896 (t. IX).

GUILLEMIN (Henri), *Zola, légende ou vérité ?* René Julliard, Paris, 1960, 187 pages.

HEMMINGS (F. W. J.), *Émile Zola*, The Clarendon Press, Oxford, 1953, 308 pages.

HURET (Jules), *Enquête sur l'évolution littéraire*, Bibliothèque Charpentier, Paris, 1894, 455 pages.

— *Tout yeux, tout oreilles*, Bibliothèque Charpentier, Paris, 1901, 428 pages.

Job (Thomas), *Thérèse*, drama in two acts, Samuel French, New York, 1946.

Josephson (Matthew), *Zola and his Time*, The Macaulay Company, New York, 1928, 558 pages.

Jullien (Jean), *le Théâtre vivant, essai théorique et pratique*, Bibliothèque Charpentier, Paris, 1892, 421 pages (of which pp. 3-91 comprise the *essai théorique*, and pp. 93-421 are the *pratique*, consisting of the five plays : *l'Échéance, la Sérénade, le Maître, la Mer, Vieille Histoire*).

Kuhn (Gottfried), *Zola als Dramatiker*, Abhandlung zur Erlangung der Doktorwürde der philosophischen Fakultät I der Universität Zurich, Imprimerie Alsacienne, Strasbourg, 1926, 73 pages.

Lanoux (Armand), *Bonjour Monsieur Zola*, Amiot-Dumont, Paris, 1954, 398 pages.

Le Blond (Maurice), *Notes et commentaires*, in his edition of Zola's Les Œuvres complètes, particularly his notes to the following volumes : *Théâtre II* (containing a summary of Zola's dramatic work and excerpts from reviews of his plays) ; *le Rêve* (containing a summary of Zola's collaboration with Alfred Bruneau and excerpts from reviews of their operas) ; *Mélanges, Préfaces et Discours* (containing a summary of Zola's newspaper work, and a bibliography of studies on Zola).

Le Blond-Zola (Denise), *Émile Zola raconté par sa fille*, Fasquelle, Paris, 1931, 264 pages.

Lepelletier (Edmond), *Émile Zola, sa vie, son œuvre*, Mercure de France, Paris, 1908, 492 pages.

Lucas (Dr Prosper), *Traité philosophique et physiologique de l'hérédité naturelle dans les états de santé et de maladie du système nerveux*, 2 vol., J.-B. Baillière, Paris, 1847-1850.

Mallarmé (Stéphane), *Dix-neuf lettres de Stéphane Mallarmé à Émile Zola*, avec une introduction de Léon Deffoux, un commentaire de Jean Royère, une lettre de Mallarmé en fac-similé et des notes. Jacques Bernard, " la Centaine ", Paris, 1929, 74 pages.

— *Œuvres complètes*, Bibliothèque de la Pléiade, Paris, 1945. (Appreciations of Zola are at pp. 320-321 and 344-345.)

Mantle (Burns), *Best Plays of 1945-1946*, Dodd, Mead & Co., New York, 1946.

Martino (Pierre), *le Roman réaliste sous le second Empire*, Hachette & Cie, Paris, 1913, 311 pages.

— *le Naturalisme français (1870-1895)*, Librairie Armand Colin, Paris, 1923, 220 pages.

Massis (Henri), *Comment Émile Zola composait ses romans*, Bibliothèque Charpentier, Paris, 1906, 346 pages.

Matthews (J. H.), *les Deux Zola, science et personnalité dans l'expression*, Librairie E. Droz, Genève ; Librairie Minard, Paris, 1957, 101 pages.

Melcher (Edith), *Stage Realism in France between Diderot and Antoine*. A dissertation presented to the Faculty of Bryn Mawr College in

partial fulfilment of the requirements for the degree of Doctor of
Philosophy. Bryn Mawr, Pennsylvania, 1928, 189 pages.

MICHELET (J.), *l'Amour*, Hachette & Cie, Paris, 1859, 4e éd., 464 pages.

ŒHLERT (Richard), *É. Zola als Theaterdichter mit einer Einleitung
über den Naturalismus im französischen Drama*, Romanische Studien,
Heft 17, Berlin, 1920, 145 pages.

PARDO BAZÁN (Emilia), *le Naturalisme* (translation by Albert Savine
of *la Cuestión palpitante*), Giraud & Cie, Paris, 1886, 316 pages.

REQUE (A. Dikka), *Trois auteurs dramatiques scandinaves — Ibsen,
Björnsen, Strindberg — devant la critique française, 1889-1901*,
Librairie ancienne Honoré Champion, 1930, 227 pages.

REWALD (John), *Cézanne et Zola*, éd. A. Sedrowski, Paris, 1936, 202 pages.

ROBERT (Guy), *la Terre d'Émile Zola, Étude historique et critique*, thèse
principale pour le doctorat ès lettres soutenue le 27 mai 1950 à la
Faculté des Lettres de l'Université de Paris, Société d'Édition les
Belles-Lettres, Paris, 1952.

— *Émile Zola, Principes et caractères généraux de son œuvre*, Société
d'Édition les Belles-Lettres, Paris, 1952, 207 pages.

ROD (Édouard), *A propos de l'Assommoir*, Marpon & Flammarion,
Paris, 1879, 106 pages.

SARCEY (Francisque), *Quarante ans de théâtre (feuilletons dramatiques)*,
t. VII, Bibliothèque des Annales politiques et littéraires, Paris, 1902.
(Pages 1-84 contain articles on Zola.)

SCHILBBACH (Werner), *Die Dramatisierung des naturalistischen Romans
bei Émile Zola.* Inaugural-Dissertation zur Erlangung der Doktorwürde der Hohen Philosophischen Fakultät der Martin Luther-
Universität Halle-Wittenburg, Halle (Saale), 1937, 177 pages.

SEILLIÈRE (Ernest), *Émile Zola*, Bernard Grasset, Paris, 1923, 354 pages.

SHERARD (Robert Harborough), *Émile Zola, a Biographical and Critical
Study*, Chatto & Windus, London, 1893, 288 pages.

SONDEL (Bess Seltzer), *Zola's Naturalistic Theory with Particular Reference to the Drama.* A part of a dissertation submitted to the Faculty
of the Division of the Humanities (University of Chicago) in candidacy for the degree of Doctor of Philosophy. Group Studies in the
Humanities : Literature 1938. Private edition distributed by The
University of Chicago Libraries, Chicago, 1939, 57 pages.

THALASSO (Adolphe), *le Théâtre-Libre, Essai critique, historique et
documentaire*, Mercure de France, Paris, 1909, 2e éd., 299 pages.

VAN TIEGHEM (Philippe), *Introduction à l'étude d'Émile Zola : Germinal*,
documents inédits de la Bibliothèque Nationale, Centre de Documentation universitaire, Paris, 1954, 116 pages.

VIRTANEN (Reino), *Claude Bernard and his Place in the History of Ideas*,
University of Nebraska Press, Lincoln, 1960.

VIZETELLY (Ernest Alfred), *Émile Zola, Novelist and Reformer*, John
Lane : The Bodley Head, London and New York, 1904, 560 pages.

WAXMAN (Samuel Montefiore), *Antoine and the Théâtre-Libre*, Harvard
University Press, 1926, 247 pages.

WILSON (Angus), *Émile Zola, An Introductory Study of his Novels*, William Morrow and Company, New York, 1952, 148 pages.

XAU (Fernand), *Émile Zola*, Marpon & Flammarion, Paris, 1880, 68 pages. (An interview with Zola.)

ZÉVAÈS (Alexandre), *Zola*, éd. de la Nouvelle Revue critique, Paris, 1945, 313 pages.

F) NEWSPAPERS AND PERIODICALS

1. *Prior to Zola's death*
and which have not been reprinted in the " Notes et commentaires " of Zola's
LES ŒUVRES COMPLÈTES

1879

COURRIER DES THÉATRES, *le Figaro*, 18 janvier : announcement of the opening of *l'Assommoir*.

UN MONSIEUR DE L'ORCHESTRE, *le Figaro*, 20 janvier : account of *l'Assommoir*.

VITU (Auguste), *le Figaro*, 20 janvier : review of *l'Assommoir*.

1881

SARCEY (Francisque), *le Temps*, 31 janvier : review of *Nana*.

UN MONSIEUR DE L'ORCHESTRE, *le Figaro*, 30 janvier : account of *Nana*.

VITU (Auguste), *le Figaro*, 30 janvier : review of *Nana*.

1885

CRI DU PEUPLE (le), Articles relating to the censorship of *Germinal* in the issues of 31 octobre, 1 and 6 novembre.

DUMAS fils (Alexandre), *le Figaro*, 9 novembre : reply to Zola concerning the censorship.

MAGNARD (F.), *le Figaro*, 27 octobre : article on the censorship.

SARCEY (Francisque), " Chronique à propos de la censure ", in *la Revue des Journaux et des Livres*, 2e année, n° 55, 8-14 novembre 1885, pp. 42-44.

SPECTACLES ET CONCERTS, *le Temps*, 28 octobre 1885 : notice concerning the censorship of *Germinal*.

1887

CALMETTE (Gaston), *le Figaro, Supplément littéraire*, 19 février : interview of Zola.

COURRIER DES THÉATRES, *le Figaro*, 18 février : announcement of the opening of *le Ventre de Paris*.

GANDERAX (Louis), " Revue dramatique " *(le Ventre de Paris)*, in *Revue des deux mondes*, LVIIe année, troisième période, t. quatre-vingtième, 15 mars 1887, pp. 453-461.

SAINT-CÈRE (Jacques), " Un Poète du Nord ", in *Revue d'Art dramatique*, t. V, janvier-mars 1887, pp. 277-282 and t. VI, avril-juin 1887, pp. 20-24.

SPECTACLES ET CONCERTS, *le Temps*, 19 février : announcement of the opening of *le Ventre de Paris*.

— *le Temps*, 20 février : account of *le Ventre de Paris*.

1888

COURRIER DES THÉATRES, *le Figaro*, 21 avril 1888 : announcement of the opening of *Germinal*.

FOUQUIER (Henry), " la Pitié ", in *le Figaro*, 23 avril.

SARCEY (Francisque), *le Temps*, 23 avril : review of *Germinal*.

UN MONSIEUR DE L'ORCHESTRE, *le Figaro*, 22 avril : account of *Germinal*.

VITU (Auguste), *le Figaro*, 22 avril : review of *Germinal*.

WOLFF (Albert), *le Figaro*, 24 avril : review of *Germinal*.

1891

DUMAS fils (Alexandre), *le Figaro*, 12 mars : testimony before a parliamentary commission investigating stage censorship.

UN MONSIEUR DE L'ORCHESTRE, *le Figaro*, 19 juin : account of *le Rêve*.

VITU (Auguste), *le Figaro*, 19 juin : review of *le Rêve*.

1893

DARCOURS (Charles), *le Figaro*, 24 novembre : review of *l'Attaque du moulin*.

1897

BRUNEAU (Alfred), " Messidor expliqué par les auteurs : la Musique ", in *le Figaro*, 20 février.

FOURCAUD, *le Gaulois*, 20 février : review of *Messidor*.

— *le Gaulois*, 25 février : " Réponse à M. Émile Zola. "

1901

CHARPENTIER (Gustave), *le Figaro*, 30 avril : review of *l'Ouragan*.

2. Subsequent to Zola's death

BRISSON (Adolphe), " Chronique théâtrale ", *le Temps*, 30 septembre 1912.

BROWN (Calvin S.), " Music in Zola's Fiction, especially Wagner's music ", *PMLA*, vol. 71 (March 1956), pp. 84-96.

— " Wagner and Zola Again ", *PMLA*, vol. 73 (Sept. 1958), pp. 448-452. (Two comments by Robert J. Niess with rejoinders by Calvin S. Brown.)

CRESSOT (Marcel), " Zola et Michelet ", *Revue d'Histoire littéraire de la France*, 35e année, 1928, pp. 382-389.

Gauthier (E. Paul), " New Light on Zola and Physiognomy ", *PMLA*, vol. 75 (1960), pp. 297-308.

Grant (Elliott M.), " The Political Scene in Zola's *Pot-Bouille* ", *French Studies*, vol. 8 (1954), pp. 342-347.

Hemmings (F. W. J.), " The Origin of the Terms, Naturalisme, Naturaliste ", *French Studies*, vol. 8 (1954), pp. 109-121.

— " Zola on the Staff of Le Gaulois ", *Modern Language Review*, vol. 50 (Jan. 1955), pp. 25-29.

— " The Present Position in Zola Studies ", *French Studies*, vol. 10 (1956), pp. 97-122.

— " Zola, le Bien public and le Voltaire ", *The Romanic Review*, vol. 47 (April 1956), pp. 103-116.

— " Zola's Apprenticeship to Journalism (1865-1870) ", *PMLA* vol. 71 (June 1956), pp. 340-354.

— " Zola, Manet and the Impressionists (1875-1880) ", *PMLA*, vol. 73 (Sept. 1958), pp. 407-417.

Kanes (Martin), " Zola and Busnach : The Temptation of the Stage ", *PMLA*, vol. 77 (March 1962), pp. 109-115.

Lapp (John C.), " The Play Germinal : an Unpublished Letter of Zola ", *French Studies*, vol. 15 (1961), pp. 47-48.

Leblond (Maurice), " Les Projets littéraires d'Émile Zola au moment de sa mort, d'après des documents et manuscrits inédits ", *Mercure de France*, vol. 199 (1er octobre 1927), pp. 6-25.

Leblond-Zola (Denise), " Zola et Cézanne ", *Mercure de France*, vol. 225 (1931), pp. 39-58.

Lote (G.), " La Doctrine et la Méthode naturalistes d'après Émile Zola ", *Zeitschrift für französische Sprache und Literatur*, vol. 51 (1928), pp. 193-224 and 389-418.

Moore (Charles H.), " A Hearing on Germinal and Die Weber ", *The Germanic Review* (Columbia University Press, vol. 33 (Feb. 1958), pp. 30-40.

Niess (Robert J.), " Wagner and Zola Again ", *PMLA*, vol. 73 (sept. 1958), pp. 448-452. (Two comments by Robert J. Niess with rejoinders by Calvin S. Brown.)

Pryme (Eileen E.), " Zola's Plays in England, 1870-1900 ", *French Studies*, vol. 13 (1959), pp. 28-38.

Robert (G.), " Zola et le classicisme ", I and II, in *Revue des Sciences humaines*, nouvelle série, fasc. 49 (janvier-mars 1948), pp. 1-24 and fasc. 50 (avril-juin 1948), pp. 126-153.

— " Trois textes inédits d'Émile Zola ", *Revue des Sciences humaines*, nouvelle série, fasc. 51 (juillet-décembre 1948), pp. 181-207.

Tancock (L. W.), " Some Early Critical Work of Émile Zola, Livres d'aujourd'hui et de demain (1866) ", *Modern Language Review*, XLII (1947), pp. 43-57.

Triomphe (Jean), " Zola collaborateur du Messager de l'Europe ", *Revue de Littérature comparée*, XVII (1937), pp. 754-765.

ADDENDA

I would like to add to my bibliography the following publications which have recently come to my attention :

MITTERAND (Henri), *Zola journaliste, de l'affaire Manet à l'affaire Dreyfus*, Paris, 1962, 311 pages.

ZOLA (Émile), *Lettres inédites à Céard*, edited by Albert J. SALVAN (publication of Brown University), Les Livres essentiels, Paris.

ZOLA (Émile), *Salons*, recueillis, annotés et présentés par F. W. J. HEMMINGS et Robert J. NIESS et précédés d'une étude sur « Émile Zola, critique d'art », de F. W. J. HEMMINGS ; Librairie E. Droz, Genève ; Librairie Minard, Paris, 1959, 277 pages.

INDEX